T0260693

The IT Value Quest

Wiley Series in Information Systems

PREVIOUS VOLUMES IN THE SERIES

The IT Value Quest

How to Capture the Business Value of IT-Based Infrastructure

THEO J.W. RENKEMA

JOHN WILEY & SONS, LTD
Chichester · New York · Weinheim · Brisbane · Singapore · Toronto

Copyright © 2000 by John Wiley & Sons Ltd,
Baffins Lane, Chichester,
West Sussex PO19 1UD, England
National   01243 779777
International   (+44) 1243 779777
e-mail (for orders and customer service enquiries):
cs-book@wiley.co.uk
Visit our Home Page on http://www.wiley.co.uk
or http://www.wiley.com

Other Wiley Editorial Offices

John Wiley & Sons, Inc., 605 Third Avenue,
New York, NY 10158-0012, USA

WILEY-VCH Verlag GmbH, Pappelallee 3,
D-69469 Weinheim, Germany

Jacaranda Wiley Ltd, 33 Park Road, Milton,
Queensland 4064, Australia

John Wiley & Sons (Asia) Pte Ltd, 2 Clementi Loop #02-01,
Jin Xing Distripark, Singapore 129809

John Wiley & Sons (Canada) Ltd, 22 Worcester Road,
Rexdale, Ontario M9W 1L1, Canada

Library of Congress Cataloging-in-Publication Data

Renkema, Theo J.W.
     The IT value quest : how to capture the business value of IT-based infrastructure / Theo J.W. Renkema.
     p.   cm. – (Wiley series in information systems)
Includes bibliographical references and index.
     ISBN 0-471-98817-0 (alk. paper)
     1. Management information systems.   2. Capital investments.
     3. Decision support systems.   I. Title.   II. John Wiley series in information systems.

British Library Cataloguing in Publication Data

A catalogue record for this book is available from the British Library
ISBN 0-471-98817-0

Typeset in 10/12 pt Palatino by C.K.M. Typesetting, Salisbury, Wiltshire.

Printed and bound by Antony Rowe Ltd, Eastbourne

Wiley Series in Information Systems

Editors

RICHARD BOLAND Department of Management Information and Decision Systems, Weatherhead School of Management, Case Western Reserve University, 10900 Euclid Avenue, Cleveland, Ohio 44106-7235, USA

RUDY HIRSCHHEIM Department of Decision and Information Systems, College of Business Administration, University of Houston, Houston, Texas 77202-6283, USA

Advisory Board

NIELS BJØRN-ANDERSEN Copenhagen Business School, Denmark

D. ROSS JEFFERY University of New South Wales, Australia

HEINZ K. KLEIN State University of New York, USA

ROB KLING Indiana University, USA

TIM J. LINCOLN IBM UK Limited, UK

BENN R. KONSYNSKI Emory University, Atlanta, USA

FRANK F. LAND London School of Economics, UK

ENID MUMFORD Manchester Business School, UK

MIKE NEWMAN University of Manchester, UK

DANIEL ROBEY Georgia State University, USA

E. BURTON SWANSON University of California, USA

ROBERT TRICKER Warwick Business School, UK

ROBERT W. ZMUD University of Oklahoma, USA

In memory of my father
and in dedication to my son

The ideas of economists and political philosophers, both when they are right and when they are wrong, are more powerful than is commonly understood. Indeed the world is ruled by little else. Practical men, who believe themselves to be quite exempt from any intellectual influence, are usually the slaves of some defunct economist—John Maynard Keynes.

The General Theory of Employment, Interest and Money.

Contents

Foreword

This book is timely. Why do I say this? Firstly, because despite the growing and now massive importance of getting IT infrastructure right, in the last decade there have been all too few books seriously devoted to the subject. Among these, Peter Keen, in *Shaping The Future* (1990) provided a founding conceptualization, defining the business functionality of the corporate IT platform in terms of reach and range. In *Leveraging The New Infrastructure* (1998) Peter Weill and Marianne Broadbent provided insights into fifty-four businesses and their infrastructure practices, produced four views of infrastructure, and were able to show why some firms were consistently achieving more business value for their information technology investments.

Subsequently it has become recognised, not least through such high profile books as Bill Gates' *Business@ The Speed of Thought* (1999), that e-business hardly gets off the ground, let alone being based on anything like the 'digital nervous system' posited by Gates, without detailed attention to rethinking and reinventing infrastructure. In the present book Theo Renkema makes several new, worthwhile contributions. Not least of these are the provision of a comprehensive, closely argued, and neatly conceptualized approach to how to assess and prioritize infrastructure projects, and the deft harnessing of insights from case studies to produce guidelines on how to manage the IT based infrastructure for business value.

A little history provides the second reason for this book's timeliness. During 18 years of working and subsequently researching in information systems, I have always been struck by the fact that, whatever you touched, at the back of IT there was always something grumbling away, variously alluded to as 'legacy' and 'maintenance' problems, or less generously 'spaghetti systems'. The 1990s have seen various attempts to redevelop infrastructure. In terms of business value, moves to replace the mainframe and also react against the often unmanageable proliferation of stand-alone computers — for example standardising the desktop, and adopting client/server architecture — have not always proved successful. From 1995 organizations have also increasingly recognised the need to start on yet another cycle involving internet/intranet and extranet solutions. Indeed business and technical managers are told on a daily basis, in no uncertain terms, that this present cycle is truly inescapable.

The Year 2000 (Y2K) problem then quickened the pace with a vengeance as corporations and government institutions alike sought to patch up, develop or replace their legacy systems and address infrastructure questions. I know several global corporations that have spent upwards of $US400 million each on attempting to deal with this problem. For many the solution — and not just to Y2K issues — lay partly in enterprise systems — in terms of technology, services and consultancy a $US40 billion market in 1998. This involves stripping out legacy software and systems as much as possible and putting in place a new, and Y2K compliant, suite of software, that, somewhat unfortunately, also needs to be aligned with the surviving infrastructure, technologies and applications, and also requires considerable business reengineering if what has been called the 'second wave' of maximising business value for the enterprise resource planning (ERP) investment is to be caught. These different initiatives and cycles of investment have in some organizations straightened out the infrastructure problems, but more often have piled complexity upon complexity and left all too many practitioners wondering — how do we manage this? And which way to business value? Renkema provides more than a good starting point in this situation; indeed he provides a detailed road map that makes success much more likely.

And so we come to the final reason why this book is timely. One of the alarming findings from studying IT evaluation techniques in firms and government institutions over the past 10 years has been how patchy evaluation practices continue to be. In *Beyond The IT Productivity Paradox* (1999) our companion text in the Wiley Information Systems Series, a range of studies underline how perennial and widespread is the lack of integrated, life-cycle IT evaluation for business value. That book offers detailed ways forward and provides a chapter on Infrastructure investments, but cannot hope to give the subject the attention it demands — if the above argument is valid — and which Theo Renkema really now does provide.

If, as I did, you want to know how to treat IT-based infrastructure as a strategic business asset, how to define different aspects of IT infrastructure, how to set up an Infrastructure governance approach — called controlled dynamics by the author — how to make Infrastructure decisions, define value metrics, and use the product, process, participation and politics model for strategic investment control, then this book by an experienced manager and academic — provides well articulated, well researched, grounded ideas that can be implemented in practice. The book is not just timely, it's actually rather good.

Leslie Willcocks
Templeton College, Oxford
November 1999

Series Preface

The information systems community has grown considerably since 1984, when we began publishing the Wiley Series in Information Systems. We are pleased to be a part of the growth of the field, and believe that this series of books is playing an important role in the intellectual development of the discipline. The primary objective of the series is to publish scholarly works that reflect the best of the research in the information systems community. We are specifically interested in those works which are relevant to the practice of IS. To this end, Theo Renkema's text *The IT Value Quest: How to Capture the Business Value of IT-Based Infrastructure* is an excellent example.

The book offers an empirically driven approach for organizations to measure the value of IT infrastructural investments. This is a subject of immense interest to the field largely because it is so difficult to deal with. Organizations have historically struggled to come to grips with their significant IT expenditures, always asking 'are we getting true value for money?' Unfortunately, they have never known for sure whether they actually were. As the real benefits of IT have become increasingly difficult to quantify (especially strategic issues such as improved effectiveness, competitive advantage or preventing competitive disadvantage) the need for ever more rigorous methods to assess, control and manage investments has become vital. This text finally provides help. Renkema presents insights and instruments for organizations that want to manage their IT investments from an infrastructural perspective. This book should be of interest to practitioners and academics alike.

Rudy Hirschheim

Preface and Outline of the Book

The origins of this book can be traced back to the beginning of the 1990s when many senior business managers became concerned or even anxious about the added value of their ever-rising IT spending. In light of the many disappointed project expectations, failures to deliver real business benefits and increased interest in what came to be known as the IT 'productivity paradox', managers demanded more robust evidence of the business value of IT. Today, business managers want to know what kind of business contribution their massive investments deliver, and have particular interest in a clear business motivation of projects at the approval stage, investment justification of funding decisions, and business cases to set investment priorities.

Business value assessment of IT has become even more critical, but also more complex since many of today's IT investments are in IT-based infrastructure. In the present competitive business arena, this digital infrastructure not only facilitates successful and profitable business today, but also enables or inhibits the ability to innovate and compete in many years to come. As infrastructure touches upon the interests of many departments, business units and even individuals, investment decisions are inextricably bound up with issues of stakeholder cooperation, commitment and the possibility to capture business synergy. Although many investment methods and techniques are already available, infrastructure investment evaluation remains an issue that is poorly covered or even deliberately ignored.

This book's prime purpose is to give guidance to managers who want to have control over their IT-based infrastructure investments and who want to maximize their return on investment. It discusses investment issues and management decisions from a clear view of IT-based infrastructure as a management tool for getting the full benefits of IT. Business value assessment of IT-based infrastructure is considered to be a highly organizational and communicative process, in which 'hard' financial appraisals and strategic evaluations interact with 'softer' issues of managing the assessment process in terms of stakeholder agreement, management ownership, conflicts of interest, power and politics. This book does not offer a recipe-like, ready-to-use investment approach as a substitute for finance-based justification techniques. The basic premise is that every organization that has the ambition to install tighter management control of IT-based infrastructure investment will have to design and implement its own type of investment method, tailored to its particular business strategy, style of management and investment priorities. Recipes simply cannot be given, but there are generic insights and instruments which can be of help in this process of change.

Many persons, in business, academia and consulting have contributed to this book, especially in the period when the academic research underlying this book was conducted and published in an earlier book in 1996. I acknowledge all of their comments and many interesting discussions that have shaped and sharpened the final contents. Also special thanks is warranted for the many participants in graduate, masters, and executive management courses in which I lectured over the last few years. I am constantly aware that their collective experience is much more valuable than my personal views and opinions. I hope some of their experience and expertise has been captured in this book, and that it may suit the educational purposes of others.

This book is decomposed into five parts, each consisting of a number of chapters. Figure 1 on p. xx gives an outline of the book.

Part I: Investment Issues and Management Challenges
The first part of this book introduces the theme of investing in IT-based infrastructure, with a focus on the organizational issues surrounding these investments. The problems, challenges and managerial dimensions of business value assessment and creation will be discussed in Chapter 1. In Chapter 2 a first introduction will be given of the main changes that are currently taking place in business with respect to both the role of IT-based infrastructure and the management decisions underlying investments in this infrastructure.

Part II: The New Digital Infrastructure
The theme of the second part of this book is the nature and role of corporate IT-based infrastructure. Before looking at investment decisions in more detail, the notion of IT-based infrastructure is explored

in Chapter 3 through some interviews with business practitioners and a review of important theoretical views. Also, the notion of IT-based infrastructure is more narrowly defined in Chapter 4 and translated into operational terms by means of an overview of generic infrastructure components. This overview is used to describe the actual IT-based infrastructure in two case studies.

Part III: Investment Governance and Control
The third part of this book addresses corporate control of investments in IT-based infrastructure. First, the governance approach underlying IT-based infrastructure investment is discussed in Chapter 5. A choice will be made of an approach that centers on the control of separate infrastructure investment projects with their own specific business value proposition. In order to find appropriate control options the existing methods of IT investment evaluation and project appraisal are reviewed and critically assessed in Chapter 6. Next, elaborating on established decision-making theories, a model—coined the 'P4 model'—for managing decision-making on infrastructure IT projects is proposed in Chapter 7 and applied in the description and analysis of a number of project case studies in Chapter 8.

Part IV: The Business Case for Investment
The fourth part of this book addresses the definition of business cases for investment decisions regarding IT-based infrastructure, through a study of theory and practice. This business case consists of a set of value metrics, which is used for evaluating and selecting project proposals and lies at the heart of the P4 decision-making model. First the metrics for justifying a proposed project are reviewed in Chapter 9. Chapter 10 subsequently looks at metrics for evaluating the full infrastructure impacts of investments in terms of synergy.

Part 5: Concluding Management Perspectives
The fifth and final part of this book gives concluding management perspectives on how to assess and control the business value of IT-based infrastructure. First the book's results are integrated in the form of an investment methodology in Chapter 11, addressing the question of how an organization can proceed when designing an appropriate investment methodology for IT-based infrastructure. Chapter 12 provides a summary of the key messages for senior executives as put forward in this book and gives some concluding thoughts.

Part I: Investment Issues and Management Challenges

> 1: IT-Based Infrastructure: Value for Money?
> 2: Refocusing the Search for IT Value

Part II: The New Digital Infrastructure

> 3: Strategic Dimensions of IT-Based Infrastructure
> 4: The Business Role of IT-Based Infrastructure

Part III: Investment Governance and Control

> 5: Infrastructure Governance Through Investment Decisions
> 6: Appraisal Methods for IT Investments
> 7: Investment Decisions with the P4 Model
> 8: The P4 Model in Practice

Part IV: The Business Case for Investment

> 9: Assessing Infrastructure Projects
> 10: Assessing Infrastructure Synergy

Part V: Concluding Management Perspectives

> 11: An Investment Methodology for IT-Based Infrastructure
> 12: Managing IT-Based Infrastructure for Business Value

Figure 1   *Outline of this book*

About the Author

Theo J.W. Renkema is working in the IT Strategy department of the Rabobank and is employed as a Research Fellow in the Department of Technology Management of Eindhoven University of Technology, both in the Netherlands. He previously worked with a large financial services firm and was a management consultant in the Corporate IT department of Philips Electronics. As well as gaining a 'cum laude' Masters degree in Business Economics Theo Renkema has a Ph.D. in Industrial Engineering & Management Science.

Dr Renkema has authored several books, numerous articles, and regularly lectures in the areas of IT investment appraisal, business value assessments, and benefits management.

Part I
Investment Issues and Management Challenges

1

IT-Based Infrastructure: Value for Money?

1.1 INTRODUCTION

Throughout the second half of the twentieth century, information technology (IT) has been permeating virtually every part of modern society. It has even been suggested that this marks a digital revolution which will have far-reaching and profound consequences, perhaps even more than the well-known industrial revolution (see, for example, Negroponte, 1995; Tapscott, 1997). It seems we are only at the start of a radical digitalization of business activities, which will have a profound impact on virtually every organization, both in the private and public sectors. Organizations have become increasingly dependent on IT in their search for corporate success and survival. Until recently, IT was mainly used to rationalize routine business processes in the corporate 'back office' (e.g. payroll automation or electronic inventory control). IT was considered an administrative expense or a liability and the main thrust was to improve efficiency through cost savings and cost displacements.

Today, long-term and capital-intensive business investments are made in the corporate 'front office' in order to improve effectiveness, to gain and sustain competitive advantage and to transform entire business processes. IT has a become a critical asset, and plays an essential role in building an infrastructure that enables important business improvements, for instance (building on Farbey et al., 1993):

- Product and market diversification: globalization, widening business scope, entering new markets, offering new products.

- Marketing strengthening: improving cross-selling, customer service, customer loyalty, targeting marketing efforts, adding value to products.
- Effective management control: improving order and delivery information, getting new products to market faster, improving cycle-time, providing just-in-time services.
- Streamlined communications: improving decision-making, providing up-to-date planning data, bypassing time and place constraints.
- Competitive positioning: e.g. increasing bargaining power in the competitive arena, creating entry barriers, locking in customers.
- Cooperative advantage: strategic alliances enabled by IT with suppliers, customers and partners in the business chain.

For many contemporary organizations, investing in IT-based infrastructure has become nothing less than a sheer necessity. Nowadays, it is not so much the question of whether to invest, but more the question of how and where to invest in order to get maximum business value and to increase return on investment. Well-known examples of firms that report IT-based infrastructure success are for instance:

- Verifone, a software company in credit-card verification, that shifts software development projects around the world electronically, enabling almost 24-hour workdays.
- Mrs. Field, a US bakery chain, who centrally monitors its production and sales at several hundreds of outlets, enabling huge price discounts in material supply and firm top management control.
- Bally, a firm specializing in the manufacture of building constructions, that has direct interconnections between the design department and sales representatives, enabling client-order-driven design in a few hours.
- Benneton, a clothing company, that has electronic connection with all its retailers and commercial agents, enabling fast customer information and up-to-date production and distribution plans.

Infrastructure Investments and IT-Based Infrastructure

Recently, increased emphasis has been placed on the role of infrastructure investments in order to obtain the full benefits of large-scale IT deployment (Scott Morton, 1991; Luftman, 1996). Various sources point out that the infrastructure part of IT capital expenditures might well be more than one-third of total expenditures and rising (McKay and Brockway, 1989; Keen, 1991). Broadbent and Weill (1997) even claim that infrastructure investments now cover the majority of all IT-related expenses and account for more than 58% of the total IT budget of large firms and about 4% of revenues. They state that infrastructure investments have increased by about 11% annually and that this increase is likely to continue.

Infrastructure investments are closely related to what has come to be known as the emergence of a corporate IT-based infrastructure. Although the notion of infrastructure has been used since the advent of business computing, there is a lack of clarity with respect to the present role of this IT-based infrastructure for profitable IT deployment in organizations. Many executives still see this infrastructure as a technological artifact, merely consisting of shared hardware equipment, systems software and telecommunications facilities. It has in fact become more a business asset of the modern enterprise, which can enhance competitiveness and generate sustainable competitive advantage (Feeny and Ives, 1989; Ross *et al.*, 1996). Without exaggeration, authors such as Lucas (1995) speak of the 'T-based organization' (in which 'T' stands for 'Technology') and Martin (1996) of the 'Cyber corporation', to illustrate that the right infrastructure for IT probably is the most important element of the organization of the future.

Infrastructure investments are known for their high and often unpredictable cost-of-ownership and the intangible nature of their benefits (Parker *et al.*, 1988; Banker *et al.*, 1993). They also have far-reaching consequences in terms of business efficiency, effectiveness, competitive positioning and the ability to innovate. Infrastructure investment decisions are amongst the most complex, delicate and perilous business decisions. Many managers do not even try to justify their expenditures or try to assess the business value of proposed investments. Senior executives therefore find it particularly difficult to make IT-based infrastructure decisions that are aligned with the current and future needs of their business.

Financial Importance of Information Technology

The increased importance of IT-based infrastructure has meant that in many firms, IT investment claims a major and increasing part of the available financial resources. It is estimated that large organizations spend up to 50% of their total capital expenditure on IT, while they constitute between 1% and 10% of sales turnover (Weill and Olsen, 1989; Bakos and Kemerer, 1992; Banker *et al.*, 1993). Information-intensive organizations—e.g. in financial services or many governmental organizations—have the highest spending figures compared with other organizations. Figure 1.1 gives an overview of the estimated IT

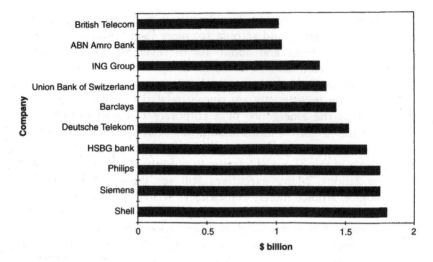

Figure 1.1   Estimàted IT expenditures of major European companies in 1997 (from Computable, 1997)

expenditures of several major European commercial enterprises in 1997 (Computable, 1997). Although subject to a slight downward trend in the 1980s, IT budgets rising with double-digit percentages a year should not be considered as rare, while still up to half of the total IT costs are not part of formal budgets. In many cases, IT spending is on a comparative level with spending on, for instance, research and development (R&D) and marketing (Ballantine *et al.*, 1995).

US government statistics indicate that as of 1994 computers and related IT resources make up about half of all business spending on equipment, even excluding the massive spending on programming and software (Sager and Gleckman, 1994). In industrialized economies, for instance the United Kingdom and the Netherlands, total recorded business and public sector spending in 1995 was estimated at £3.6 billion and *f* 21 billion, respectively (Willcocks, 1994; CBS, 1996). It was estimated that in 1997 European businesses would spend about $210 billion on IT products and services. Developing economies such as China, India and Brazil are expected to increase their IT expenditures considerably in the coming years (Engardio, 1994). At the turn of the century, the IT industry might well account for some 10% of world economic activity, a doubling of the 1990 figure (Willcocks, 1994). The financial importance of IT makes it clear that investment issues with respect to IT can no longer be ignored. Businesses that really want to get 'value for money' from IT-based infrastructure need to pay active attention to the process of assessing and creating business value.

1.2 FROM PRODUCTIVITY PARADOX TO MANAGERIAL PARADOX

The value for money to be obtained from investments in advanced IT-based infrastructure is far from guaranteed. IT investments have repeatedly been the subject of disappointed expectations and their evaluations raise many questions. The increased financial importance of IT and of IT-based infrastructure contrasts considerably with the difficulties encountered when trying to assess the potential business benefits and measure the realized contribution to business performance. Many IT-based improvement projects are known for their overshoots in time and budget, and for insufficient quality or unclear business contribution. Although not all unsuccessful IT projects are likely to be publicly known, there is a well-documented history of unsuccessful or even clearly failed investments and of their inability to generate sufficient business value, e.g:

- The cancellation of the Taurus project of the London Stock Exchange in 1993, cost £80 million and over £400 million of abandoned system development costs to the securities industry.
- In 1994 the British insurance firm Prudential stopped their Plato project to migrate to a client-server IT architecture, costing £40 million.
- In 1997 the US Internal Revenue Service admitted that their attempt to build a single integrated system for processing 200 million tax forms was a failure, and had already cost several billions of US dollars.

Organizations estimate that around 20% of their IT spending is wasted and that 30% to 40% does not contribute to business performance (Willcocks and Lester, 1993). Around 70% of all firm IT investment seems to give no adequate return on investment (Hochstrasser and Griffiths, 1990). Only around 50% of completed projects are considered to be a true success (Lyttinen and Hirschheim, 1987). Even the Gartner Group, one of the prime commercial IT research firms, sees only a 1% net average return on IT in the years 1985–1995. The reported failure rates of IT infrastructure enabled reengineering programs are also high. Belmonte and Murray (1993) think that less than 45% of companies that try such business process redesign are successful at achieving their intended goals. Hammer and Champy (1993) estimate that up to 70% of these programs fail.

Strategic Questions for Senior Executives

In addition to the troublesome history in demonstrating the return on and value of investments, the general investment climate towards continued investment in IT-based infrastructure has been under severe pressure from what has been called the 'IT productivity paradox' (see Chapter 2 for a more detailed treatment). This notion refers to the observation that economic data give no conclusive answer as to what the contribution of IT to organizational performance is, notwithstanding the fact that the general investment level continues to rise (see, for example, Loveman, 1988; Strassmann, 1990). This is what made Nobel laureate Robert Solow say: 'You see computers everywhere except in the productivity statistics.'

Although the debate regarding IT productivity is expected to continue, from a business perspective it is important to note that the productivity paradox has a very profound managerial counterpart. In light of the many controversial findings regarding the impact of IT on business performance and the many disappointing IT investments, senior management has become highly unreceptive towards 'act of faith' investment decisions. Illustrative in this respect is the comment by the top manager of the large Dutch NMB bank in 1992:

> They told us that computers would bring cost savings, but they did not. They told us that our work would become easier, but our work did not become easier. Up till now, the IT industry has only in few cases been able to demonstrate the advantages of IT deployment.

Today, senior management is expecting more definitive answers to such strategic questions as:

- How can we evaluate the business benefits of proposed investments?
- Which decision criteria are most appropriate to set priorities between competing projects?
- What is the contribution of our investments to improving the corporate strategy and business leverage?
- How can we manage the decision-making process that underpins our investment appraisal?
- How can we create commitment to a decision and establish a shared mind-set?
- How can we monitor the progress and performance of investments, in order to identify improvement actions?
- How can we get evidence of adequate returns on the funds invested?

The Need for New Assessment Methods

Assessing investments in terms of their financial return and business value is easier said than done. Conventional, accountancy-based techniques no longer suffice, due to their sole focus on effects that can easily be translated into short-term financial figures. Using strictly financial methods only makes sense when trying to justify IT investments that are aimed at reducing costs and increasing efficiency. This makes it very difficult to produce evidence for the strategic potential and business contribution of today's infrastructure-driven IT investments, which are more and more targeted at improvements that go beyond clear cost containment. The limitation of the classical financial techniques are well reflected in the saying: 'you measure what is measurable, not what is important.'

Competitive conditions increasingly force contemporary organizations to have a proactive, offensive strategy instead of a reactive, defensive strategy (Earl, 1989; Baskerville *et al.*, 1994). The types of investment that result from proactive strategies generally have uncertain and often diffuse business impacts, which cannot easily be quantified. Infrastructure projects typically do not deliver benefits *per se*, but rather generate business value through facilitating innovations and business process changes (see, for example, Earl, 1992; Ward *et al.*, 1996b). Also, the risks of these investments are substantial, hard to assess beforehand and difficult to manage, both in financial, technological and organizational terms. Therefore, the call for more rigorous methods to assess, evaluate and manage the consequences of investments in IT-based infrastructure is apparent.

The paradoxical situation many firms encounter arises from their conviction that investments in IT-based infrastructure—although difficult to justify—do play an essential role in the achievement of their corporate strategies. They often find themselves in a 'Catch-22' situation (Willcocks, 1994). Not investing in IT might severely jeopardize their organization's future viability, even though the expected investment outcomes are highly uncertain beforehand. Keen (1991) expresses the dilemma many senior managers face as:

> Senior executives are caught in a worrisome double bind (...); economically, companies cannot afford to increase capital spending on IT; competitively, they cannot afford not to do so. The economics of information capital is firmly on the top management agenda, and corporate managers are clamoring for help.

1.3 PURPOSE OF THIS BOOK

The central theme of this book is the assessment and creation of business value from corporate investments in IT-based infrastructure. More and more it is recognized that an ever-greater part of today's business investment is in IT-based infrastructure. We are in the midst of a shift in the application of IT that can be considered as fundamental.

From limited use to rationalized routine business processes, the role of modern IT has evolved to a widespread enabling business infrastructure. Investments in this infrastructure are simply too important in terms of their impacts and expenditures, and the risks of making the wrong decisions simply too great to let them simply take their course. These generally capital-intensive investments have the potential, for example, to radically improve product development, to restructure interaction with suppliers and customers, to redesign manufacturing and distribution processes and to add new features to a company's products and services. The purpose of this book is to give general guidance to managers who want to have control of their IT-based infrastructure expenditures and who want to maximize their return on investment.

Business Role of IT-Based Infrastructure

For most firms and their management it is not yet clear what the precise business role of an IT-based infrastructure is and, more importantly, which implications it has for exploiting IT in the most profitable way. Before discussing investment issues in detail, managers should have a clear view of the role of this digital infrastructure as a business asset for successful IT deployment and for leveraging business improvements. This book aims to clarify and also somewhat demystify the role of IT-based infrastructure. After reading this book the reader should have more insight into what precisely an IT-based infrastructure is and how it can be of help in getting the full benefits of IT.

Assessing Business Value

Investments in IT-based infrastructure constitute a major and increasing portion of the capital expenditures of the modern enterprise. These investments not only determine a firm's efficient and effective business operations today, but also to a large extent the ability to improve its future performance. Top management no longer wants to treat the value prospects of proposed investments as articles of blind faith. Traditional financial methods, however, cannot cope with the need for well-founded investment decisions and for measurement techniques that take account of the strategic potential of infrastructure investments. The call for more robust assessment approaches and principles is louder than ever before.

The assessment approach presented here should be considered as a generic management-based instrument for successfully identifying, evaluating and managing the business impacts of infrastructure investments. The focus is on the use of value metrics for estimating the total life-cycle costs, appraising the business benefits and assessing the risks of proposed investments. It has become increasingly clear that there is no single reliable method for evaluating and managing investments but that organizations need a better view on a range of balanced techniques, taking into account their own specific characteristics and priorities. This makes it virtually impossible to develop a cut-and-dried, recipe-like investment method. Also the importance of life-cycle assessment will be stressed. Investment appraisal should not be an isolated act in order to justify expenditures at the feasibility stage, but be part of a continuous process of managing business impacts across an investment's life-cycle.

Corporate Decision-Making

Investment appraisal is more than simply calculating financial returns and assessing hard, measurable business impacts. If this were the case, managers could easily take refuge in one of the many standard capital budgeting textbooks. Above all, it is an organizational process, in which multiple stakeholders interact to agree upon the value of an investment (Symons, 1991; Butler *et al.*, 1993). As such, the hard C of Calculation is surrounded by a number of softer C's, Communication, Cooperation, Consensus and Commitment, which underpin and guide the appropriate use of calculations in decision-making (see Figure 1.2). Evaluation methods and measurement techniques are not only tools for justifying expenditures or calculating benefits, but also important in order to be able to:

- inform all stakeholders of the consequences of a decision;
- commit stakeholders to the route to be followed;
- create a shared, value-focused view of an investment amongst stakeholders;
- control investment outcomes after the decision stage, in order to maximize business value;
- foster organizational learning, by learning from both the successes and failures of previous investments.

Apart from appraisal criteria, important organizational elements of decision-making are, for instance, the steps to be taken in the investment process and the responsibilities of the persons involved in this process. Evaluation stakeholders, whether they are individual persons or interested parties, almost by definition have different judgments regarding the value and desirability of a proposed investment

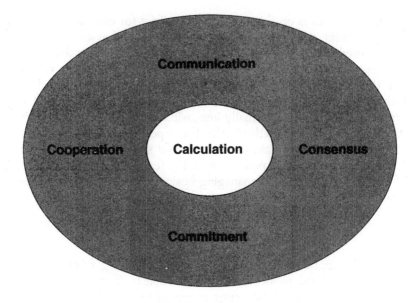

Figure 1.2   The 'hard' center C and its surrounding softer C's

(Legge, 1984; Walsham, 1993), especially when this concerns an infra-structure investment. Managing investments therefore also means managing conflicts of interests and managing power relations. If managed well, these decision-making elements provide the basis for good communications and mutual consultations amongst stakeholders. It is increasingly recognized that this is bound to increase decision-making quality and ultimately business performance.

1.4   APPROACH OF THIS BOOK

The approach of this book is design-oriented, i.e. it is directed towards delivering knowledge that can be used to improve organizational practice. As such, this more instrumentalist approach differs from the 'traditional' academic research approach which usually has an empirical orientation, i.e. to describe, explain and ultimately predict organizational behavior (Aken, 1994a). Although following the rigor of academic research (e.g. regarding data collection, analysis and use of literature; see Miles and Huberman, 1984; Yin, 1989), this book's approach has a close relationship with the practical, result-driven orientation of engineering and social intervention disciplines. The main thrust is to provide scientifically sound, generic knowledge in order to support business professionals[1] in their day-to-day business tasks. The advantages of using this knowledge are exemplified by giving practical illustrations and by providing a logically consistent framework for action.

The context-bound and managerial nature of IT-based infrastructure investments makes it virtually impossible to give quantitative predictions of the effects of using the approach presented in this book. In line with the developments in the contingency theory of organizational design (see, for example, Mintzberg, 1983b; Daft, 1986) and postmodern management thinking (see, for example, Remenyi *et al.*, 1997), the basic supposition is that there is no 'one best way' of assessing and managing IT-based infrastructure investments. Or, in the words of Strassmann (1997): 'Computers have relevance only in the context of a particular organization.' Recipes cannot be given, but there are lessons to be learnt and there are important generic concepts, which can be shared to get real value out of corporate investments in IT-based infrastructure.

Hard and Soft Designs

Any attempt to improve the way IT-based infrastructure investments are assessed and managed is inevitably influenced by some underlying values and assumptions. This book is underpinned by the belief that improvements in organizational practices should always take account of two types of designs, referred to as 'hard' and 'soft' designs.[2] 'Hard' designs refer to content-, or goal-driven, technical—economic solutions to organizational problems. 'Soft' designs refer to social and political processes that take place in organizations. In the former type of design, a problem is solved or prevented by prescribing how an organization should function in an improved situation, in terms of structure, formal procedures, responsibilities, etc. In the latter type, the goal is that

---

[1] A professional, like an architect, a lawyer, an IT or a management consultant, is someone from a clearly identified profession who, with the aid of creativity and application skills, uses scientific knowledge to deliver value to his or her client (Schön, 1983; Aken, 1994a).

[2] This closely relates to the distinction between what has been called 'hard systems thinking' and 'soft systems thinking' (Checkland, 1985; Rosenhead, 1989). The difference between hard and soft designs is also inspired by two fundamentally different 'paradigms' of traditional academic research (see, for example, Orlikowski and Baroudi, 1991). In the dominant positivist tradition, often called quantitative research, mathematical and statistical techniques are applied to analyse 'hard' data that were obtained through experiments and surveys. The interpretative tradition (or qualitative research) is trying to increase understanding of organizational reality as 'soft' social constructions, in which continuous processes of 'sensemaking' take place (for a detailed treatment, see Weick, 1979).

people learn to think and work, in terms of social interactions, shared meaning, mutual learning, etc. in such a way that this in the end will lead to an improved situation.

The distinction between 'hard' and 'soft' designs often seems artificial, when working on concrete organizational change. Although frequently the subject of academic debate, firms do not really have much to gain from extensive debates concerning 'the truth' of the starting-points that are being employed in a change process.[3] What organizations do need are practical, result-focused solutions. In practice, hard and soft designs are generally used in an integrated and pragmatic way in order to give recommendations that deliver added value. Therefore, hard and soft designs go hand in hand. A soft design, exclusively focusing on social and political processes, is not really useful if it is not underpinned by a goal-driven course. On the other hand, the development of a hard, content-driven design only has a chance of being successful if the abilities and will to change of involved stakeholders have been sufficiently mobilized.

Role of Case Studies

Since the advent of capital budgeting theory, much is known about financial appraisal methods and investment measurement techniques. This knowledge, however, is often of a highly mechanistic, prescriptive and context-free nature (see, for example, Bierman and Smidt; 1984; Lumby, 1991). It hardly addresses the important context-bound issues of investments in IT-based infrastructure such as intangibility, uncertainty, subjectivity, multiple stakeholder perspectives and conflicting interests. Also the many studies on IT productivity generally do not give much guidance as to how investments should be assessed and managed, but merely analyze macro-economic, industry-level or aggregated firm data (see, for a review, Brynjolffson, 1993; Hoogeveen, 1997). The social-constructive or interpretative perspective on evaluation draws attention away from metrics and measurement towards organizational processes, but is more a research philosophy than a practical business tool (see, for example, Hirschheim and Smithson, 1988; Symons, 1991).

---

[3] Within traditional academic research there usually is not much room for maneuvering between a positivist and an interpretative approach. The philosophical starting-points with respect to ontology (what is the nature of reality?) and epistemology (what are the possibilities of gaining knowledge of reality?) (see Guba and Lincoln, 1989), too much serve as 'religious truths' of the researcher.

In accordance with the design approach of this book, the approach presented here is built around the belief that real improvements in business value assessment and creation can only be made if these are grounded in, and guided by, real-life case studies,[4] in which both 'hard' and 'soft' aspects receive sufficient attention. The words of Hogbin and Thomas (1994) give good justification for the role of case studies: 'success in determining the value of IT lies in the more consistent and diligent application of what is known and practiced, rather than in new or complex methods of appraisal.' Our role in conducting case studies was inspired by the attitude of what Schön (1983) calls a 'reflective practitioner', who studies a series of cases in which proposed designs are applied. He or she then tries to translate these into more generic instruments by reflecting on the lessons learnt.

Apart from building on well-articulated business experiences and challenging views, the ideas and instruments covered in this book are inspired by the practical experiences of four large organizations. One is a government organization and three are multinational commercial enterprises: an insurance firm, a commercial bank and an industrial firm. In the framework of the research that underpins this book, the author had the opportunity of working with them to learn from their experiences, to apply proposed thinking and instruments and to improve their investment assessment approach. For reasons of confidentiality, the full identity and specific investment details of these case study organizations will not be revealed, but more detailed case study experiences will be discussed in the remainder of this book.

1.5   CONCLUSIONS

Although the business potential of IT is beyond dispute, it proves to be very difficult to evaluate its true business value. IT spending has increased considerably and now represents one of the largest capital items of many firms, across many industries. In the present competitive business arena, modern IT provides the enabling infrastructure for efficient and effective business operations, leveraging business improvements and securing a competitive edge. Capturing the value of this IT-based infrastructure is often considered as the most critical

---

[4] In research methodology, case study research is recommended in the case of studying 'sticky, practice based problems, where the experiences of the actors are important and the context of action is critical' (Benbasat *et al.*, 1987, p. 369). Yin (1989) states that case studies are particularly appropriate when seeking an answer to research questions such as 'how' and 'why'.

and yet the most complex part of managerial decision-making. Given the increasingly faster technology developments, making the right decisions at the right moment will be more important than ever before. Many managers do not try to justify their expenditure or measure whether their money was well spent. This situation has become unacceptable in the light of the rising costs and uncertain benefits of this increasingly important type of business investment. The risk of making the wrong decisions, selecting the wrong projects or — in broader terms — of misalignment of IT-based infrastructure and the business — is simply too great. The call for more financial returns and more 'value for money' can no longer be ignored.

Building on well-researched practical case studies, the purpose of this book is to give guidance to managers who want to have control over their IT-based infrastructure expenditures and want to maximize their return on investment. The starting point for this is the basic recognition that IT-based infrastructure is critical to obtain the full benefits of IT. IT-based infrastructure has become much more than a mere technology artifact with equipment and telecommunications provisions. Today, IT-based infrastructure is a strategic business asset which, when exploited in a successful way, can enhance competitiveness and generate sustainable competitive advantage. In order to achieve this, organizations and their senior management should be prepared to make well-articulated and motivated investment decisions, and have in place clear business procedures to manage an investment across its entire life-cycle. Business value assessment of IT-based infrastructure is above all seen to be a communicative stakeholder process in which 'hard' strategic appraisals interact with 'softer' issues of mutual agreement, management commitment, power and politics. This requires rigorous, yet relevant insights and instruments, which cannot be supplied by taking refuge in the standard, finance-oriented appraisal techniques. These type of insights and instruments will be discussed in the remainder of this book, with allowance for organization-specific adaptations to reflect a particular business strategy, investment priorities, and styles of decision-making and management control.

2
Refocusing the Search for IT Value

2.1 INTRODUCTION

The previous introductory chapter sketched the managerial background and main business issues of investing in IT-based infrastructure. This chapter takes a more detailed look at the changing focus of the business computing infrastructure of today's enterprises and of the management decisions underlying investments in this infrastructure. First, in Section 2.2 the emergence of IT-based infrastructure will be discussed, emphasizing the main business implications it has for successfully managing IT. Then in Section 2.3 a short review will be given of the IT productivity paradox, since this has in many cases triggered the present business focus on benefits delivery and value management, instead of mere cost control. Subsequently, the focus moves in Section 2.4 to investment decisions regarding IT-based infrastructure, especially why they are critical to organizations, but also difficult to take. The conclusions are summarized in the final Section 2.5.

2.2 THE EMERGENCE OF IT-BASED INFRASTRUCTURE

The notion of 'infrastructure' is not entirely new in the IT/IS field. Until recently the notion of infrastructure had a rather narrow, technological connotation. In this 'traditional' view an infrastructure was considered to include all basic technological resources, often organized in a centralized information systems department. This technical infrastructure encompassed all technological means such as mainframe computers, data communications equipment and operating systems.

Also the personnel (e.g. operators and system designers) and organizational procedures in the IS department were considered to be part of the infrastructure. More modern views use the notion of an infrastructure in a broader sense, increasingly referred to as IT-based infrastructure. This IT-based infrastructure has been drawn to attention from notably two directions, which will be discussed in the following two sections.

IT-Based Infrastructure and the Electronic Information Highway

First of all, the IT-based infrastructure has emerged as a focal point of national or even international IT policies. From this perspective, infrastructure investments are seen to provide the telecommunications-based 'information superhighway' that allows for the interconnection of and communication between individuals and organizations on a grand scale. The main influencing factors are the ever-decreasing costs of computerized data storage and the turbulent developments in telecommunications (particularly the worldwide computer network Internet or World Wide Web). In the United States this has come to be known as the National IT-based infrastructure initiative, with vice-president Al Gore as the main protagonist, while the European Union published the 'Bangemann' report (European Union, 1994). Several other countries initiated projects, e.g. the Dutch government published a report, called 'Action plan Electronic Highways' (Dutch Ministry of Economic Affairs, 1994). These developments can for the larger part be traced back to what has been called the emergence of the 'wired society' (Rockart, 1988). Questions surrounding the feasibility and societal impacts of such an infrastructure have also been the subject of considerable public debate. As Cairncross (1997) convincingly argues, the overarching and most profound effect of the emergence of a worldwide IT-based infrastructure will be 'the death of distance.' The development of 'raw' computing power and networking capabilities is only one of the driving forces, or what she calls 'roots of revolution', next to increased carrying capacity and development of mobility regarding telephony, and more channel capacity for television.

These developments often culminate in reflections regarding the 'information revolution' and the rise of the 'information economy' or 'information society.' It is expected that access to the right information might well be the right means for societal and economic control. Kling (1994), for instance, concludes:

> An information revolution is clearly underway. The exponential growth in computational capability per unit dollar will continue at least for the next several

decades. Communication bandwidth is undergoing simultaneous exponential growth. Connectivity among individuals, companies and nations is forming what some are calling cyberspace and virtual communities and new forums and formats for electronic publishing, communication and commerce. These combined trends are leading us into an Information Society in which wealth, power and freedom of action derive from access to, and effective use of, information.

IT-Based Infrastructure and IT Management

The notion of IT-based infrastructure has also gained prominence as a key element in the strategic management of information technology. The apparent trend in surveys of the most important IT management issues is the increased interest in infrastructure issues (see, for example, Niedermann *et al.*, 1991; Watson *et al.*, 1997). Many of the top 10 issues touch upon IT problems and management challenges with an infrastructural nature. From this corporate level perspective, it is advocated that organizations should direct their IT strategy primarily towards building and maintaining an IT-based infrastructure that provides the basic, shared facilities for IT deployment. The reason for this can to some extent be found in the rapid technological developments, which enable more intense and faster data exchange. More and more, however, it is realized that users are very well able to deploy IT in the most appropriate way to meet their own, specific needs. This is not only a consequence of an increasingly skilled and empowered workforce, but also of the trend to create flatter, less-hierarchical and agile organizations that can cope with the increasingly turbulent organizational environment.

Consequently, senior management does not need to take decisions regarding all possible IT issues, but can focus its attention and decisions on the corporate IT-based infrastructure, which is of strategic importance for the entire organization. This IT-based infrastructure has a much broader content and impact than the 'old' and well-known technical infrastructure. In addition to basic technological resources such as mainframe computers and operating systems, shared business applications, key databases and core knowledge are part of the IT-based infrastructure. Infrastructure resources enable improved communication and collaboration between:

- *Individual employees*, e.g. for electronic mail, task and meeting scheduling, group decision support or videoconferencing.
- *Functional departments* and *business units*, e.g. for just-in-time manufacturing, identifying cross-selling options or standardizing the customer interface.

- *Partners in the business chain*, e.g. for telemarketing and teleshopping of customers, shared business intelligence systems or integral supply chain management.

Several authorities consider such a business-driven view of the notion of infrastructure as a breakthrough in information systems thinking or even as a paradigm shift in IT management (see, for example, Tapscott and Caston, 1993; Applegate, 1994). From this perspective, strategic management of IT-based infrastructure serves as an alternative to the approach embedded in the more classical IT 'blueprint' planning methodologies. These methods generally are aimed at the firm-wide, top-down planning and prioritization of the IT applications portfolio (Martin, 1989; Ward et al., 1996a). In an infrastructure-based planning methodology not all possible IT investments are planned, but key decisions are made regarding a limited, yet strategic, set of infrastructure investments. Users of this infrastructure have substantial degrees of freedom in extending this infrastructure, taking their own business specific needs, priorities and value prospects into account.

Perspective of this Book

What both of the aforementioned perspectives of the IT-based infrastructure have in common is that they stress the increasingly shared, coordinated nature of today's IT investments. A comparison can be made with public infrastructures such as roads, public transport and facilities in the fields of education or social services. This book's perspective is on the IT-based infrastructure as a tool of strategic management, in line with the development discussed in the previous section. Modern enterprises face the challenge of how to build and exploit this IT-based infrastructure in the most successful and profitable way. However, there are very few structured and proven methods that give guidance in this process, which is bound up with many uncertainties. If firms truly want to use the notion of infrastructure to formulate better IT investment strategies, we first need to know more of the precise meaning, role and business implications of this infrastructure.

2.3 THE IT PRODUCTIVITY PARADOX

The present business focus on getting more value from IT-based infrastructure has to a large extent been triggered by, and become bound up in, the inconclusive findings of economic studies regarding the productivity effects of IT. These studies receive much attention in the more popular business press and frequently are the subject of intense public debate. This also influenced top management perceptions of IT value and has made many senior managers ask why they should commit themselves to continued IT investment. Lester Thurow of the Sloan School of Management (MIT) sketches the following situation (Thurow, 1991):

> Organizations have invested enormous sums of money in the hardware and software of the new electronic technologies. There are many examples of extraordinarily useful systems that now exist that could not have existed only a few years ago. Specific cases in which the new technologies have permitted huge increases in output or decreases in costs can be cited, but when it comes to the bottom line there is no clear evidence that these technologies have raised productivity or profitability.

The IT Price/Performance Ratio

The debate concerning IT productivity markedly contrasts with the conclusion that the improved price/performance ratio of IT has made it much more attractive to invest in IT. In 1991 it was estimated that a computer performance of 1 MIPS ('Million Instructions Per Second') that cost about US$1 million in 1980, will cost about US$2000 at the turn of the century (Scott Morton, 1991). Data storage capabilities have also developed in a similar, spectacular manner. The improvement factor of IBM computer memory in the years from 1955 to 1985 is about 100 000. According to Intel forecasts, by 2006 chips will be 1000 times more powerful and cost 10% of what they did in 1996 (Cairncross, 1997). The astonishing ongoing improvements in computing capacity is driven by 'Moore's law' (after Intel co-founder Gordon Moore): the number of integrated circuits of transistors that can be put on a silicon chip will double every 1.5 years.

Thus, it can at least be called surprising that the massive IT investments do not yield any clear, measurable advantages, notwithstanding the impressive price/performance improvements in recent years. This conclusion seems to go against the intuition and common sense of many of us (Landauer, 1995). Fitzgerald (1998) says in this respect:

> There are some people, who suggest that the benefits are so dramatic that it does not need to be proven, it is obvious simply by casual observation and that sophisticated studies would be manipulations to confirm what everybody intuitively already feels.

In spite of the puzzling figures, the seemingly paradoxical situation should as yet not be taken as too definitive: 'a shortfall of evidence is not necessarily evidence of a shortfall' (Brynjolfsson, 1993). A closer look at the IT productivity paradox reveals that this paradox has several dimensions. The following three subsections try to demystify this paradox somewhat by showing that the precise nature depends on whether the level under consideration is the macro-economic level, the industry level or the organizational level.

National Economy Level: Disappointing Productivity Growth

When speaking about the IT productivity paradox on a macro-economic level, one generally refers to the observation that a decrease in the productivity growth of developed countries coincides with a strong increase in IT investment spending levels (see, for example, Diebold Group, 1990). Since the 1960s productivity growth in Europe has, for instance, decreased from an average of 4.5% in the period 1960–1968, to 1.4% in the period 1990–1992; see Figure 2.1.[1] This coincided with an exponential growth of IT investments.

Thus, at first glance, the suggested 'information economy' does not seem to bring any clear financial returns. This conclusion should, however, be treated with care, at least for the time being. It proves to be very difficult to find a precise relation between IT investments and national economic productivity. This is due to several factors. It is, for

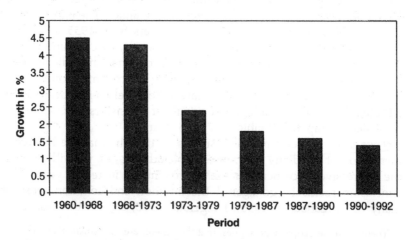

Figure 2.1   *Productivity growth in the European Union (after OECD, 1992)*

---

[1] In order to increase the readability of Figure 2.1, it gives average figures for each period. Consequently, the diagram visualizes a stronger decline than the growth rates. During the same period the estimated growth in the United States decreased from 2.6% to 0.7% and in Japan from 8.8% to 2.9% (Huppes, 1990; Pruijm, 1992).

instance, very difficult to isolate discrete IT effects from all factors that influence productivity growth. Also, the available figures are based upon very rough estimates and generally represent the mere measurable effects that easily can be translated into monetary terms. Therefore, it is better to speak of contradicting trends than of a given, well-specified negative relation between IT investments and productivity growth.

Industry Level: Disappointing Performance of Service Industries

Industry-level productivity figures suggest that the apparent decrease in productivity growth is largely due to a limited growth in productivity of office work in the service industry (see Figure 2.2 for representative figures from the United States).[2] In particular, the service industry has had the highest IT spending levels. Strassmann (1990) also claims that there is no positive correlation between IT spending and productivity or profitability in the service sector. Some studies seem to be more positive, varying from possible performance improvements in the insurance sector (Harris and Katz, 1989) to even a return on investments of 60% (Brynjolfsson and Hitt, 1993). Especially Roach has stressed the importance of improving the productivity of office work (see, for example, Roach, 1991). He also suggests that this may imply a drastic reconstruction of the service industry.

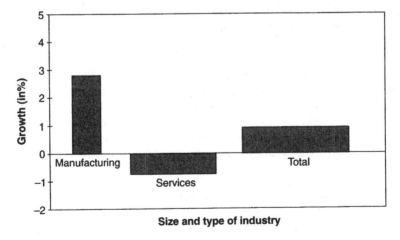

Figure 2.2 *Lagging productivity growth in the service industry (Pruijm, 1992)*

---

[2] Productivity figures from the manufacturing industry are not solely positive. One of the earliest productivity studies (Loveman, 1988) showed, for instance, no IT contribution to performance improvements in manufacturing.

Organizational Level: Possible IT Success

Notwithstanding the rather disappointing results from productivity studies at the national economy and industry levels, it has been shown that some organizations are able to gain large benefits with IT. Classical US-based examples of successful IT projects that received a lot of attention in the 1980s are, for instance: ASAP, the ordering and inventory system of American Hospital Supply; Economost, the order-processing system of the distribution firm McKeson; and Sabre, the American Airlines system for airplane bookings.

Apart from this rather anecdotal evidence, of which many examples can be found in the popular business press, several studies point out that there are substantial differences between organizations that deploy IT in a successful versus an unsuccessful way. Weill (1990) suggests this is due to differences in what he calls 'conversion effectiveness.' This notion refers to the organizational conditions regarding top management commitment, organizational experience, organizational satisfaction and political turbulence that are present in deploying IT in the most profitable way. It was shown that some firms were able to increase their performance, in contrast to others with about the same IT spending level, because they managed IT in a better way. Related to this is what Cron and Sobol (1983) speak of as the 'amplifier' effect; IT reinforces existing management practices, differentiating high performers from low performers. Landauer (1995) suggest that more user-centered computerization is the key factor for IT productivity. In this respect, Strassmann (1990) speaks of 'management value added'; or, in other words, the added value of well-performed management tasks.

In a broader sense 'good management' implies above all that all involved stakeholders continuously strive for the actual realization of investment goals. Explanations for the existence of the IT productivity paradox are increasingly sought in the realm of evaluation practices and management of the investment process. These generally come down to two suggestions (Brynjolfsson, 1993; Wilson, 1993):

1. Successful IT investment processes will lead only to differential advantages, at the cost of close competitors. On an aggregated industry or macro-economic level this has no effect on productivity growth. The overall benefits can also be transferred to the 'consumer surplus', indicating that consumers are the main beneficiaries of IT investments (Brynjolffson and Hitt, 1994).
2. A lack of relevant decision criteria makes it difficult for firms to find the right arguments to appraise IT investments and to justify expen-

ditures. Possible consequences of this are that IT is being used merely to create organizational slack (which negatively influences productivity) or that decision-makers keep their own interests and the political agenda in mind rather than the overall organizational interests.

Other explanations of the IT productivity paradox focus on the way productivity is being measured:

- There are essential measurement problems with respect to the used input and output measures and unreliable data. From an IT value perspective this means, for instance, that increased customer service and organizational flexibility through IT are difficult to measure. Also the organizational change efforts that accompany IT investments are difficult to capture.
- IT productivity is measured at the wrong moment: IT benefits are not measurable yet, but only after organizations have learned to cope with the impacts and dynamics of IT. David (1990) has shown that it has taken almost 40 years to get productivity gains from electric motors in factories, and it might be the case for IT and business performance.[3]

It can be concluded that the apparent commotion surrounding the IT productivity paradox is less alarming for managers than it might look at first glance. There are no definitive conclusions to be drawn yet, and both the problems with measurement techniques and questionable evaluation practices stand in the way of reaching a final conclusion. The doubt about the value of IT is likely to continue in the coming years; Strassmann (1997) still speaks of the 'squandered' computer. From a managerial perspective, it is however important to note that, for individual organizations, there are still many opportunities for an innovative and profitable IT deployment. Research findings suggest that a well-structured investment decision-making and evaluation process could contribute to this. 'Well-structured' means in this respect first of all that the ambitions of a project are articulated as much as possible, and that a well-focused effort is made to realize the ambitions of a project, in terms of both business value prospects and stakeholder processes.

---

[3] A related view is that IT investments will only deliver business value when they are accompanied with business process reengineering (BPR) activities, instead of merely automating existing processes; see, for example, Davenport (1993) and Martin (1995). This can be compared with the fact that people initially saw television as 'radio with pictures' and the automobile as a 'horseless carriage' (Cairncross, 1997).

After a review of important IT productivity Brynjolfsson and Hitt (1998) concluded that 'while the average returns to IT investment are solidly positive there is a huge variation across organizations; some have spent vast sums on IT with little benefit, while others have spent similar amounts with tremendous success.' Today, the critical question facing IT managers is not 'Does IT pay off?' but 'How can we best use computers?' Apart from the conclusion that investing in IT does bring benefits, this stresses the importance of good evaluation practices. The key differentiating factor between IT success or failure may well be the ability to evaluate the benefits and strategic potential versus the cost and risks of proposed investments, and having the right investment management processes in place, before, during and after project execution.

2.4   CORPORATE INVESTMENT DECISIONS

Organizational decision-making with regard to IT investments has been a recognized problem area for the last four decades; in fact from the start of computerization in business. Many studies of investment issues can be found, although these generally do not take the infrastructure nature of many of today's IT investments into account. Very diverse approaches can also be found, partly due to different views on how organizations behave or should behave (Stone, 1991). Already in 1961 the International Federation of Information Processing (IFIP) devoted its first conference to IT evaluation issues (Frielink, 1961). In 1968 Joslin wrote his book on computer selection and proposed several methods for investment evaluation (Joslin, 1968). Several other IFIP conferences were held in the following years (see, for example, Frielink, 1975; Bjorn-Andersen and Davis, 1988). Since 1994 the European Conference on IT Investment Evaluation has been held yearly (see, for example, Brown and Remenyi, 1994, 1995), bringing together researchers and practitioners.

From Cost Control to Benefits Management

Notwithstanding the many research efforts of the preceding years, IT investments are still considered as very difficult to evaluate and manage. Over the years the research focus has been shifting from cost and efficiency related issues to the more fundamental question of how to get maximum business value from IT. Rapid technological developments have continued for many years. The dynamic characteristics of IT differ so much from what economists are used to that concepts and techniques from both macro-economics and business economics are not really appropriate for a good understanding of the economic and financial impact of IT. Technological progress has proceeded much faster than the progress in IT investment evaluation techniques. Clemons (1991), however, draws attention to the importance of the evaluation process when he concludes: 'Of course, the most important question is determining *what* to build.'

Today, IT professionals are increasingly required to deliver IT benefits, in contrast to the early days of business computing in which they were only asked to complete IT projects within time and budget constraints. This might work in a period where investment merely had automating effects, which could easily be justified on the basis of efficiency improvements, but has become unacceptable today, when investments have 'informating' and 'transformating' effects (see Zuboff, 1988) that go beyond efficiency. Therefore, benefits management of IT-based infrastructure should be the prime concern, and not merely cost control. Table 2.1 gives, building on the work of Bolwijn and Kumpe (1990), a historical overview of the range of business performance criteria that IT is expected to support. On the price-driven markets of 1960s, IT was mainly used to increase efficiency. Over the last three decades, as a consequence of changing market demands, IT has additionally been used to improve the quality, flexibility and innovative ability of organizations.

Organizations generally consider it difficult to take the right investment decisions concerning IT-based infrastructure, particularly how to evaluate the advantages, disadvantages and risks of proposed investments. The problems with measuring the possible contribution to the business are nowadays seen as one of the major barriers to successful IT strategy formation (Wilson, 1991). The way in which organizations appraise, control and measure their IT investments raises many questions. Around 50% of organizations do not use formal evaluation

Decade	Market demands	Ideal firm	IT performance criteria
1960s	price	the efficient firm	efficiency
1970s	price, quality	the quality firm	efficiency + quality
1980s	price, quality, choice/delivery time	the flexible firm	efficiency + quality + flexibility
1990s and beyond	price, quality, choice/delivery time, uniqueness	the innovating firm	efficiency + quality + flexibility + innovative ability

Table 2.1   *Market demands, firm goals and IT performance criteria (adapted from Bolwijn and Kumpe, 1990)*

procedures (Hochstrasser and Griffiths, 1990; Bacon, 1992). *Ad hoc* arguments or even indifference seem to dominate current decision-making practices (Deitz and Renkema, 1995). If attempts are made to quantify the business impacts of IT projects, the use of financial calculations is almost ritualistic (Currie, 1989; Symons, 1990). In this respect it is useful to be reminded of what Ackoff (quoted in Aken, 1994b) calls the 'corporate raindances' of strategic decision-making: much 'noise and showing-off', but highly uncertain effects on the weather. Although many of the competitive advantage applications of the 1980s are known for bypassing the standard management approval process, and are based more on 'strategic insight' (Earl and Runge, 1987), an act of faith attitude towards investments will certainly give no adequate guarantees of successful infrastructure deployment. This has become increasingly true today, when the risk of investing in the wrong business areas, processes and projects is too great, and when firms have to compete on tight margins and distinctive competencies. More-over, many senior executives who have been confronted with disappointing project track records and pay-off simply enforce scrutiny and tight management control of major infrastructure projects. Strategic decisions regarding IT-based infrastructure require specific senior management attention for three main reasons (Oosterhaven, 1990):

- for *social* reasons, since many individual users will have to change their behavior if the infrastructure is changed;
- for *technological* reasons, since many local IT applications have to be changed if the infrastructure is changed;
- for *economic* reasons, because of the difficulties with quantifying business benefits and the long-term nature of these benefits.

Why is Investment Evaluation Critical?

Until recently, investment projects were often justified on the basis of technology-driven arguments, which themselves were in many cases influenced, or even dictated, by supplier promises or future prospects. Nowadays, decision-makers look for business-driven arguments, which give more concrete and robust evidence of how proposed investments can really improve their business. The added value of investments should be evidenced by achieving business goals in an improved and more successful way, e.g. cheaper, faster, easier or with higher quality. There are four major reasons why investment evaluation with respect to IT-based infrastructure is important to organizations (see Table 2.2).

Investment evaluation: why critical?	Investment evaluation: why complex?
• Preventing misallocation of financial resources	• Benefits are difficult to assess, measure and manage
• Improving business performance	• Costs are high and difficult to predict
• Creating a shared investment vision and capturing learning opportunities	• Large uncertainties and major risks
• Profitable exploitation of IT-based infrastructure	• Communication problems and stakeholder politics

Table 2.2   Importance and difficulties of investment evaluation

Preventing Misallocation of Financial Resources

Investments in IT-based infrastructure constitute a major part of the available financial resources of modern firms. Therefore, the costs of misallocating these resources have become very high. When capital rationing is employed, it is essential to set the right priorities between competing projects. Scarce funds can also be spent on other business opportunities with more guarantees of future pay-off. Without good grounds to invest in new project initiatives, investment decision-making will be reduced to what Shank and Govindarajan (1992) refer to as 'technology roulette: place your bet, spin the wheel, and hope!' Given the high spending levels of today, no organization can permit itself to be in such an uncertain or even risky situation.

Improving Business Performance

Taking the right infrastructure investment decisions has an important impact on future corporate strategies and business performance. Investments not only have financial consequences, but also influence, for example, the structure, culture, working conditions and style of management of organizations (Harrington, 1991b; Glasson *et al.*, 1994). With the permeation of IT throughout the entire organization, we have witnessed the emergence of what Zuboff (1988) coined the 'informated organization.' The IT-based infrastructure has become an inextricable part of contemporary business operations, and its role in shaping future strategies, processes and thus business performance is likely to increase. In this situation it is essential to take well-founded and well-motivated investment decisions concerning the IT-based infrastructure that enables business improvements.

Creating a Shared Investment Vision and Capturing Learning Experiences

All stakeholders involved in project initiation and justification will have an—often implicit—personal assessment of the desirability and expected business value of an investment. By paying explicit attention to investment evaluation and by speaking out at these different assessments, an organization will better be able to create a shared vision on what is considered to be advantageous or harmful to its future existence. This in turn offers the opportunity for mutual commitment to the successful business outcome of an investment and to learn from collective experiences. These learning experiences provide important input for establishing an organizational process of continuous improvement.

Profitable Exploitation of IT-Based Infrastructure

Last but not least: recent research findings suggest that good evaluation and decision-making practices might well contribute to the ultimate value to be gained from investments (see, for example, Weill and Olsen, 1989; Willcocks, 1994). It is therefore likely that firms who better assess what they expect from their infrastructure deployment and also manage and control investments from this perspective will be more successful than others who do not have formal evaluation procedures in place.

Why is Investment Evaluation Difficult?

Although the importance of implementing a well structured and explicit investment evaluation process seems evident, only a few organizations manage to do so. Four major difficulties can be identified (see also Table 2.2).

Benefits are Difficult to Assess, Measure and Manage

Organizations have found it difficult to appraise all possible advantages of their IT-based infrastructure projects. Increasingly these investments are not targeted at achieving mere cost savings, which often can be translated into financial terms. From planned 'second-order' business improvements (Farbey *et al.*, 1993), such as increased customer service or improved product quality, it has proved to be almost impossible to calculate a direct pay-back period, let alone the return on investment (ROI). Nonetheless, these generally are the techniques used in practice to justify most IT investments, although the more advanced capital investment appraisal techniques are not used extensively (see, for example, Yan Tam, 1992; Ballantine *et al.*, 1994). The historical legitimacy of financial calculations makes it difficult to systematically use non-financial valuations. It is also very difficult to adequately assess whether the potential outcomes of investments have indeed been realized. This requires the use of performance indicators that take into account the chiefly qualitative character of investment goals.

Infrastructure investments are particularly hard to justify because of largely indirect, long-term business benefits (see, for example, Parker *et al.*, 1988; Hogbin and Thomas, 1994). Coleman and Jamieson (1994) articulate this as: 'infrastructure projects are therefore "enabling the enabler" and are thus one step further away from the cold realities of profit generation.' What is characteristic of infrastructure investments is that they constitute the long-term foundation of successful local applications of end-users of the IT-based infrastructure. This rather complicates investment planning and project evaluation. On top of this, business benefits of infrastructure are generally based upon synergy arising from the shared exploitation of common facilitates. Potential synergy is only realized and thus only increases if several users make use of the infrastructure ('network externalities'). This requires clear business choices for stable, technology proven investments, which guarantee long-term use.

Costs are High and Difficult to Predict

Apart form difficulties on the benefits side, the costs of proposed infrastructure projects are also not easy to assess. Investment costs are usually high and cost dynamics cause them to be rather unpredictable. Despite the many available methods and automated tools for cost estimation, keeping a project between budget constraints often remains wishful thinking. On top of this, the total costs of a project are often underestimated at the time of the initial project proposal. Sometimes this is due to the fact that someone would like to see the project approved; but this can also be due to a lack of attention to full life-cycle costs (the 'total cost of ownership'). Maintenance of existing infrastructure facilities generally covers a substantial part of total expenditures (Swanson and Beath, 1989). Keen (1991) estimates that these might well be 2.5 times the development costs of IT projects. Also, firms tend to forget that investments engender all kinds of side-effects. Indirect organizational costs emanate from, for instance, the integration of new working methods into existing practices and from learning to cope with new, innovative technologies.

Infrastructure investments also exploit the phenomenon that the costs of an infrastructure facility or service generally decrease with intensified use (economies of scale) and with use for several user purposes (economies of scope). Infrastructure costs have to be financed and preferably recovered in collaboration between several involved units or departments. A complicating factor in this respect is that costs are not necessarily incurred at the same place where this infrastructure is most beneficial. If discussions get a too political nature, this may severely jeopardize the success of an investment.

Large Uncertainties and Major Risks

The difficulties with the evaluation of benefits and costs of investments already show that almost every investment is accompanied by substantial uncertainties. Both the possible advantages and disadvantages of proposed investments move between wide margins. These uncertainties entail a degree of risk for achieving the intended investment outcomes, turning investments often into 'high-risk/high-reward' projects. Project risks can be broken down into several risk categories. Resistance to change is, for instance, a risk factor that should be taken into account when implementing a new type of infrastructure. An innovative type of technology may give technical problems, which have not been experienced before. Also there is the risk that an organization reaches its project ambitions, but still is outperformed by its main competitors. Dealing with risk means that one tries to recognize them and, if possible, tries to manage them. Also there is a need to have a balanced portfolio of IT investments in terms of risks and rewards in place. Both things are, however, not easy to do.

Communication Problems and Stakeholder Politics

A final issue that deserves special attention concerns the organizational alignment between all stakeholders involved with investment evaluation. Often communication problems arise from differences in the background knowledge and expertise of the different people working on a project (e.g. line management, project management, users, IT professionals and financial executives). Consequently, it is not always clear whether everyone has the same judgment concerning relevant costs, benefits and risks, and therefore whether the investment is a good thing to do. This necessitates special attention to the use of clear and unambiguous terminology in the evaluation process. Conflicting interests might also complicate the cooperation between involved stakeholders. Every decision is usually made against the background of different intentions, wishes and preferences of different parties (Pfeffer, 1981; Mintzberg, 1983b). Depending on the precise constellation of interests with respect to an investment, decision-making will always have a political nature to some extent.

2.5 CONCLUSIONS

This chapter has discussed the changing nature and focus of business investments in IT-based infrastructure. This IT-based infrastructure has become much more than a collection of mere technical equipment and tools. It is nowadays a strategic asset which, if deployed appropriately, can be used to improve business operations and profitability. Well-directed management of IT-based infrastructure also allows senior executives to focus on those issues that are of strategic importance for the entire organization, instead of taking decisions on all of the many IT issues. The IT productivity paradox lies at the heart of the apparent difficulties in demonstrating IT value and productivity. This has prompted the need for appropriate benefits management of IT-based infrastructure, instead of only trying to keep projects within time and budget constraints, without addressing the business contribution of projects. This productivity paradox does not, however, stand in the way of—and in fact reinforces the need for—a well-articulated and managed investment appraisal process. This is important to prevent misallocation of limited funds, to be able to improve business performance, to create a shared investment vision, to capture learning opportunities, and to really profit from IT-based infrastructure. Difficulties that will have to be overcome lie in the areas of benefits assessment and management, cost analysis, risk management and, last but not least, stakeholder communications and organizational politics.

Part II
The New Digital Infrastructure

3
Strategic Dimensions of IT-Based Infrastructure

3.1 INTRODUCTION

As argued in the previous chapter, the notion of an infrastructure is not totally new to corporate management of IT, but has undergone important changes in terms of its business role and managerial implications. As such it has become 'the new infrastructure' (Weill and Broadbent, 1998) for organizations, exploiting the possibilities of today's digital technologies. This chapter explores these changes in more detail by combining practical insights gained in case studies and important insights from the business-oriented IT literature. Several literature sources will be discussed, which were found particularly useful for illustrating the most important infrastructure changes in managerial and broadly applicable terms. Building on this, the next chapter will offer a more precise definition and detailed view of IT-based infrastructure and how this notion can be translated into more operational terms. Together, this and the following chapter form Part II of this book, which centers around the role and meaning of the notion of an IT-based infrastructure for successful IT deployment in organizations. The focus of the remaining parts of the book is more on the strategic decision-making and investment issues surrounding this infrastructure. First, Section 3.2 gives the results of a number of interviews that were held with practitioners, and in which the meaning of the notion of IT-based infrastructure was discussed. The following sections all review important insights from the literature. Section 3.3 examines the development of the traditional view of a 'technical infrastructure' towards the more modern view of an 'IT-based infrastructure.' This section also takes a brief look at what can be learned from an analogy with public infrastructures. Subsequently, Section 3.4 looks deeper into the main business and IT factors surrounding the new role of IT-based infrastructure, thereby discussing several of the more modern views. Finally, the conclusions of this chapter are given in Section 3.5.

3.2   PRACTITIONERS' VIEWS ON THE MEANING OF INFRASTRUCTURE

This section presents the results of a survey of empirical views of the notion IT-based infrastructure. Survey data were collected by interviewing several employees from the case study organizations discussed in Chapter 1, all of whom were responsible for a specific part of the IT-based infrastructure. Two issues were addressed: the meaning of the notion of an IT-based infrastructure and the importance of investments in this infrastructure. The interviewees' view of the purpose of investing in an IT-based infrastructure will be discussed in Chapter 9.

With respect to the meaning of the notion of infrastructure, both the perceptions regarding this notion and an appropriate definition of this notion were discussed. The perception of the notion of IT-based infrastructure was expressed in several different ways. Some interviewees preferred a rather broad description, others mentioned a number of components which they definitely considered to be infrastructure. Also sometimes there was a focus on a certain part of the infrastructure (e.g. shared data definitions, databases or master data) and other parts were seen in relation to this. A number of general conclusions can be drawn:

1. The emphasis on the nature of infrastructure flows in two main directions:
    *   infrastructure as a coherent system of all organizational IT resources;
    *   infrastructure as a system of technological facilities, with specific references made to developments in the fields of networks and telecommunications.
    The respondents working in a centralized IT department slightly preferred the second line of thought.
2. An element, which was considered of increasing importance, was the improved organizational communication enabled by the IT-based infrastructure. This improved communication had its impact both internally (between employees and internal departments) and externally (linking with customers, suppliers, industry partners).

3. It was emphasized that an IT-based infrastructure should be structured according to the needs of its customers, i.e. the end-users of infrastructure-based IT systems. Business needs, not technology should be the driving force.

4. Several respondents pointed out that what might best be called 'wider organizational arrangements' are of great importance to the IT-based infrastructure. Examples mentioned are data standards and data procedures, but also an explicit senior management vision of the role of the infrastructure in business.

5. Within the group of interviewees there seemed to be no fundamental differences regarding the meaning of the notion of IT-based infrastructure. The discrepancies found were in fact due to different accentuation, and could generally be traced back to differences in background and formal position in the organization.

3.3 THE RISE OF IT-BASED INFRASTRUCTURE

Although the importance of well-directed investments in an IT-based infrastructure is becoming increasingly clear, there is very little agreement in the business-oriented IT literature concerning the precise meaning of this infrastructure. In the IT management literature the notion of infrastructure is used in a variety of meanings usually without defining it and delineating it very narrowly. The following citations give a good illustration of some of the different perspectives taken:

- 'Investments in IS infrastructure are built around the central precepts of corporate-wide networks, central data collections, common business practices, common application systems, and standardized hardware, operating systems, and databases' (Allen and Boynton, 1991, p. 440).
- 'It is becoming increasingly clear that the successful exploitation of IT stems from a co-alignment between the strategic context and the IT infrastructure of a business' (Venkatraman, 1991, p. 151).
- 'That is why a learning information infrastructure—a human/technology partnership that enables global collaboration and knowledge leveraging—is at the core of every organization's future success and survival' (Brown and Watts, 1992, p. 245).
- 'The central IS function will be increasingly responsible for managing the infrastructure for decentralized or dispersed computing, that includes telecommunications, office systems, software and hardware' (Clark, 1992, p. 63).

- 'IT infrastructure is the base foundation of IT capability in the form of reliable services shared throughout the firm and (usually) provided by the IS function' (Weill *et al.*, 1996, p. 365).

Traditional Views: 'Technical Infrastructure'

In traditional views an infrastructure is considered to contain all the technically enabling IT facilities that are needed for the use of IT-based systems in the end-user environment. This is generally referred to as the 'technical infrastructure' or the 'infrastructure of technological facilities.' Relevant elements to be included are, for instance, 'technological' facilities such as hardware equipment for data operations (e.g. mainframe computers, minicomputers, host computers, and servers); communication devices and basic systems software (e.g. connectors, routers, operating systems, and interconnectivity software). Originally, this system of technological facilities was often centrally organized in the specialized IT unit (the 'computing center' or 'data center'). Also the personnel operating and using the technological facilities (e.g. system operators and system development specialists) and organizational procedures were considered to be infrastructure in this traditional view. Usually, the combination of technology components, personnel and organizational procedures results in the delivery of a relatively stable set of services (Weill and Broadbent, 1998). It is from this essentially technological viewpoint that the notion of infrastructure has entered the information systems discipline and the practice of IT management. For many, it still has a rather technological connotation.

Modern Views: 'IT-Based Infrastructure'

In more modern views, infrastructure is considered to include all basic, shared IT provisions that have long-term availability for the end-user of IT. An IT-based infrastructure in this view is seen as a tool of (senior) management, to guide the appropriate design of a comprehensive, organization-wide system of IT resources (Bemelmans, 1994; Berg and Renkema, 1994). Although their view still is rather technology-driven, McKay and Brockway (1989) define infrastructure therefore as 'the enabling foundation of shared information technology capabilities upon which business depends.' Infrastructure in this sense has become a real business term, and has left the purely technological domain, dominated by specialist views. The modern view looks at infrastructure from a much broader perspective than the merely technological perspective of the traditional view. As Ross *et al.* (1996) argue, a value-driven IT-based infrastructure can be thought of as being a combination of three interdependent IT assets and can therefore be a source of competitive advantage:

- The *human* asset: highly performing IT professionals who have technical skills, business understanding, and a problem-solving orientation.
- The *technology* asset: a well-defined technology architecture and sharable platforms and databases.
- The *relationship* asset: shared risk and responsibility between IT and the business.

Often a connection is made with developments in the realm of the information superhighway and the rise of the 'information economy.' Darnton and Giacoletto (1992) express this as follows:

> The previous major paradigm shift to an industrial economy required the development of massive manufacturing infrastructure. Similarly, a paradigm shift to an information economy requires the development of a massive information infrastructure which must be designed and constructed, that is architected, carefully.

The development of the Internet, the World Wide Web and more recently of Intranets and Extranets, have increased senior executives' interest in issues that relate to building and exploiting their infrastructure for IT. Many publications have recently covered this from a business perspective, some in the context of the emerging possibilities for 'electronic commerce' (see, for example, Hagel and Armstrong, 1997; Schwartz, 1997).

Although technological developments, be it Internet technology based or not, cannot be ignored, it is important to illuminate the overall strategic consequence of the rise of a corporate IT-based infrastructure. For senior managers the most prominent consequence of this shift to a business-based, IT-based infrastructure is that their firm's IT deployment should be integrated with their business structure and overall strategy. The central premise of this view is that a firm should manage the linkages between its business strategy and IT strategy on the one hand and its business infrastructure and IT-based infrastructure on the other hand. The process by which this is done has in recent years become known as the 'strategic alignment' process (Scott Morton, 1991; Henderson *et al.*, 1996; Luftman, 1996). Figure 3.1 gives a visual representation of this 'strategic alignment model' in basic terms. 'Functional integration' stands for aligning the business and IT domain, while 'strategic fit' stands for aligning external strategies with internal structures.

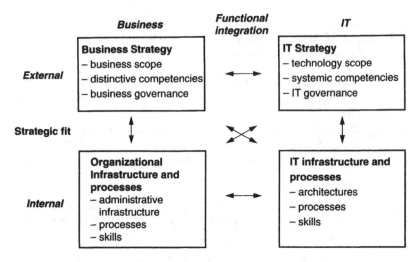

Figure 3.1   The 'strategic alignment' model (from Henderson and Venkatraman, 1993)

Characteristics of IT-Based Infrastructure

As discussed previously, the IT-based infrastructure as suggested here has much more content and range than the well-known 'technical infrastructure.' Next to technological facilities, for instance shared or standardized application systems, databases and knowledge bases are considered to be part of the IT-based infrastructure. The characteristics of IT-based infrastructure can be described in terms of its components, distinctive features and quality standards (see Figure 3.2).

Truijens *et al.* (1990) introduce the following division into infrastructure components:

- The *computer configurations infrastructure* (hardware platforms and related software, e.g. operating software, system software).
- The *communications infrastructure* (all facilities for electronic communication and related communication standards, e.g. protocols).
- The *data infrastructure* (common databases, data definitions and procedures).
- The *applications infrastructure* (shared and standardized IT systems).
- The *organizational infrastructure* (all organizational procedures to plan, build and use the IT-based infrastructure).

Within this modern view several features are seen as being characteristic of IT-based infrastructure (elaborating on Maes, 1990):

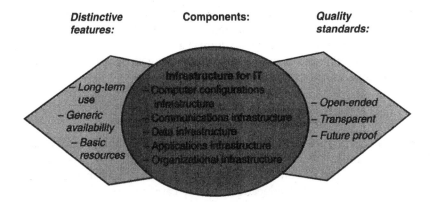

Figure 3.2   *Characteristics of IT-based infrastructure*

- *Long-term use*: this characteristic ensues from the fact that it is not very wise to continuously change IT provisions that are used by many different users, that are located on different business locations and often part of different organizations.
- *Generic availability*: infrastructure IT resources have a generic availability both in terms of their breadth (crossing organizational and departmental boundaries) and in terms of their depth (direct responsiveness, large-scale availability).
- *Basic resources*: the resources of the IT-based infrastructure cover the basic business operations of organizations. Generally supporting systems are built on and 'plug into' this infrastructure, and by doing so add to the total IT structure of a firm.

These characteristics also imply three basic quality standards of information infrastructure (also elaborating on Maes, 1990):

- *Open-ended*: it should be possible to extend the capacity of the infrastructure easily and without limitations in order to cope with increasing user demands. These demands are generally unknown at the time of creating an infrastructure, which necessitates design and technology choices that account for future flexibility.
- *Transparent*: the internal complexity—which undoubtedly is there—should remain invisible to the user. An important element of this is a user-friendly man–machine interface, which hides all the modules and elements of the infrastructure when using the infrastructure 'anywhere, anytime, and anyhow.'
- *Future proof*: the infrastructure should allow for new business opportunities and new technologies to be easily fitted into the

infrastructure. This is extremely difficult since a compromise between stability and flexibility is needed. Falling short on this compromise will lead to an infrastructure that is either to rigid (new developments are slowed down instead of stimulated) or to unstable to guarantee a permanent use.

Learning from Public Infrastructure

From a societal perspective, the notion of infrastructure is well known in the context of the total system of transport facilities of a country or region. Also, the notion of infrastructure has been used in the context of public facilities for education, health care and social security for example. During the 1990s there has been much public debate concerning the infrastructure for technological 'know-how' (increasingly referred to as the 'knowledge infrastructure'). The term infrastructure originates from the military domain, where it was used to refer to all facilities for the transport of military equipment and armed forces. In contemporary parlance, infrastructure is considered to include all physical facilities for the transport of substances, energy, goods, persons, and information (Sanders, 1994). Next to more obvious elements, such as roads, railroads, and seaways, this also covers elements such as cables, wires, power stations, airports, harbors, and stations. Several reasons can be identified to extend the infrastructure for transport (Sanders, 1994):

- To enable new types of transport, which was done, for instance, when railways were built to replace carriages and vessels.
- To increase the capacity of existing transport needs, e.g. when building a second bridge on a place with too much traffic congestion.
- To displace or relieve traffic streams, e.g. through creating a ring road surrounding a village or city.
- To influence the choice of transport, e.g. by building a dedicated railway for the transport of freight materials that would otherwise be transported by road (which will actually be done in the Netherlands by building the so-called 'Betuwe line').
- To stimulate the economic development of a specific region, e.g. by building highways to remote areas.

The main thrust behind the creation of public infrastructure is that the users of this infrastructure have several advantages which would be lost if there were no infrastructure. In many cases it would, for instance, simply be too expensive if every potential user were to create his or her own infrastructure. Essentially, the common interest of all users would not be addressed if everyone strove to optimize his or her own infrastructure.

In public choice theory this is known when considering the choice between public versus private facilities. If the total of external effects of individual decisions (i.e. the negative effects on other individuals) regarding a certain facility are considered to be harmful, it is wise to make a facility part of the public infrastructure (see, for example, Samuelson and Nordhaus, 1985).

Since an infrastructure serves common interests, individual users do not always recognize the advantages of infrastructure as such. Some public infrastructures, for instance, are created to establish a more just income distribution or to prevent a polluted environment. Creating the right public infrastructure also stimulates private investment. Infrastructure investments contribute to economic success in several ways; reviews of their contribution show that (see McKay and Brockway, 1989; Weill, 1993):

- There is a strong correlation between investment in public infrastructure and the overall productivity of a country.
- Infrastructure investments increase private investments, and are likely to improve the return on private investments. In turn, private investments may again stimulate investments in public infrastructure, e.g. through higher tax revenues.
- Investments in a regional public infrastructure increase the growth of a region as measured by personal income, and regions are likely to have an improved competitive position if they have a good infrastructure, e.g. through attracting new businesses. They increase manufacturing output in metropolitan areas, and have a greater impact on net capital formation in distressed areas than in growing cities.

It can be concluded that, given the characteristics of public infrastructure, there are important lessons to be learnt for managing and capitalizing on corporate IT-based infrastructure. A closer look at both infrastructures shows that there are important similarities (based on Weill *et al.*, 1996):

- Both infrastructures are generally governed by some type of central agency, and funded by some form of taxation. The infrastructure provided by this agency provides some sort of essential service that users would generally not be motivated or able to provide.

- Both infrastructures enable user-level business activities, which without the infrastructure would not be viable or would underperform.
- Both infrastructures generally have to be created without prior knowledge of all relevant future business activities, which places high demands on the flexibility of the infrastructure.
- Deciding on the size of the infrastructure is matter of balance; not enough infrastructure may lead to the duplication of facilities, incompatibilities and a suboptimal use of resources; too much infrastructure may however discourage user investments.

3.4   THE NEW ROLE OF IT-BASED INFRASTRUCTURE

Notwithstanding the developments sketched in the previous section, the modern view of IT-based infrastructure can hardly be called a homogeneous view. The section gives a further illustration of this observation by examining a number of factors driving the present interest in the role and implications of the notion of IT-based infrastructure. These factors are at the heart of the present business opinion that contemporary IT investments increasingly influence directly the basic infrastructure for IT, and indirectly current business operations and future business strategies. Figure 3.3 sketches this by identifying the main driving business and IT factors.

New Organizational Forms

Driven by increased time-based competition, organizational dynamics, demanding customers and the need for flexible, agile business structures, we have witnessed the rise of new organizational forms for division and coordination of work activities (see, for an overview, Drucker, 1988; Handy, 1994). The traditional organizational hierarchy is replaced by 'flat' organizational designs, often referred to as 'net-

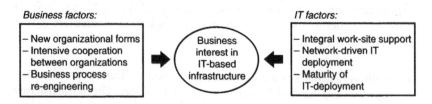

Figure 3.3   Business and IT factors driving the interest in infrastructure issues

worked organizations.' Popular themes in this respect are, for instance, decentralization, empowerment, and internal entrepreneurship. A common theme is the emergence of organizations consisting of units that are to a large degree autonomous in their management, strategy formulation and business operations. The different units also depend upon each other within a larger, overall organizational structure. The driver, however, is to have responsibilities and resources at the lowest organizational level possible; in other words, with the employees that fulfill market needs directly, and engage in and manage client contacts themselves. This type of organization requires a culture in which employees take many initiatives in order to meet the performance targets that were agreed upon collectively. This is taking place without many rules and policies or much management intervention.

The degree of interdependence of the semi-autonomous organizational units is reflected in the extent to which use is made of shared facilities, among which possibly the most important is the IT-based infrastructure. This infrastructure encourages and supports organizational coherence, and preserves common interests, resources, strategies and plans. Oosterhaven (1994) suggests that this infrastructure is a result of the 'organizing principles' (agreements regarding control and coordination) and the 'business cohesion' (the division of the contributions of the different units). These two elements in turn are the result of the overall business strategy.

Intensive Cooperation Between Organizations

In conjunction with the trend to break down traditional hierarchies within organizations, firms have also been refocusing their strategy on the elements they want to excel in ('back to core business'). As a consequence of this trend there has been increased cooperation between organizations in areas that they do not consider to be their respective core business. Successful management and control of all these organizational collaborations requires an adequate IT-based infrastructure. In recent years this has been accelerated by the improved opportunities to share data and to integrate IT systems in and between organizations. The deployment of Web technologies for using the Internet and related Intranet/Extranet applications has certainly contributed to this. In manufacturing industries, Enterprise Resource Planning systems have made it possible to bypass traditional intermediaries and to send orders, quotations, invoices, etc. directly to suppliers and customers. Financial services firms can interact directly with their customers, e.g. for electronic payments, equity dealing, insurance quotations, claim processing, etc. without the need for specialized agents or offices. Similar examples can be found in, for example, the areas of holidays, real estate and publishing.

Reengineering of Business Processes

Investments in IT-based infrastructure are increasingly being undertaken as part of what has become known as business process reengineering (BPR) exercises (Renkema and Dolan, 1995).[1] BPR has been receiving a lot of interest in the business and academic press, basically since it initially was considered as the final business trend to move the search for IT business value one step forward, and to make the claims for competitive advantage from IT much more plausible. Although the concept seems to have lost its sharp edges over the last few years, and there are still many different views on what BPR is or should be. The common elements generally are (Grover *et al.*, 1993; Hammer and Stanton, 1995):

- The rethinking and restructuring of business processes, focusing on the end-to-end transfer of a client need to a product or service.
- The typical employment of infrastructure-type IT as an enabler, capturing opportunities for information sharing and for bypassing the constraints of time and place.
- The attempts to achieve dramatic improvements in operational performance (e.g. in costs, quality of outcomes, throughput and delivery times, and customer satisfaction), in contrast to the more incremental approach of earlier quality improvement programs.

Table 3.1 gives an overview of what can be seen as the main characteristics of traditional versus reengineered organizations.

In order to gain a more in-depth insight into the characteristics of different BPR approaches, Jones (1994) distinguishes between five dimensions of BPR, depending on the scope of the main processes, namely the scale of change, the means of achieving change, the source of the change model, and the role of IT. These dimensions can be used to characterize eight main BPR schools; for a further review see the Appendix to this chapter.

It can be concluded that although the currently available BPR approaches still exhibit a large variety on several dimensions, the key role of IT-based infrastructure seems to be as a binding element.

---

[1] The precise name differs from author to author; BPR has, for instance, also been called Business Engineering (Meel *et al.*, 1994), Process Innovation (Davenport, 1993) and Core Process Redesign (Kaplan and Murdock, 1991).

Traditional organization	Reengineered organization
• Departmental, hierarchical structure	• Client-driven organization, built around core processes
• Restraining, control-oriented style of management	• Coaching and facilitating management
• Functional responsibilities of employees, focusing on (parts of) a task	• Empowered employees with resultant accountabilities for clear 'start-to-end' process steps
• IT used to support and automate manual or mechanized tasks	• IT used as enabler to reengineer new processes from scratch
• Fragmented IT-based infrastructure with 'islands of automation' and lack of interconnectivity	• Solid, process-driven IT-based infrastructure, with maximum generic functionality

Table 3.1   Differences between the 'traditional' and the 'reengineered' organization

By embarking on BPR programs, organizations will almost always be confronted with the need to create a long-term enabling infrastructure for IT. As such, a BPR program will try to exploit the 'recursive relationship' between IT and business processes (Davenport and Short, 1990; Davenport, 1993). In order to really be able to capitalize on the potential of modern IT to innovate business processes, firms should inevitably be prepared to make long-term commitments to creating and funding a shared IT-based infrastructure. This will become even more true today, since the need for continuous business innovation extends the boundaries of single organizations, and has introduced supply chain management, electronic commerce and networked organizations as the new corporate paradigms.

Integral Work-Site Support

In contrast to the early days of business IT deployment is no longer the sole domain of a centrally coordinated IT unit. Modern enterprises increasingly decentralize all or part of their IT facilities into their organization. In accordance with the trend of flat organizational designs, organizational units, departments and even individual work sites are given the opportunity to apply and develop IT support to their own specific, local interests. In order to be able to do this there generally is a need for a set of standardized, commonly used, and therefore infrastructural tools and facilities. Examples are for instance:

- Communication facilities, e.g. backbone network, messaging and e-mail facilities, and Intranet/Internet access facilities.
- Facilities for overall security and recovery, and standard contingency plans.
- Modern programming languages and tools for computer-aided software engineering (CASE), e.g. C++, Visual Basic or Java.
- Standard templates software packages which can easily be adapted to local circumstances (e.g. for ERP packages such as Baan, SAP, and Peoplesoft).
- Reusable software components for tailor-made software development (component libraries).
- Standardized systems and data definitions for key applications (e.g. for financial reporting, intra-organizational transactions, pricing or general office support) and common data (e.g. for products, services, key accounts, suppliers, or customers).

An important consequence of this trend is that the traditional division between 'applications' versus 'infrastructure' is not as relevant as it used to be. CSC Index (1993) has discussed extensively how the traditional application-based use of information systems has undergone important changes. Their view is that building an infrastructure essentially means deploying IT functionality where possible as a shared facility: 'the "application" is really the way that a user deploys the infrastructure, rather than a substantial piece of software.' This development leads to a type of work-site support in which a user is connected, through a transparent user–machine interface, with an infrastructure with integrated facilities, e.g. for information retrieval, calculations and communications (Gunton, 1989). Figure 3.4, elaborating on earlier work of Cullen (1995), sketches a picture of what a work site with these kinds of support facilities may look like. A work site like this is not necessarily based in a traditional office, but can also, for the whole or in parts, be available at home, accessible from other places or through mobile access. The related infrastructure coordinates the work activities of highly skilled employees (increasingly referred to as 'knowledge workers'), that operate in a relatively autonomous manner. This way the 'protective walls' (Rodden *et al.*, 1992) that were built between end-users in the past are broken down.

Telecommunications and Network-Enabled IT Deployment

Organizational control based on increased autonomy, increased co-operation between organizations, and integral work-site support, have meant that good communications and information exchange

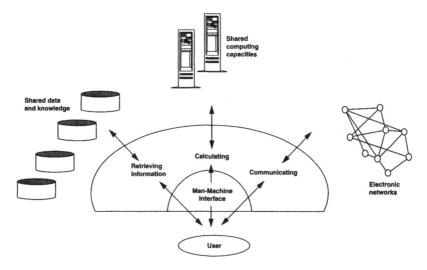

Figure 3.4 *A model of integral work-site support (after Cullen, 1995)*

have increased in importance. In turn, rapid developments in the field of telecommunications, electronic data interchange, chipcards/smart-cards, distributed databases and networks, including Intranets, Extranets and the Internet, have enabled work activities that rely on intensive communications, often bypassing time and place constraints. From the perspective of an individual organization, this has greatly changed the shape of the IT function with its traditional 'technical infrastructure' of equipment and telecommunications facilities. From centralized, monolithic batch processing of administrative tasks of the early days of business computing, the IT function has nowadays become responsible for facilitating a communication-oriented infra-structure, including rapidly evolving technologies, e.g. for personal and groupware computing, real-time processing, distributed database management and application interconnectivity.

In recent years, organizations have in fact had no other choice than to adopt the 'client/server' architecture for computing. In this architec-ture several hardware platforms (personal computers, midrange com-puters, mainframes) are connected through computer networks, where 'clients' make requests to 'servers' for data storage, transport and processing tasks. A task is allocated to the server that seems most appropriate, which is done in a user-transparent way. This architecture abandons the former 'master/slave' concept, in which computer terminals ('slaves') were connected to a centralized mainframe com-puter (the 'master'). In recent years the client/server architecture also has started to cover the client and server standards for using Web technologies and Intranets/Extranets (e.g. TCP/IP and HTTP protocols, firewalls, Web host computers, browser software).

According to Keen and Cummins (1994), the development towards an IT-based infrastructure based on telecommunications and networks, has three important characteristics, see Figure 3.5:

- *Reach*: how far inside and outside the organization can we directly link people and organizations? This ranges from 'within a single location' to 'anyone, anywhere.'
- *Range*: what information can directly and automatically be shared across business processes? This ranges from 'simple messages' to 'cooperative transactions.'
- *Responsiveness*: what level of service can be guaranteed? This ranges from 'non-immediate response' to 'perfect service.'

A common theme of the telecommunications and network based IT-based infrastructure is integration (Tapsott, 1997; Cairncross, 1997).

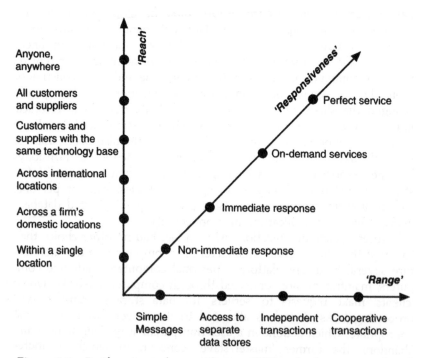

Figure 3.5   *Reach, range and responsiveness of IT-based infrastructure (adapted from Keen and Cummins, 1994)*

From a business perspective, integration in the context of IT-based infrastructure covers three main domains:

- Integration of different types of *media*: where IT was formerly used for storing, transporting, processing and presenting structured data, multimedia applications have made it possible to extend this to unstructured text, speech, sound, etc. The expected digital integration of the Internet, television and telephony will certainly contribute to this development.
- Integration of different *IT application areas*: where IT was formerly used for the large-scale 'back-office' processing of administrative data, IT applications are nowadays extended to primary production processes, such as manufacturing, distribution, and marketing, and embedded in the products (e.g. consumer electronics, cars, professional equipment) and the services of firms (e.g. ATMs, chipcard services, Internet-based selling and configuration services).
- Integration of different *organizational cooperation levels*: where IT was formerly used to create internal 'islands of automation', IT applications are nowadays used to link individuals (e.g. through electronic mail or Groupware), departments (e.g. through systems for enterprise resource planning, interface-based integration of local systems or standards for interoperability), and business partners (e.g. linking with systems of suppliers or partners in the supply chain, electronic marketing and sales).

It can be expected that in the near future organizations will create and invest in IT-based infrastructures with rapidly increasing reach, range and responsiveness. If there are barriers for specific firms, these will not be technological, but will lie in the strategic choices that firms are willing to take, the amount of funding they want to devote to such capital-intensive decisions, and the amount of change they are able absorb.

Maturity of IT Deployment

In the course of time, organizations have been following a growth path of IT deployment which makes the need for capitalizing on infrastructure more and more apparent. The role of infrastructure becomes clearer when looking at the 'stages theory' of Nolan as described by Nolan (1979) and Nolan and Koot (1992). The model makes a distinction between the 'initiation', 'contagion', control', integration', 'architecture', and 'deconcentration' phases. Although originally defined from a descriptive perspective, this model has increasingly become a prescriptive model, and is one of most frequently cited models when addressing IT management issues.[2] For managers, it has proved to be particularly useful for gaining an insight into, and finding management tools for the control of, the IT evolution in their organization. The basic premises of the stage theory are:

- A firm should have a balanced development throughout the subsequent phases. Important elements of the learning curve may be missed when skipping a phase. Nolan and Koot (1992) make an analogy with the development of an infant to a grown-up. A phase like puberty cannot be skipped in order to have a good personal and intellectual development.
- For each phase, a balance is needed between the type of IT application, used resources, the role of management, and the role of end-users.

Critics of the Nolan stages model indicate that the model should be refined for a particular type of technology and a particular type of business (see, for example, Earl, 1989). The strength of the stage model lies in the focus on the dynamics of IT, both from the technological and organizational perspectives. The phase that is considered as the most mature one by Nolan and Koot (1992) gives a compendious account of how important the infrastructure dimension of IT exploitation has become. If organizations—and more importantly senior executives—do recognize the importance of an infrastructure approach to managing IT, and grow towards incorporating this approach, this means:

- Creating organization-wide infrastructures for intensive information sharing, crossing the borders of the individual organizational units and the overarching organizational level (e.g. holding or parent company).
- Investing in infrastructure facilities for developing and exploiting IT-based systems. These facilities are generally organized within a federal structure of centralized and decentralized facilities.
- IT management is undertaken within a dialogue between top management and the lower echelons of a firm. The top creates the

---

[2] The Nolan stages model has been criticized quite extensively. The main criticisms are that it is essentially a deterministic model, thereby suggesting that there is only one best way of managing IT, that it has strong managerial bias, and that it mixes prescriptive and descriptive elements (Zuurmond, 1994). However, it cannot be ignored that, for many organizations and senior managers, the Nolan stage model does bring some structure into their thinking and actions regarding IT deployment.

conditions and sets boundaries, while the business units decide on the actual IT deployment. In relation to this, IT strategy formation and business strategy formation are interdependent and well-aligned.

- The end-users of IT pursue a collective interest in the successful exploitation of the shared infrastructure, instead of merely attending to their own interests.

3.5   CONCLUSIONS

This exploratory chapter has made clear that the notion of an infrastructure in the context of organizational IT deployment has undergone a shift in both content and tenor. Until recently, the notion of infrastructure had a rather narrow, technological connotation, generally referring to centralized computing equipment and facilities for telecommunications within the firm (the 'technical infrastructure'). In accordance with increased usage of the term infrastructure in the context of the 'electronic superhighway', more modern views of IT-based infrastructure use it to refer to all long-term IT elements that are in common use in an organization or between organizations. As such, the notion of an IT-based infrastructure reflects the increasingly shared and coordinated nature of today's IT investments. The infrastructure provides the base foundation that enables subsequent local application of IT, tailored to users' own characteristics and preferences. The contemporary role of IT-based infrastructure can be compared with public infrastructures such as roads, railroads, seaways, electricity supply and also facilities in the field of education or social services. The main business factors influencing the role of IT-based infrastructure are the emergence of new, less-rigid and less-hierarchical organizational forms, intensified cooperation between organizations and the need to redesign the business processes in order to maintain and improve competitive positioning. The main IT factors are the rise in integral work-site support, telecommunications and network-enabled IT deployment, and the current position of many organizations on their growth path of IT deployment.

APPENDIX: APPROACHES TO BUSINESS PROCESS REENGINEERING

This appendix reviews the main approaches to business process re-engineering (BPR), based on a study of Jones (1994). The dimensions used to characterize BPR approaches are:

Author	Scope of main processes	Scale of change	Means of achieving change	Source of change model	Role of IT
Hammer (1990)	Organization	Radical	Inspiration	Novel	Essential enabler
Davenport and Short (1990)	Organization/dept./task	Incremental	Systematic	Industrial Engineering (IE)	Recursive relationship
Harrington (1991a)	Department/task	Incremental	Systematic	Kaizen	Automation (secondary)
Kaplan and Murdock (1991)	Organization	Radical	Systematic	Total Quality Management (TQM)	Key enabler
Business Intelligence (reported in FinTech, 1992)	Department/task	Incremental	Systematic	Kaizen	In theory, not necessary
Davenport (1993)	Organization	Radical	Systematic	TQM + IE + 3 others	Primary enabler
Johannson et al. (1993)	Organization	Radical	Systematic	TQM	One of several 'Break-Points'
Morris and Brandon (1993)	Organization/dept./task	Incremental	Systematic	Industrial Engineering	Not necessarily based on IT

Table 3.2 Characteristics of different BPR approaches (from Jones, 1994)

- *The scope of the main processes.* The scope of the main processes refers to the level where the focus of process analysis lies. This can for instance be at the individual task level, at the department level, or be concerned with organization-wide and boundary-crossing activities.
- *The scale of change.* The scale of change considers whether the approach advocates an incremental change of existing processes, or a radical, fundamental reappraisal of the way work is carried out.
- *The means of achieving change.* The means for achieving BPR can be either based on a proposed systematic BPR methodology or can be more inspirational.
- *The source of the change model.* The source of the change model underlying a BPR approach relates to the concepts on which the approach is considered to be based. Jones (1994) assumes that '... approaches which see themselves as developing out of particular established techniques or concepts will reflect a similar approach to change as their predecessors...'.
- *The role of IT.* The final dimension to be considered, and as Jones (1994) argues possibly the most significant one, is the contribution of IT to BPR. The author contends that with respect to the role of IT as the engine of organizational change there is a considerable divergence of opinion. It seems to us however that in cases where the role of IT is not considered central, the actual role of IT in reengineering business processes will not be much different from the more explicit IT-enabled BPR approaches (see Table 3.2).

4

The Business Role of IT-Based Infrastructure

4.1 INTRODUCTION

The previous chapter presented a first exploration of IT-based infrastructure in general terms, based on several relevant strategic perspectives. Elaborating on this, this chapter will examine in more detail what is meant by IT-based infrastructure in the context of this book. First, Section 4.2 further delineates the contents of the notion of IT-based infrastructure by giving a definition. Since not all infrastructure assets are alike and will have different business purposes, a distinction is made between the two main types of infrastructure: 'direct' and 'indirect.' Subsequently, Section 4.3 discusses how this definition of IT-based infrastructure can be translated into more operational terms in order to get a clear view of what the infrastructure of a particular organization or organizational unit looks like. Section 4.4 then discusses the general structure and rationale of a tentative checklist with key infrastructure components, which was designed as part of the research study underpinning this book and can be found in this chapter's appendix. Section 4.5 present the results of two case studies in which the applicability of using checklist-based instruments for infrastructure description was validated. This chapter's conclusions are given in Section 4.6.

4.2 WHAT EXACTLY IS IT-BASED INFRASTRUCTURE?

The previous chapter made clear that the notion of IT-based infrastructure is increasingly used in the context of organizational IT deployment and management, but that it is not always clear what exactly is meant by it. A more unambiguous meaning of IT-based infrastructure is needed in order to discuss infrastructure investment issues in a meaningful and structured way. In order to arrive at a more precise definition of IT-based infrastructure, this chapter follows the approach of Verschuren (1992), who proposes a two-step approach for defining notions (see Figure 4.1). In this approach, a word is first translated into a notion through a 'concept definition' and a notion is then associated with a practical phenomenon through an 'operational definition.' The concept definition is covered in this section, while the next section addresses the translation of this definition in more operational terms.

Definition of IT-Based Infrastructure

Building on more modern views of IT-based infrastructure, see Chapter 3, an IT-based infrastructure of an organization is defined here as *the shared system of staff/skills, tools and procedures in the field of IT which is used for a longer period of time, and as such is underpinned by organizational commitment and top management ownership.* This definition requires some further explanation.

Organization and the Layered Nature of IT-Based Infrastructure

The notion of organization is context-bound and therefore is a relative notion: it refers to a number of stakeholders or actors (for instance employees, departments, units or autonomous organizations) who decide to cooperate to achieve certain common goals. Consequently, an IT-based infrastructure is a layered notion: every organization can be part of one or more other organizations or be dependent upon the regulation of another organizational level (see Figure 4.2). This also implies that what is considered to be infrastructure on one level, can be local for another level, depending on the level of analysis. Therefore, one has to be very explicit about the precise organizational level for which the infrastructure is defined. It is possible to speak of, for

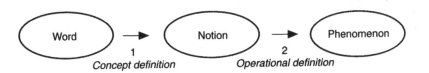

Figure 4.1 *The two-step definition approach of Verschuren (1992)*

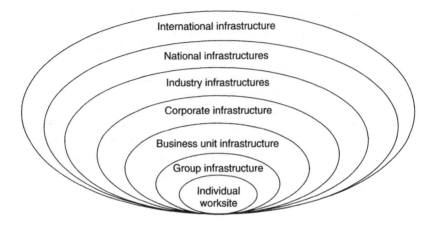

Figure 4.2   *The layered nature of IT-based infrastructure*

example, a group infrastructure, a business unit infrastructure or a corporate infrastructure that are all interdependent. These different organizational levels will also have to take into account the infrastructures of the industries and nations they are working in, established international infrastructures (e.g. the Internet) and even the infrastructure standards of international bodies (e.g. ISO standards).

Elements of IT-Based Infrastructure

The aforementioned definition refers to 'staff/skills, tools and procedures' as elements of IT-based infrastructure. These elements, evident in capacities and capabilities, correspond to what traditionally is considered to be the part of an information system (see, for example, the definition of Davis and Olsen, 1985). The IT-based infrastructure is the shared and long-term part of the entire information system of an organization, if conceptualized on a high level. The notion of *staff/ skills* (e.g. information analysts, system designers, and operators) does not only have a material content, but also refers to available knowledge and expertise, both in technical and business terms. *Tools* can be further divided between structured and unstructured databases and knowledge bases, hardware (essentially equipment) and software. *Procedures* concern business procedures with respect to the elements people and tools, i.e. work and use procedures, and to the acquisition and construction of these elements, i.e. standards.

Information Technology

The elements of IT-based infrastructure cover information technology in a broad sense. IT covers all technological tools for electronically acquiring, processing, storing, disseminating, and presenting information, together with the knowledge to be able to use these tools. As such, this refers to both the more traditional technologies such as microfiche or other archive technologies and to more advanced applications, e.g. data warehousing or multimedia technologies.

Shared and Long-Term Use

Since an infrastructure is always used by more than one interested person or party, shared use is a key characteristic of IT-based infrastructure. This shared use reflects the provision of infrastructure as a basic, enabling resource. Furthermore, different users use the infrastructure for many different purposes. This means that infrastructure facilities should be stable, and not subject to frequent change. This also explains why an IT-based infrastructure is used for the longer term. It is important to note that this does not mean that an IT-based infrastructure is purely static: the infrastructure will change as certain elements are no longer considered infrastructure and other elements will be added to the infrastructure.

Direct and Indirect Infrastructure

Not all investments in IT-based infrastructure have the same impact on business processes or on the products and services of a business. In order to be able to illustrate the main differences in business impact, two main types of infrastructure can be discerned: indirect and direct. The first type of infrastructure concerns the 'traditional' infrastructure of shared technical computing facilities. The second type of infrastructure concerns the shared applications of software, databases and knowledge bases of an organization. The first type of 'indirect' facilities create the enabling conditions for well-directed deployment of the second type of 'direct' facilities, while in turn the use of direct infrastructure necessitates the use of indirect infrastructure. Direct infrastructure facilities generally have a much more tangible business impact than indirect infrastructure facilities, therefore it is often easier to identify promising new investment opportunities and to measure investment results for direct infrastructure than for indirect infrastructure. Table 4.1 summarizes the main characteristics of both types of infrastructure.

Direct infrastructure	Indirect infrastructure
Focus: Integrated within the business processes and products/services of an organization	*Focus:* Enables the use of IT in business processes and products/services of an organization
Objects: Manifests itself in shared IT applications, databases and knowledge bases	*Objects:* Manifests itself in shared technological and organizational facilities
Character: Demand: uses facilities of the indirect infrastructure	*Character:* Supply: offers facilities to the direct infrastructure

Table 4.1   *Direct and indirect infrastructure*

Direct Infrastructure

The direct infrastructure consists of all shared, relatively permanent capacities and capabilities in the field of IT, which are business-specific, i.e. to a large extent integrated within the business processes or embedded in the product and services of a firm. As argued in the previous section, the direct infrastructure manifests itself in the application infrastructure and the infrastructures of data and knowledge bases, including the organizational procedures that are needed for adequate use. These organizational procedures cover, for instance, application management, access and change authorization; they are often referred to as facilities for 'application control.' Users can often benefit directly from the direct infrastructure—hence the term 'direct'—by making day-to-day business operations, for instance, faster, cheaper and more accurate. Deploying direct infrastructure will trigger a demand for the facilities of the indirect infrastructure.

Indirect Infrastructure

The indirect infrastructure is defined here as all shared, relatively permanent basic capacities and capabilities in the field of IT, which enable business-specific use of IT in the business processes or products and services of a firm. The indirect infrastructure is manifest in the infrastructures of basic technological and organizational facilities. As such, the indirect infrastructure resembles most the well-known 'technical infrastructure', including the adjacent personnel facilities (human resources, skills and expertise). Examples of indirect infrastructure are, for instance: processing equipment, telecommunications networks and tools, database management systems, and the system designers and system operators that have the necessary skills and expertise to secure appropriate use. These facilities are generally of no direct benefit to end-users (which can often be seen by the degree of outsourcing), but are indispensable for successful IT deployment. The supply of general facilities of the indirect infrastructure enables the use of more business-specific IT through the direct infrastructure.

4.3   IT-BASED INFRASTRUCTURE IN MORE OPERATIONAL TERMS

Although the previously discussed definition of IT-based infrastructure gives a further delineation of what exactly an IT-based infrastructure is, this definition and its explanation are not concrete enough to get a clear view of what an IT-based infrastructure precisely looks like in practice. This requires that this definition be translated into more operational terms. In the case study research that underpins this book, a generic checklist of key infrastructure components (see the Appendix to this chapter) was used to facilitate the organizational conception of which IT elements were considered to be part of the IT-based infrastructure and which elements were not. This operational conception sketches a picture of the existing IT-based infrastructure at a given moment in time; in other words, of where the actual division lies between infrastructure components on the one hand, and local components on the other hand (see Figure 4.3).

The actual infrastructure of an organization or organizational unit will almost always show a dynamic behavior, since decisions to change the infrastructure will be taken continually. The actual infrastructure is the result of top management decisions to invest (or divest) in infrastructure projects, which are executed in the course of time. The division line of Figure 4.3 will thus be in constant motion. Before elaborating on the use of a checklist of infrastructure components, and the checklist presented in the appendix of this chapter, several issues deserve specific attention.

Organizational Level

A particular IT-based infrastructure can refer to several organizational levels (see Section 4.2). Within one autonomous organization, there can even be several levels. Using a checklist to describe an existing infrastructure can, for instance, be done for: a corporate-wide infrastructure, a divisional infrastructure, a business unit infrastructure, the infrastructure of a subsidiary, the infrastructure of a staff department or even the infrastructure of a group of employees that work together.

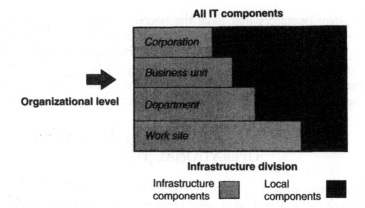

Figure 4.3   *The division between infrastructure components and local components*

Level of Detail

When using a checklist of infrastructure components for infrastructure description, experience shows that it is advisable to use a rather elaborate list of possible infrastructure components, which is further divided into main and subcategories. In order to arrive at a business-oriented description, these categories should reflect the previously made distinction between direct and indirect infrastructure. A description of the actual IT-based infrastructure is generally made easier and faster if a description is made in several steps, instead of making a detailed description all at once. These subdescriptions can then be put together later to get an overall view.

Treating 'External' Infrastructure as a Black Box

In many practical cases certain infrastructure elements are delivered by external suppliers, which falls outside the organizational scope of the infrastructure under consideration. These infrastructure components are however in use, but detailed knowledge concerning their characteristics is often not available. When this is the case, it is generally more feasible to denote these infrastructure elements as 'external infrastructure' and treat them as a black box.

Using Local Language

A checklist with infrastructure components should cover a large number of sample components, which together give a more or less complete overview of the way in which an IT-based infrastructure can be manifest in an organization. This does not mean, however, that all components should be present or that no infrastructure components can be added to the list. A checklist should not be considered a 'strait-jacket' for all sorts of infrastructure components, but should offer a supporting and facilitating framework for getting an operational view of the actual state of the IT-based infrastructure as a prelude to assessing infrastructure capabilities. Depending on the kind of terminology and the type of technology already in use, the definition of components should be adapted to the local language of an organization in order to ensure that everyone involved knows what is meant by a certain component.

Formal and Informal Infrastructure

A checklist with infrastructure components can be a powerful tool to get a clear view of the actual infrastructure of a firm, business unit or organizational department. Both the formal (i.e. authorized by corporate directives and policies) and informal infrastructure can be covered by such an exercise. If considered appropriate, a further distinction can be made between:

- infrastructure that is compulsory always and for everyone;
- infrastructure that is compulsory, unless motivated counter-arguments can be given;
- free supply of infrastructure: this can be used, but there is no formal obligation to do so.

4.4 A TENTATIVE LIST OF KEY INFRASTRUCTURE COMPONENTS

As discussed in the previous section, the Appendix to this chapter gives a checklist of infrastructure components as developed in the framework of the research study that underpins this book. Since it was developed during a particular period in time and within specific organizations it can only be considered a tentative list of key infrastructure components. It therefore merely serves as an example and a starting point; repeated use of a checklist will require adaptations in terms of (new) information technologies used and organizational characteristics and preferences. The infrastructure components are based on a generic, descriptive model of a business firm and of IT deployment. These components are structured into main categories that can be found in almost every case to some extent. This section will focus on the reasoning behind the structure of the main categories.

A subdivision between the 'primary' and 'secondary' process of a firm has served as the starting point of the structure of direct infrastructure (see Figure 4.4). Every organization will have a primary process: creating and adding value to products and services. Usually the work in this primary process is divided into different process steps: from purchasing in supply markets, to product/service development, to manufacturing to inventory or order fulfillment, until sales or order acquisition in demand markets. The primary processes will always be managed by a controlling process (often called the planning and control process), which also can be divided into subprocesses for the purpose of adequate work divisions. This can be seen in the different levels of management control (e.g. operational, tactical, and strategic; Anthony, 1965), and the staff functions of organizations (e.g. personnel or finance) that support management processes. By combining the production processes and the controlling processes in a business-specific way an organization designs and manages its 'value chain' which eventually defines its competitive competencies and chance of survival in competitive markets (Porter, 1985). What the direct infrastructure ultimately will look like depends on the extent to which the different processes require infrastructure support (i.e. information intensity) and the choices made with respect the level of infrastructure support (i.e. infrastructure coverage).

When using a checklist of direct infrastructure components based on the basic division of primary and controlling processes it became clear that two potential types of infrastructure components were not identified immediately. In the first place this concerns all kinds of infrastructure facilities used for organizational communication. Within every firm there will be communication structures and patterns amongst employees, which are increasingly supported by modern IT. Secondly, the initial

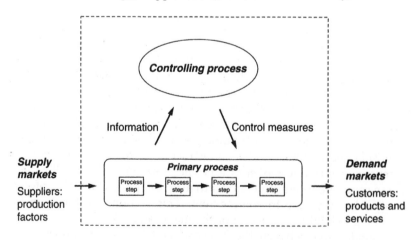

Figure 4.4   *The primary and the controlling processes of a business*

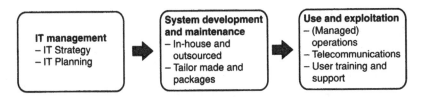

Figure 4.5   Categorization of indirect infrastructure based on the IT life-cycle

structure of the checklist based on primary and controlling processes did not sufficiently reflect the IT support for office activities (e.g. word processing, calculations support with spreadsheets, print facilities, etc.). In order to facilitate identification of both types of direct infrastructure the list of key infrastructure components should be extended with a category 'communication and office support.'

The components of indirect infrastructure will vary from organization to organization, since technological, organizational and procedural choices will not always be the same. Figure 4.5 gives an impression of the IT life-cycle to which the different components refer. To identify key infrastructure components a distinction is made between staff/skills, tools and procedures.

4.5   CASE STUDIES OF INFRASTRUCTURE DESCRIPTION

Two case studies were used in the research that underpins this book to illustrate the applicability and advantages of using a checklist with key infrastructure components for infrastructure description. The first case concerns the departmental infrastructure of a department of a large, internationally operating insurance firm, here referred to as 'InsuraCo.' The second case concerns the IT-based infrastructure which a large bank uses in all its local banking offices (about 500), which will be referred to as 'BankCo.' Both case studies are static descriptions, which sketch a picture of the IT-based infrastructure at a given moment in time. Since the IT-based infrastructure will in reality have a dynamic character, it is very possible that certain components have disappeared, been changed or added to the infrastructure. For reasons of confidentiality the infrastructure description will not be given in full detail, but in both cases it will be discussed how the instrument of a checklist with key infrastructure components was used, what the results of using a checklist are, and what the overall conclusions are.

InsuraCo: Financial Control Services

The initial checklist of infrastructure components was the result of an interactive, action-driven process in which the existing infrastructure of the Financial Control Services department of InsuraCo was described in operational terms. At the start of this exercise there was a checklist available which covered the main infrastructure categories discussed in the previous section (excluding the category 'communication and office support' which was added during the description) and a limited number of sample components. The main purpose of this case study was to check whether the use of a checklist of infrastructure components as suggested was a feasible management instrument. The Financial Control Services department of InsuraCo appeared to be a good candidate for a first attempt to describe an IT-based infrastructure in more operational terms. The reasons for this were the fact that high-quality IT support played a key role in the business processes, and that the general manager had good knowledge of and experience with the possibilities and limitations of infrastructure investments. Moreover, the general manager was very interested in an assessment of the existing IT-based infrastructure and its capabilities. At the time of the case study the department had about 50 employees and offered mainly financial services to the five internal business units and other organizational units (e.g. subsidiaries). The main activities were payment processing, managing accounts payable and customer registration.

When using the checklist it became clear that the categories of Research & Development and Purchasing & Supply were not considered specific parts of the production process. Therefore, these processes were not covered during the case study. Also a choice was made to combine the category Product & Services with Manufacturing & Logistics.

The results of the case study show that a large part of the infrastructure is provided as external infrastructure. The external direct infrastructure is delivered to a large extent by staff functions of InsuraCo's headquarters. This concerns Human Resource Management, a part of Finance & Accounting, and a part of Legal Compliance. Infrastructure components for Communication & Office Support are delivered by a specific InsuraCo department and the centralized IT department. The external indirect infrastructure for System Development & Maintenance is delivered by a department specializing in system development for staff functions and the headquarters within InsuraCo. The central IT department of InsuraCo mainly delivers the staff/skills, tools and procedures for IT Use and Exploitation (e.g. processing, managed operations, telecommunications).

The direct infrastructure of the department further covers 'own' applications and databases for Strategic Management (especially consolidated management information), Finance & Accounting, and Legal Compliance (e.g. fiscal information regarding intermediaries and information needs emanating from privacy legislation). There is no IT-based infrastructure for Marketing & Sales. Manufacturing & Logistics is supported by a relatively extensive direct infrastructure. Separate infrastructure facilities can be found for invoicing, payment processing, control of accounts receivable, control of intermediaries, administration of intermediaries, and administration of end-customers. Also several employees, tools and procedures for application control (e.g. application managers, authorization procedures, and system management tools) are used. The existing indirect infrastructure covers facilities for IT Strategy and Planning (e.g. IT policy meetings and service contract management), User Training & Support, and a PC-based telecommunication network (Local Area Network).

The overall conclusion of this case study is that a checklist of key infrastructure components can be a very efficient and effective tool for obtaining a clear view of IT-based infrastructure in operational terms. Also this case study has made clear that a very descriptive infrastructure tool should be adapted to local circumstances. Some terms were re-formulated, some elements were added to the list and some ignored, in order to reflect department-specific ways of working and terminology.

BankCo: Local Banking Infrastructure

After the initial case study within InsuraCo, which focused on the feasibility of working with a checklist of key infrastructure components, a second case study was started within a banking firm, here referred to as BankCo. The case study covers the infrastructure used within all local banking offices, about 500 legal entities dispersed all over The Netherlands. This infrastructure is provided to standardize IT deployment as much as possible within the different banking offices, all of which have the possibility to design and build their own specific IT support. Two elements justified the choice of including this case study in the research study that underpins this book. Firstly, this case study offered the opportunity of using a checklist-based instrument for infra-structure description in another business environment, with new facilities, new terminology, and new people who had to make themselves familiar with such an instrument. Secondly, the existing IT-based infra-structure seemed to be rather complex at first glance, but also there seemed to be many infrastructure knowledge available with subject experts and within documents. As such, describing the IT-based infra-structure in operational terms was considered to be a good exploration of the applicability of using a checklist with key infrastructure components.

In line with the InsuraCo case study, a number of changes were made in the initial checklist to reflect the specific characteristics of BankCo and to reflect the preferences of the participants in the description exercise. The checklist used speaks for instance of 'technical infrastructure', which concerns the infrastructure components for IT Operations and Telecommunications. Relatively speaking, this infrastructure covered a large part of the existing infrastructure, which prompted the need for an additional restructuring of the initial checklist. This was realized by using a specific model, based on the 'Open Systems Interconnection' (OSI) model for standardized communication between computer systems. Again a choice was made to combine the categories Manufacturing & Logistics with Product & Services.

The results of the case study show a large number of IT-based infrastructure components, which are categorized according to the structure of the main categories of the checklist used. The level of detail of this description can be qualified as very high; the described direct infrastructure, for instance, consists of a total of 184 components related to standardized applications and data/knowledge bases. These are further categorized to reflect the specific application components and systems for specific tasks. The larger part of the infrastructure is supposed to support the day-to-day operations for Manufacturing & Logistics. These concern processes such as credit accounts (e.g. bank savings, insured savings, employee savings), payment services (e.g. payment accounts, automatic payment transfers, speed payments), and finance transactions (e.g. loans and mortgages).

Other large direct infrastructure components cover Strategic Management (mainly for financial management information), Finance & Accounting (mainly for financial planning and general ledger), Marketing & Sales (mainly market information and invoicing), and Communication & Office Support (mainly electronic media and worksite support). Relatively small infrastructures for Human Resource Management, Legal Compliance & Research and Development can be found. The direct infrastructure for Human Resource Management is partly an external infrastructure, delivered by a supporting organizational unit. A number of facilities are used for application control of the direct infrastructure, mainly for the purpose of internal audit.

The description of the indirect infrastructure of BankCo covers to a large extent what the bank refers to as 'technical infrastructure.' A distinction is made between the local platform (the personal computers, the network and the servers within the different local banking offices), the central platform (the mainframe computing equipment within the bank headquarters), and telecommunication facilities (the facilities for electronic communication between the different locations). In the local platform description several infrastructure components are identified: personal computing facilities (configuration standards, log-in screens, connection facilities), local network servers, database servers, transaction servers and communication servers). The central platform consists of two types of mainframe computers. Regarding tele-communications facilities, a distinction is made between a cabling infrastructure (within-building and to connect locations), a connection infrastructure (including the communication protocols), and a communication infrastructure for connecting the main offices with smaller offices and the main offices with central computing platforms. The latter connection is further divided into four partial infrastructures within the infrastructure description of BankCo, which support different communication functions (e.g. software connections, data transfer). Next to technical infrastructure, the infrastructure description pays attention to IT Strategy & Management (e.g. IT managers, strategic choices), System Development & Maintenance (e.g. system developers, development languages and workbenches, implementation guidelines), IT Operations and Managed Operations (e.g. system operators, types of system management tools), and User Support & Training (e.g. people and tools for support, training manuals).

The overall conclusion of this case study is that the use of a checklist of key infrastructure components gives a quick insight into the IT provisions that are considered to be part of the IT-based infrastructure of a business. Using a checklist as a descriptive and diagnostic tool is experienced as helpful and easy. It was quite simple to categorize the different infrastructure components into different categories. Again it was very important to adapt the list with infrastructure components to structures and terminology already used within BankCo. The main added value of this exercise was seen to be to use a checklist-based instrument to establish a re-confirmation and re-commitment of all earlier made infrastructure decisions. In particular, those employees who have no, partial or limited knowledge of the IT-based infrastructure can benefit from this.

4.6 CONCLUSIONS

This chapter has defined an IT-based infrastructure of an organization as being all relatively permanent IT capacities and capabilities that are for common use, resulting from organizational agreement and top management mandate. What should be considered infrastructure in a specific situation depends on the organizational level under consideration. An IT-based infrastructure therefore is a context-bound and layered notion; one can, for instance, speak of the infrastructure of a group of employees, of a business unit, and so forth, up to an international infrastructure. Two main types of infrastructure can be discerned: direct and indirect. Direct infrastructure consists of all commonly used, long-term IT provisions which are very much integrated within the business processes and products and services of a firm. This infrastructure manifests itself in the application infrastructure and the infrastructure of data and knowledge bases, including specific facilities for application control. Indirect infrastructure consists of all commonly used, long-term IT provisions which enable the use of IT in the business processes and products and services of a firm. This infrastructure manifests itself in the infrastructures of basic technological and organizational facilities. Using a checklist with key infrastructure components can be very helpful in describing the existing IT-based infrastructure of an organization or organizational unit in operational terms. Such a description will be a sketch or picture of the infrastructure at a given moment in time; the actual infrastructure has a dynamic nature and will change continuously since management decisions to invest or divest will also be made continuously.

APPENDIX: CHECKLIST OF KEY INFRASTRUCTURE COMPONENTS

This checklist gives a (tentative) overview of key infrastructure components in general terms. It is based upon research conducted within several large organizations within the public, services and manufacturing sectors. Given the generic nature of the checklist, it should not be considered as normative. Also this checklist does not cover specific hardware or software products, nor their suppliers, since these will change rapidly and depend greatly on a company's preferred technology, product and supplier base. The checklist should be seen as a starting point for company-specific identification of available, existing infrastructure components and appropriate new infrastructure capabilities. When using it as reference material, allowance should be made for:

- the type of industry (e.g. public, not-for-profit, manufacturing, financial services, utility, retail, transport, etc.);
- the technological maturity (e.g. IT intensity, degree of automation, infrastructure coverage, degree of innovation);
- the degree of IT outsourcing (e.g. none, selective), leading to internal versus external infrastructure;
- the locally required level of detail and local terminology and conventions.

Direct infrastructure

Controlling Processes

Strategic Management	• Overall planning and control • General management information • Financial/commercial reporting and consolidation • Environmental scanning • Strategic scenario analyses • Competitor analysis • Product/market portfolio analysis • Knowledge and competence management • Technology capability management
Finance & Accounting	• General ledger • Budget reporting • Cash and treasury management • Fixed asset management • Financial asset management • Customs and foreign exchange management • Cost calculation and cost recovery • Accounts receivable and invoicing • Accounts payable • Leasing and credit management • Tax management
Human Resource Management	• Staff and social policies • General employee characteristics • Payment guidelines and fringe benefits • Standards for functioning and performance evaluation • Employee insurance • Standards for laying off • Management development • Training and education
Legal Compliance	• Financial and fiscal reporting • Annual reporting and external financial auditing • Privacy legislation • Environmental legislation

Primary Processes

Research & Development Development and Product/Service Creation	• Innovation management • Patents and trademarks • Product design ('Computer Aided Design') • Piloting and simulation • Product development management • Product/engineering data management
Purchasing & Supply	• Supply market research • Suppliers' quotation and invoice management • Initial purchasing

(Continued)

Direct infrastructure (Continued)

Primary Processes

	• Purchase orders
	• Supplier and vendor rating
	• Purchasing performance management
	• External services and consulting
	• Interim management
Manufacturing & *Logistics*	• Production capacity management
	• Production and materials requirements planning
	• Procurement and materials management
	• Order management
	• Assembly planning
	• Production process management
	• Shop floor control/manufacturing execution management
	• Production quality assurance
	• Inventory management
	• Waste and defects
	• Warehousing and distribution management
	• Customer service management/after sales support (e.g. spare parts/installed base management)
	• Equipment management
Products & Services	• Product automation/embedded software
	• Information services
	• Barcoding
	• Chipcards and smartcards
	• Electronic Data Interchange services
	• Videotext/Internet services
Marketing & Sales	• Public relations and corporate communications
	• Interactive client marketing
	• Market research and sales forecasting
	• Customer base and order management
	• Quotation management
	• Key account administration
	• Sales targets and performance

Communication and Office Support

Communication & *Information Exchange*	• Internal transaction and transfer systems
	• Dedicated interorganizational systems
	• Video conferencening and groupware systems
	• Workflow and document archiving systems
	• Electronic mail and bulletin board systems
	• Naming resolution and directory services
	• Intranet/Internet/Extranet systems
Office Support	• Text processing systems
	• Drawing and publications systems
	• Spreadsheets
	• Databases and query languages

- Scheduling systems
- Graphical user interfaces
- Desk top standards (e.g. monitor, floppy/hard disk, optical media/CD-ROM, peripherals)

Application Control

Staff/skills
- Data managers
- Application managers
- Application control specialists

Tools
- User manuals
- Data definitions and (master) data models
- Application functionality models
- Application management tools
- Configuration and management tools
- Information architecture tools

Procedures
- Access procedures and authorizations
- Change procedures and authorizations
- System ownership procedures
- Configuration and version management procedures

Indirect infrastructure

IT strategy and planning

Staff/skills
- General IT management (team)
- IT steering groups and IT policy committee
- User/customer councils
- Platforms for exchanging IT experiences
- Strategic IT planners/IT policy support staff
- IT capacity and capability planners
- Technology assessment specialists/trend analysts

Tools
- IT strategy and planning tools
- Architecture modeling tools
- Capacity planning tools

Procedures
- IT assessment and planning methods (e.g. Information Systems Planning, SWOT analyses, Quick Wins assessments)
- IT audit and business control procedures
- User/customer satisfaction methods
- IT project call procedures
- IT standardization procedures
- IT capacity and capability methods
- IT investment justification and prioritization procedures (financial and non-financial methods)
- IT funding and budgeting procedures
- IT contracting procedures
- IT cost allocation and recovery procedures

(*Continued*)

Indirect infrastructure (Continued)

IT Strategy and Planning

- IT security and privacy procedures
- Contingency procedures
- IT piloting procedures (e.g. for technological explorations and experiments)

System Development and Maintenance

Staff/Skills

Project management
- Project managers
- Quality assurance specialists
- Risk management specialists
- Supplier selection specialists
- Contract managers for external project management

Tools
- Project management and planning tools

Procedures
- Planning and contracting procedures
- Development methods and techniques (e.g. waterfall, prototyping, rapid application development)
- Quality assurance procedures
- Risk management procedures
- Milestone procedures
- Budgeting procedures
- Supplier selection and management procedures
- Contracting and quotation procedures

Staff/Skills

Information Analysis and Systems Design
- Information analysts
- System analysts
- Functional designers
- Technical designers

Tools
- Computer-aided design tools
- Development workbenches
- Tools for building interfaces

Procedures
- Milestone procedures
- Process, data or hybrid modeling procedures
- Specific analysis and design tools
- End-user participation procedures

Staff/Skills

Tailor-made Software Engineering
- Technical designers
- System programmers
- Test specialists

Tools
- Reusable software components (software repositories)

- Computer-aided software engineering (CASE) tools
- Programming workbenches/application generation tools
- Software configuration management tools
- Development languages
- Programming and test platforms
- Expert system shells
- Internet technology toolsets
- Interface tools

Procedures
- Milestone procedures
- Programming quality procedures
- Testing procedures
- Interfacing procedures

Selection and Procurement of Software Packages

Staff/skills
- Package market researchers
- Package selection specialists
- Package contracting specialists

Tools
- Feasibility assessment tools
- Package evaluation tools

Procedures
- Milestone procedures
- Package evaluation criteria
- Selection procedures
- Request for information/proposal procedures

Systems Conversion and Implementation

Staff/Skills
- Conversion specialists
- Implementation specialists
- Organizational change specialists

Tools
- Conversion tools
- Tools for data clean-up
- Temporary interface tools
- Organizational communication manuals

Procedures
- Milestone procedures
- Shadow processing procedures
- Organizational change and communication procedures

IT Use and Exploitation

IT Operations

Staff/Skills
- System operators
- Transactions operating specialists
- Database specialists

Tools
- Supercomputers
- Mainframe equipment
- Minicomputers/midrange platforms
- Desktop and mobile computing equipment

(Continued)

Indirect infrastructure (Continued)

IT Operations

	• Terminal emulation tools • Dedicated servers (e.g. file, communication, transaction or print servers) • Disk and tape units • Operating systems for central servers, local servers and desktop computing • Time sharing systems/compilers/assemblers/monitors • Logging systems • Back-up and recovery systems • Databases and database management systems • Data dictionary tools • Database query and reporting tools • Data warehouse tools
Procedures	• General operating procedures • User procedures for operating tools

IT Managed Operations

Staff/Skills	• Equipment management specialists • Operations quality specialists • System management specialists • Problem management specialists • Change management specialists • Reliability and recovery specialists • Operations contracting specialists
Tools	• Equipment management tools • Operations quality tools • System management tools • Problem management tools • Change management tools • Reliability and recovery tools
Procedures	• Equipment management procedures • Operations quality procedures • System management procedures • Problem management procedures • Change management procedures • Reliability and recovery procedures • Operations contracting procedures

Telecommunications

Staff/Skills	• Network specialists • Network managers • Specialists for operations management of telecommunications • Firewall specialists • Internet technology specialists

Tools	• Connection tools (e.g. bridges, gateways, hubs, routers) • Cables and wires (e.g. coaxial or glass fibre) • Ether and telephone connections and operating equipment • Wide area and local area network tools • Telecommunications operating software • Internet technology tools • Firewall tools • Interconnectivity/middleware tools
Procedures	• Planning procedures for telecommunications resources • Operations management procedures for telecommunications • Network architectures • Telecommunications standards and protocols • Interconnectivity procedures

IT User Training and Support

Staff/Skills	• Training and education specialists • PC support specialists • Helpdesk/incident specialists • Installation and configuration specialists
Tools	• Course and instruction materials • Incident management tools • Installation and configuration tools
Procedures	• Training plans and procedures • User support procedures • Support service level agreements

Part III
Investment Governance and Control

5
Infrastructure Governance
Through Investment Decisions

5.1 INTRODUCTION

After looking at the business role and managerial implications of
IT-based infrastructure in Part II, the focus of Part III moves to investment decisions concerning this infrastructure. The present first chapter
of this part is meant to build a bridge between the role and implications of the notion of infrastructure on the one hand and assessing
infrastructure investments on the other hand. It will be argued that top-
down planning of all IT functionality, as proposed in many of the
classical strategic IT planning methodologies, is not suitable for
corporate governance of IT-based infrastructure. These methodologies
more or less assume that investments can be planned, without taking
much account of the infrastructure in place. For the majority of contemporary organizations this is not the case. Having already made
massive investments in infrastructure in the past, their main investment
issue is how to gradually, step-by-step, improve their infrastructure by
making the right investment decisions. This will be further elaborated
on in Section 5.1. One of the most important business implications of
IT-based infrastructure is that it not only encompasses much more than
technology (see Part II of this book), but also that it is accompanied by
a specific type of control philosophy and governance style. This means
that the shared and relatively permanent part of all IT provisions (the
'substructure') is realized by investing in diverse investment projects
that bring about improvement in the total infrastructure. The remaining part of the total system of IT provisions, i.e. all local applications
(the 'superstructure'), builds on this in all freedom and extends

organizational IT deployment to cover the local needs of separate units, distinct business processes or individual employees. This control philosophy is treated in more detail in Section 5.3. Subsequently, in Section 5.4 the discussion turns to how a checklist of key infrastructure components can be a supporting tool for identifying a portfolio of possibly desirable investment projects in a well-directed and structured way. Finally, the conclusions of this chapter are given in Section 5.5.

5.2 INVESTMENT-BASED INFRASTRUCTURE CREATION

The notion of an IT-based infrastructure was defined in Chapter 4, where it was also discussed how this definition can be translated into more operational terms. If an organization has made a deliberate choice to invest in IT-based infrastructure, a 'greenfield' approach to the design and creation of this infrastructure will generally not be feasible. Most larger organizations will already use modern IT to support much of their information needs and therefore have a *de facto* IT-based infrastructure, often being the result of past (deliberate or accidental) investment choices. The actual state of this infrastructure may however vary from moment to moment. By continuously executing investment projects, and governing and improving the infrastructure in this manner, the actual infrastructure will change continually in terms of its shape, content and capabilities. Consequently, in most organizations it is not so much a question of which overall infrastructure should be built. The prime management challenge is how to take the right investment decisions that will incrementally, step-by-step, improve the existing infrastructure. The well-known methods for strategic IT planning are hardly suitable for this.

Traditional Blueprint Methods for IT Planning

In the early days of business computing, senior managers were already well aware of the fact that IT deployment needed some type of control and coordination, or in terms of an increasingly used management concept for this, that IT investments needed governance. Notorious in this respect were the 'islands of automation', which meant that every department designed and developed its own IT systems, which consequently led to a system of IT provision with little cohesion and integration. In the course of time, all kinds of methodologies for strategic IT planning have been proposed (see, for example, Martin, 1989; Ward *et al.*, 1996a). Traditional strategic planning methodologies for IT are however not suitable for managing IT from an infrastructure perspective. Classical methods focus on an integral design of information systems, without much consideration given to the distinction between infrastructure facilities and local facilities. To summarize, the most important reasons for the inadequacies of classical strategic planning methods are:

- The rigidity and often long throughput time of these kinds of planning exercises. The basic premise of traditional strategic planning methodologies is a corporation-wide, top-down prioritization of all IT applications that are deemed necessary. However, business reality is often much more dynamic than the planning structure embedded in these methods.
- The relatively reactive nature of these methods, with consequently little attention to innovative, groundbreaking IT exploitation.
- The exclusive attention to IT in administrative, supporting processes. Traditional planning methodologies pay little attention to IT in primary processes and in the products and services of modern organizations.
- The focus of data and application architectures within autonomous organizations with central data storage and information processing. As argued before, IT-based infrastructure planning should cover a broader range of issues and take into account the existence of relatively autonomous parts of an organization.
- The lack of sufficient aids for evaluating investment proposals in order to justify the allocation of limited funds.

The Need to Go Beyond Blueprints

Traditional methods of strategic IT planning generally sketch a rather mechanistic picture of governing IT deployment. Confronted with a large shortage of system development capacity, the focus is on designing blueprints for integrated data and application structures. The starting point is an analysis of business processes and organizational departments. The required technical and organizational facilities are then derived from this. The risk of using this approach is that investment decisions are over-monopolized by technology suppliers technical personnel. In isolation from managers and subject experts who have detailed business knowledge, 'IT architects' work on the design of an integral system of IT provision. Consequently, the required interaction with business goals and business processes is often not accomplished. This is perhaps also the most likely explanation for the fact that practical use of 'blueprint' methodologies has not kept pace with the extensive theoretical studies concerning its use (see Lederer and Sethi, 1992).

The blueprint approach for governing IT deployment will only be appropriate for organizations that work according to Morgan's (1986) 'machine' metaphor. Characteristic of these type of organizations are a stable working environment, little change of client demands and competitive structures, largely standardized formal business procedures and many hierarchical management layers with mainly centralized decision control. As Chapter 3 has argued, contemporary organizations can hardly permit themselves such a style of organizing, partly as a consequence of the rapid developments in IT capabilities. Dynamic, highly competitive markets simply dictate flexible organizational structure, not much hierarchy, and much autonomy and learning abilities at lower organizational levels. This also requires intensive cooperation with other organizations. Such a style of organizing and managing a business makes the need apparent for a new type of more dynamic control. Traditional planning methods are typically 'hard' methods focusing on the content-related and procedural aspects of governing IT projects through blueprints of the entire organization. Oosterhaven (1990) speaks in this respect of the 'one company model', in which the specific characteristics and diversity of different organizational units or departments are ignored. The success of planning and governance, however, proves to be highly dependent on attention to and room for the cooperation of all involved stakeholders (Waes, 1991; De Jong, 1994). This is what Earl (1993) refers to as the 'organizational' approach' to strategic IT planning.

5.3 'CONTROLLED DYNAMICS' AS A GOVERNANCE APPROACH

In the previous section it was argued that successfully governing IT-based infrastructure does not benefit from a rigid planning operation from a strictly top-down perspective. This fits well with the criticisms of general management methods for strategic planning as formulated by Mintzberg (1994), who convincingly argues that within firms there should be sufficient room for personal visions, experiments and learning. Many strategies can only be considered as such after execution, as a pattern in the total stream of strategic decisions ('emergent strategies'). This conclusion also has important implications for a more infrastructure-type of managing and governing IT. Not all plans concerning IT exploitation should necessarily be controlled in full detail A probably more successful approach is one in which dispersed end-applications are stimulated by building on, using and extending an IT-based infrastructure with more general functionality. This IT-based infrastructure enables and invigorates profitable IT exploitation at lower organizational levels. Governing IT in this respect is done more by triggering and stimulating business-specific decisions than directing them. Such a governance approach will be referred to here as 'controlled dynamics'.

For a good understanding of what is meant by 'controlled dynamics' a comparison with public infrastructure can (again) be very illuminating. Gerrity and Rockart (1986) define an approach for IT governance called the 'managed free economy'. This approach is a compromise between two extremes: the centrally guided integral approach and the approach in which all end-users have absolute freedom in deciding on their investment priorities. The former approach resembles in many respects the centrally driven planning economy, while the latter has many similarities with the *laissez-faire* economy. Boynton and Zmud (1987) speak in this sense of 'the information economy within the business'; a structure in which relatively autonomous organizational units partly cooperate and partly execute their own business-specific activities ('loosely coupled systems'; see Weick, 1979). The main management challenge in the governance approach of 'controlled dynamics' is to develop decision-making principles in which a balance is found between the interests of the organization as a whole and its constituent parts.

Investing in 'Substructure' and 'Superstructure'

The governance approach of 'controlled dynamics' fits well with important developments in organizational control theory. It is becoming increasingly clear that managing and governing today's firms is typically done by stimulating the ability of self-control of the different organizational parts (referred to as 'meta control' by De Leeuw, 1994). Organizations increasingly employ highly skilled professionals who continuously learn and increase their personal knowledge. This leads to a learning, knowledge-intensive organization, based upon cooperating teams, which permanently change and improve themselves (Senge, 1990; Tissen *et al.*, 1998). It has become clear that strategic management of such an organization is not likely to be successful if this is done through integrated and detailed planning, but is characterized by plotting a broad, strategic course and a 'remote control' style of management. Ciborra (1994) speaks in this respect of 'bricolage': stimulating strategies that are designed, evaluated and tested by employees with local knowledge and experience, instead of solely from a top-down perspective analyzing what the best strategy is ('from thinking to tinkering'). Governing IT deployment with

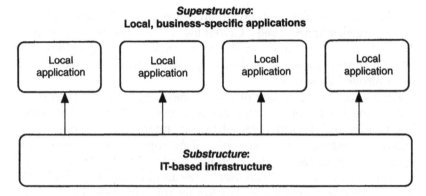

Figure 5.1   *The substructure and superstructure of IT deployment*

'controlled dynamics' as a strategic starting point means that a distinction is made between IT investments in two areas: the infrastructure 'substructure' and the business-specific 'superstructure' (see Figure 5.1).

Investing in Substructure

Investing in substructure means investing in a widely used, standardized set of infrastructure IT provisions that enables and secures coordination across relatively autonomous users of this infrastructure. For the organization as a whole and its senior executives this infrastructure is the stable factor in a dynamic business world. As such, the planning of IT-based infrastructure has replaced the integral planning of all IT provisions.

Investing in Superstructure

Investing in superstructure means investing in local, business-specific applications at the level of the users of IT-based infrastructure, which take account of, for example, 'own' client needs, working procedures and business processes. These applications build on and extend the available infrastructure provisions. These infrastructure provisions are the 'pillars' on which local applications grow and prosper.

Autonomy versus Control

Essential to these types of investment governance is that they break with the traditional way of looking at IT decision-making in business firms. Whereas the legitimacy of the central computing center used to be unquestionable, today it is very much a question of which basic facilities, such as processing servers, network standards, system development tools, are placed within the direct business environment and which will be shared among interested organizational units or even individual employees. Where the application focus used to be on developing all kinds of tailor-made systems, today the main issue is which applications and data will be shared and standardized and which will be left to the autonomy of organizational units. Consequently, the IT-based infrastructure on the one hand secures unity across different businesses by providing shared and standardized facilities, and on the other hand enables business-specific diversity by offering businesses the opportunity to freely build on and extend these facilities. As such, it serves as a governance tool to capture the business benefits of both autonomy and control.

Three Interlinked Processes

Governing IT-based infrastructure through investment projects requires managing three basic interlinked processes. These processes refer to managing an investment across its life-cycle:

- Identifying potential investments.
- Deciding on investment proposals.
- Measuring and managing investment results.

Although these processes will virtually always play a role when managing IT-based infrastructure, they also reflect the different aspects that require management attention in an investment process (see Figure 5.2). In this respect, Hogbin and Thomas (1994) speak of 'concept', 'calculate' and 'control'.

Management decisions on investment proposals have a strategic nature since they make the difference between choosing potentially successful and unsuccessful projects against the background of the desirability of a proposal. Investment decisions regarding infrastructure facilities should take account of two key assessment issues when assessing the business value of a project:

- Does investing (or even divesting) in a project deliver *added value* to the organization?
- Does the project deliver any *synergy* (or even dissynergy), by providing it as infrastructure?

Answering the question of added value means evaluating the potential benefits, costs and risks of an investment, which should give an indication of what the overall (dis)advantage is of executing a

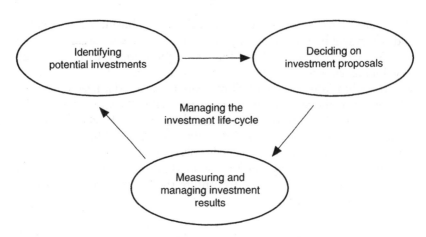

Figure 5.2   *Managing the investment life-cycle*

particular infrastructure project. Answering the synergy question means assessing the business impacts of providing the investment proposed as infrastructure, and whether these impacts are beneficial to the organization as a whole. Both questions should be answered by top management, as the strategic consequences for the entire organization need to be taken into account. Of course, the two questions are not independent; answering the question of synergy influences the evaluation of the added value of a project, and by answering both questions the overall business value of a project proposal can be assessed. Both questions also reflect the dynamic character of IT-based infrastructure. Although strategic policies may imply certain infrastructure in generic terms, an infrastructure will generally not be planned, designed and realized in its entirety but will change constantly since investment decisions will be made continuously on discrete infrastructure projects.

Infrastructure investment decisions ideally take place in an organizational context in which investments are explicitly initiated and investment results controlled. Investment decisions therefore are preceded by a phase in which a potential investment is identified, and followed by a phase in which an investment is managed. In this phase of investment management, project impacts that have previously been assessed by a clear investment evaluation are measured in terms of realized results which gives input to controlled investment outcomes. This crucial post-implementation phase of an investment project offers many opportunities for realizing previous choices and stated expectations and, more important, to learn from project experiences. This phase should be closely connected to signaling new potential investments, where the experience and knowledge gained from past successful projects is used to formulate investment initiatives based on realized investment results.

Identifying Potential Infrastructure Investments

The actual state of an IT-based infrastructure will vary as a result of the investment projects that are executed. Within a governance approach of 'controlled dynamics' investment proposals come from two directions: top-down and bottom-up. From the perceptive of planning theory, by discerning these two directions traditional methods with a largely top-down nature (see Ansoff, 1971; Steiner, 1971) and capital budgeting methods (see, for example, Bower, 1970) are brought together.

Top-Down Investments

Infrastructure assets are sometimes top-down directed and realized. One of the reasons for this is that organizations have to comply with all kinds of legal and fiscal legislation. Also agreements on industry level, national agreements, or international agreements can often not be ignored. Another reason for top-down investments is they ensue from overall strategic IT goals, intents and policies of an organization.

Bottom-Up Investments

Infrastructure assets can also be the consequence of common initiatives that are taken by local organizational units. Sometimes organizational units agree bottom-up to invest in infrastructure through mutual agreement, and without intervention from a higher hierarchical management level. Likely examples are, for instance, the purchase of a common development tool and the development of a system for coordinating mutual transactions. These types of initiatives can also be the subject of managerial decision-making at a higher level, if it seems appropriate and beneficial to endorse initiatives from the perspective of the entire firm. In all cases, it is advisable to create an investment climate in which bottom-up creativity is stimulated and to incorporate this in clear investment procedures (e.g. by subsidizing pilot projects which are expected to have an innovative infrastructure impact).

Measuring and Managing Investment Results

After deciding to invest in a proposed investment project, a post-implementation review can give very useful indications concerning the realized cost and benefits and the need to re-focus the project. The evaluation criteria used in the decision stage serve as performance metrics. This offers the opportunity to assess whether an investment really delivers 'value for money' and whether there is still room for improvement. Different studies show, however, that only few organizations pay attention and devote time to evaluations of investments after the implementation stage (Blackler and Brown, 1988; Kumar, 1991; Ward *et al.*, 1996b). Apart from performance evaluation as a prelude to benefits management, regular reviews of the investment also minimize the phenomenem of 'investment entrapment.' Investment entrapment (Van Dinther, 1993) refers to a situation in which ever-greater resource commitments are made because of too much emotional involvement, without sound evaluations of increased investment.

It can be of great value to make good use of the learning experiences gained in evaluations after the investment decision stage. Many investment decisions are still made by 'running from one project to the other'. If managed well, explicit reflections on the realized benefits, the costs incurred and the risks taken provide wonderful opportunities for organizational learning. In terms of the learning theory of Argyris and Schön (1978), investment control after the decision stage refers to 'single-loop' learning, while 'double-loop' learning refers to transferring learning experiences regarding past projects to new decision situations. Single-loop learning is aimed at managing and controlling a project in such a way that the initially stated investment goals are realized. In contrast, double-loop learning is aimed at questioning the way in which a project is managed and controlled, in order to assess whether the initially stated goals were realistic and achievable. This may result in a need to reformulate the project expectations and investment goals.

5.4   HOW TO USE A CHECKLIST OF INFRASTRUCTURE COMPONENTS

In the previous section it was argued that infrastructure project proposals can be initiated in a top-down manner and can be the consequence of bottom-up initiatives. In this process, which will lead to a portfolio of potential investments, a checklist of infrastructure components as discussed in the previous chapter can play an important supporting role. In line with the previous section such a checklist will have a dual role.

Top-Down Identification of Investment Proposals

A checklist of infrastructure components can be helpful in identifying preferred infrastructure investments from an organization-wide, top-down perspective. By modeling the existing infrastructure step-by-step, an overall view of the currently available infrastructure components can be created. Assessing these infrastructure components in terms of its status, capabilities, quality and (future) business value enables a more rigorous and goal-directed formulation of improvement, and thus investment opportunities. If an existing infrastructure component is already the result of an investment decision in which well-articulated and explicit value metrics were used, this makes it much easier to re-assess through performance evaluation whether the allocation of new funds and improvement actions are appropriate, or whether a divestment may even be appropriate. Such performance evaluations can also give valuable input to assess whether the infrastructure nature of a particular component should be maintained, or whether a more localized nature might be more appropriate. If there are no predefined value metrics available, an assessment of the existing infrastructure is likely to be of a more broad nature. Several methods and techniques have been proposed to support such an assessment, generally based on some sort of evaluation of current infrastructure support competitive needs, business process requirements, and quality standards (see, for example, Bedell, 1985, Earl, 1989). Experience shows that simple measurement scales (e.g. a five-point scale from 'poor' to 'excellent', or 'red', 'amber' and 'green' traffic lights) are much more appropriate than advanced mathematically sound, but often unpractical measurement scales. A quite straightforward yet rigorous method is to assess for each part of infrastructure:

- What the *infrastructure coverage* is, i.e. to what extent does it cover all potential opportunities for infrastructure-enabled support?
- What the *strategic importance* is, both in terms of alignment with current business strategies and enabling future business strategies.
- What the *functional quality* is, i.e. to what extent does it deliver the functionality for adequate business deployment ('fitness for use')?
- What the *technical quality* is, i.e. to what extent it conforms to technological standards and specifications, is maintainable, and meets defined service levels regarding, for example, availability, responsiveness, continuity and security.

These assessments may be combined in several graphical or tabular ways to get a clear overall picture of potentially desirable investments, for instance by using them as input for a multi-criteria or portfolio analysis (see Chapter 6). Figure 5.3 gives a synthesized illustration of this. In this example four types of basic business value profiles are identified. As such this gives a fairly rudimentary overview of the status of IT-based infrastructure, and thus sets an agenda for more detailed assessments of existing infrastructure components. The business value profiles discerned are based on the question of whether there is adequate deliverance of value or if there are still opportunities for investment increase or even a halt (see Figure 5.3):

- *Vital deliverance of value*: infrastructure importance and quality are balanced at a high level.
- *Non-critical deliverance of value*: infrastructure importance and quality are balanced at a low level.
- *Opportunities for investment increase*: high infrastructure importance but low quality level.
- *Opportunities for investment halt*: low infrastructure importance but high quality level.

In addition to this, the infrastructure coverage may be visualized, e.g. through an analysis of the present IT-based infrastructure-enabled support of the business, and the level of infrastructure capabilities

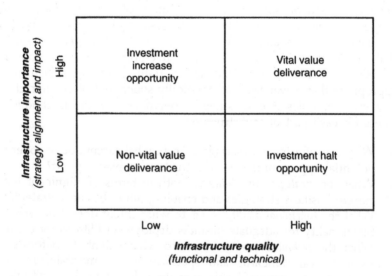

Figure 5.3   *Assessment of infrastructure status*

compared with their potential or ambition level. Essentially, these types of assessment are meant to evaluate whether the current capacities and capabilities of an infrastructure component are deemed to be problematic in terms of business value delivery, and whether this gives sufficient motivation to formulate a dedicated investment proposal.

Bottom-Up Canalization of Investment Initiatives

A checklist of infrastructure components can also be helpful in canalizing bottom-up proposals, i.e. by users of the infrastructure investment initiatives, to improve the IT-based infrastructure. By analyzing where and how a project proposal exactly impacts the existing infrastructure, a better view can be created of which infrastructure component will possibly be effected and what the business value of this may be. This can also give an indication of where the main contribution of a proposal will be: direct infrastructure, indirect infrastructure or both. If a proposed investment impacts the same infrastructure component as one which was a candidate for improvement in the top-down assessment, this gives additional reasons for formulating a potential investment.

Using a checklist of infrastructure components in a top-down and bottom-up manner makes it possible to arrive at a well-directed and well-structured formulation of potential investment projects, based on a clear view of the existing and the desired infrastructure. When taking the final investment decisions concerning these projects the evaluation criteria are analyzed in more detail and serve as value metrics to assess the business value of a proposal. Such an approach has the advantage of creating a value-driven IT-based infrastructure without extensive decision procedures, but with business value propositions on which to base the final judgments. Figure 5.4 gives a further illustration of this.

Establishing a Communication Process

When using a checklist of infrastructure components in the previously discussed manner, different views from involved stakeholders can be exchanged, discussed and—if the political context requires this—negotiated, which enables the establishment of shared mind-set for infrastructure improvement and for business value delivery. In this process the checklist offers a framework for the assessment of the existing infrastructure and for a more global sketch of the future infrastructure. If there is no knowledge available of the existing infrastructure, there is virtually no possibility of starting a communication

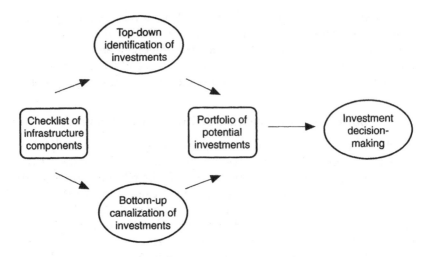

Figure 5.4   *Checklist-based identification of investment proposals*

process, which should center around the need for future investments and the appraisal of proposed investment projects in more generic terms. A first prerequisite for communicating is the existence of a common language. Everyone involved as an end-user, subject expert, IT specialist or business manager will implicitly have a limited and personal view of the IT-based infrastructure. The ability to make these informal views and judgments explicit will make the vital difference between a well-directed, value-focused change of the infrastructure and the risk of having an infrastructure with many unintended and inappropriate components. By doing so, a shared vision and mind-set is created concerning the existing and future infrastructure. This in turn is a prerequisite for taking clearly motivated investment decisions. Use of a checklist thus provides an agenda to start a communication process among all involved stakeholders.

5.5   CONCLUSIONS

This chapter has focused on the relation between the notion of IT-based infrastructure and governing this infrastructure through management decisions regarding investment projects. It has been argued that the classical, blueprint-type of methodologies for strategic IT planning do not match the more dynamic type of governance required for contemporary organizations. The most import issue for governing the IT-based infrastructure is how this can be incrementally improved. The governance approach underlying the notion of IT-based infrastructure has been typified as 'controlled dynamics'. This means that only the 'substructure' of IT provision is fixed and that the local, business-specific applications freely extend this infrastructure. Three basic processes are most important for infrastructure governance: top-down and bottom-up identification of potential investments, deciding on investment proposals, and finally measuring and managing investment results. Infrastructure investments can be both directed from a top-down perspective (e.g. emanating from the corporate hierarchy or from legislation) and be bottom-up initiated through mutual agreement of (semi-)autonomous organizational units. The use of a checklist of infrastructure components can be very useful for a well-directed and structured definition of a portfolio of potential investment projects. This checklist can be helpful for top-down identification of desirable infrastructure investments and for canalizing bottom-up proposed investment projects. The checklist then primarily serves as a communication instrument. By making the different views, opinions and judgments that ensue from different background knowledge and functions of involved stakeholders as explicit as possible, a foundation is laid for value-focused infrastructure creation.

6
Appraisal Methods for IT Investments

6.1   INTRODUCTION

In the previous chapter it was argued that taking the right investment decisions is the prime management issue for corporate governance of IT-based infrastructure. These investment decisions concern both top-down identified and bottom-up initiated project proposals. This chapter gives an overview and a critical review of the existing methods for IT investment appraisal. All too often new methods and guidelines for investment appraisal are introduced without building on the extensive body of knowledge that is already incorporated in the available methods. The purpose of this chapter is to examine the main strengths and weaknesses of existing appraisal methods.[1] First, in Section 6.2 the different concepts that are used in the evaluation are discussed and more narrowly defined. Subsequently Section 6.3 reviews the current methods and puts them into a frame of reference, reflecting the type of method and the main characteristics. Ten different methods serve as examples of a type of method. These ten methods are illustrated in more detail in Section 6.4, while Section 6.5 discusses the main short-comings of existing IT appraisal methods for investment decisions concerning IT-based infrastructure. This chapter's conclusions are given in Section 6.6.

---

[1] This chapter builds on and extends the review of IT appraisal methods as published in Renkema and Berghout (1997).

6.2 BASIC TERMINOLOGY

In order to be able to compare methods for the appraisal of IT investment proposals, one should avoid misinterpretations about the different concepts used. Also in appraisal practice the communication between stakeholders in the decision-making and evaluation processes can be improved by the use of a common language. Often when discussing IT investment notions are used, e.g. 'costs' and 'benefits', without being certain that everyone means the same thing. This section discusses and defines important investment concepts that are used in evaluation and in the remainder of the book, and that were, in the previous chapters, used more intuitively, according to daily speaking habits. Table 6.1 summarizes the main concepts and their relations.

A distinction is made between *financial* and *non-financial* impacts. Financial impacts are the impacts which can be expressed in monetary terms. Non-financial impacts cannot be expressed in monetary terms. The latter category is referred to as *contribution*. *Benefits* refer to all positive impacts of an IT investment and *sacrifices* to all negative impacts. With respect to financial impacts, a further distinction is made between *profitability* and *return*. The profitability in terms of *profits* (positive) or *losses* (negative) is defined as the accounting registration of *yieldings* and *costs*. This accounting registration reflects some accounting habits or principles. The return is determined by cash flow evaluation. Positive, incoming cash flows are *earnings*, while negative, outgoing cash flows are *expenditures*. Financial and non-financial impacts together determine the *business value* of an investment; business value therefore has a much broader content than just financial aspects. Although important, risk is not defined as a separate evaluation concept in Table 6.1. The reason for this is that risk is seen as a measure of uncertainty with respect to all specific impacts of an investment. The expected impacts can only very rarely be defined exactly, but almost always move between certain boundary values and margins. Uncertainty can, for example, be expressed in terms of the chances that

Investment impacts	Positive	Negative	Total
Financial	• Yields • Earnings	• Costs • Expenditures	• Profitability (profits or loss) • Return
Non-financial	• Positive contribution	• Negative contribution	• Contribution
Total	• Benefits	• Sacrifices	• Business value

Table 6.1 *Basic terminology*

the expected expenditures will be higher or the expected earnings will be lower. Uncertain factors that negatively influence the consequence and hence the resulting business value of an investment are referred to here as risks.[2]

When discussing investment concepts an important question that should be answered, but is often ignored, is: What is exactly meant by an investment? An investment can be defined by three main characteristics:

- An investment concerns a delineated collection of IT components, consisting of hardware (e.g. equipment and cables), software (e.g. operating system software, application packages, database software), IT staff (e.g. analysts, designers, programmers), and procedures (e.g. for system use or for new working methods).
- Scarce (financial and non-financial) resources are allocated to an investment at a certain decision moment, and these are expected to yield a positive result during several years. By doing this, financial assets are translated into real assets.
- An investment has a certain lifetime. If it is decided to stop allocating resources to an investment before the planned investment lifetime is over, the investment has become a divestment. Investments which are made after the initial decision stage, and which require separate justification, are maintenance investments.

6.3   A REVIEW OF APPRAISAL METHODS

Different authorities have given an overview of the available methods for the evaluation of IT investment projects, although often from different perspectives (see, for example, Carlson and McNurlin, 1989; Powell, 1992; Farbey *et al.*, 1993). In the context of this book more than 65 discrete methods were found, all with the purpose of assisting organizations with their IT investment decisions. An overview of these methods is given in the Appendix to this chapter. In Table 6.2 the existing methods are structured according to the type of method and the number of key characteristics, by means of discussing 10 typical methods. The different available financial methods are not analyzed in

---

[2] In more advanced mathematical theories, a division is made between 'risks' if there is uncertainty regarding decision outcomes, but a probability distribution can still be identified. 'Uncertainty' then refers to decision outcomes which do not match a predefined probability distribution. This book treats risks as commonly perceived when taking uncertain management decisions (see, for example, McGaughey *et al.*, 1994).

Characteristics		Financial methods	Multi-criteria methods		Ratio methods		Portfolio methods		
	Type of method	Financial methods	Information economics	SIESTA	Return on management	IT-assessment	Bedell's method	Investment portfolio	Investment mapping
Objects of the method	Breadth	Project-level	Project-level	Project-level	Organization-level	Project- and organization-level	Product- and organization-level	Project-level	Project- and organization-level
	Type of application area	Business investments	IT investments	IT investments	Business investments	IT investments	IT investments	IT investments	IT investments
Evaluation criteria	Financial	Earnings and expenditures	Earnings and expenditures (average accounting rate of return)	Unclear	Own measure	Yields and costs	Implicit assessment, specification of expenditures required	Earnings and expenditures (NPV)	Earnings and expenditures (IRR)
	Non-financial	None	4 business criteria 1 technological criteria	7 business criteria 6 technological criteria	Unclear	Different business criteria	Quality and importance	Business domain and IT domain separately	3 types of benefits and 3 investment orientations
	Risks	Deduction from expectations or coverage through adjusted discount rate	1 business risk 4 technological risks	4 business risks 8 technological risks	None	None	None	Deduction from expectations, spread can be specified	Spread can be specified
Support of the decision-making process		None	Discussed examples and mentions stakeholder groups	None	None	None	Maximal appraisal is once every year, mentions topmgt, users, IT staff	Discusses responsibilities, addresses role of business mgt, IT mgt. and project mgt.	None
Measurement scale		Ratio and interval	Ordinal	Ordinal	Interval	Several scales	Ordinal	Ordinal and interval	Ordinal and interval

Table 6.2 Methods for IT Appraisal

detail in Table 6.2, since the characteristics of these methods have many similarities.

Types of Method

Apart from methods that limit themselves to a purely financial appraisal of investment projects, three main non-financial approaches can be discerned. These are the multi-criteria approach, the ratio-approach, and the portfolio approach. In what follows all four approaches will be discussed.

The Financial Approach

Methods with a financial approach to investment evaluation only consider impacts which can be monetary valued. Traditionally they are prescribed for the justification and selection of all corporate investment proposals, and focus on the incoming and outgoing cash flows as a result of the investment made (see the standard accounting and capital budgeting texts, e.g. Brealey and Myers, 1988; Weston and Copeland, 1991). A calculation of yields and costs, as an estimation of the profitability of an investment, is not considered as being correct for evaluating the financial impacts of an investment proposal. When appraising a project in financial terms the purpose is to evaluate what *ex ante* (i.e. before the investment is actually implemented) the financial return is, as a consequence of the earnings and expenditures which result from the investment. Both are cash flows, as becomes clear when the terms 'cash proceeds' and 'cash outlays' are used (Bierman and Smidt, 1984). A payment to an external supplier for computing equipment is an example of an expenditure, and a reduction of staffing levels is an example of earnings. Cost and yield are essentially accounting-based terms, which are meant to report on and account for *ex post* profits or losses, and therefore open to many difficult-to-trace accounting decisions. Lumby (1991) therefore speaks of costs and yields as 'reporting devices' and of expenditures and earnings as 'decision-making' devices.

The Multi-Criteria Approach

Apart from financial impacts, an IT investment will generally have non-financial impacts, i.e. positive or negative impacts that cannot or not easily be expressed in monetary terms. Because of the differences between financial and non-financial impacts it is difficult to compare the different impacts on an equal basis. This however is a prerequisite for a comprehensive evaluation of an investment proposal and adequate prioritization of different proposals. Methods from the multi-criteria approach solve this problem by creating one single measure for each investment. Multi-criteria methods are used in many decision-making problems and are well known for their strength in combining quantitative and qualitative decision-making criteria. A good theoretical treatment of multi-criteria methods, applied in the realm of investments in advanced production technologies, is given by Canada and Sullivan (1989). Different variants of multi-criteria methods exist, but often the used methods function as follows. Before using a multi-criteria method, a number of goals or decision criteria have to be designed. Subsequently scores have to be assigned to each criterion for each alternative considered. Also the relative importance of each alternative should be established, by means of weights. The final score of an alternative is calculated by multiplying the scores on the different decision criteria by the assigned weights and adding or multiplying these.

The Ratio Approach

Economic researchers have long been paying special attention to the possibilities to compare organizational effectiveness by means of ratios. Several ratios have been proposed to assist in IT investment evaluation (Butler Cox, 1990; Farbey *et al.*, 1992). Examples of meaningful financial ratios are: IT expenditures versus total turnover and all yields that can be attributed to IS investments versus total profits. Ratios do not necessarily take only financial figures into account. IS expenditures can, for instance, be related to the total number of employees or to some output measure (e.g. products or services).

The Portfolio Approach

Portfolios (or 'grids') are a well-known decision-making tool in the management literature. A portfolio used in many strategic analyses is the 'Growth Share' portfolio for the positioning of product families of the Boston Consulting Group, which distinguishes between 'wild cats', 'stars', 'cash cows' and 'dogs.' In a portfolio several investment proposals are plotted against (sometimes aggregated) decision-making criteria.[3] Portfolio methods combine the comprehensiveness of multi-

---

[3] These portfolio types are different from the portfolios used with corporate finance, in which a portfolio refers to a set of assets, optimized from the perspective of balancing risk and return. When using this financial information for real assets (e.g. IT assets) this essentially is a refinement of the financial approach, although a similar approach can be used for risk management of the IT project portfolio (see Chapter 9, Section 9.9).

criteria methods with the graphic opportunities of portfolios. The number of evaluation criteria is generally less than in multi-criteria methods, but the result is often much more informative.

Key Characteristics of Methods

Apart from the type of method, the many available IT investment appraisal methods also differ in terms of their characteristics. This chapter distinguishes between four key characteristics to identify the main features of the different methods to be discussed: objects of the method, evaluation criteria of the method, support of the decision-making process, and the measurement scale of the method. These characteristics have the following meaning:

Objects of the Method

The objects of the method define to what extent a method limits itself to certain types of IT investments.

- *Breadth of the method*. With respect to the breadth of a method a distinction is made between 'project level assessment' (discrete investment proposals) and 'organizational level assessment' (the method takes a higher level than the project level into account, for instance by looking at the IT intensity or automation degree of certain departments).
- *Type of application area*. A method can also limit itself to a certain application area. A distinction is made between methods that are used specifically for IT investment appraisal and methods that are used for all types of business investments.

Evaluation Criteria of the Method

The evaluation criteria are the aspects that are addressed in the decision whether to go ahead with the proposed investment and to set priorities between competing projects. A distinction is made between financial impacts, non-financial impacts and risks. With respect to the financial impacts it is important to know whether the return or the profitability is evaluated.

Support of the Decision-Making Process

Support of the decision-making process refers to the extent to which a method indicates or prescribes how it should be used in evaluation practice. Complaints with respect to the evaluation of investment proposals often have to do with how difficult it is to make the possible benefits more tangible. A method might, for instance, suggest possible ways to identify the benefits of the investments, in addition to giving mere evaluation criteria. Furthermore, support could be given regarding the persons to be involved in the evaluation process and their responsibilities, data collection at the right level of detail, and the frequency of evaluations after the proposal stage.

Measurement Scale of the Method

The outcomes of an evaluation method can be measured on the following four measurement scales, with increasing meaning:

- *Nominal scale*: measurement units are used to classify on the basis of uniformity. This is done by defining 'labels' (for instance the purpose of the investment, i.e. value improvement, cost containment, risk reduction, etc., or simply type 1, 2 and 3 investments).
- *Ordinal scale*: measurement units are also used to represent a certain order. An example is to order all investment proposals from 'good' to 'bad.' The differences in this order indicate that a certain proposal is 'better' or 'worse' than another proposal, but not how much 'better' or 'worse'.
- *Interval scale*: the differences (or 'intervals') between measurement units also have a real meaning. This implies that one cannot only speak of 'better' or 'worse', but also of 'this much better' and 'this much worse.' A clear definition of a 'unity of distance' is required to be able to do this (a well-known example is the thermometer unit Celsius degrees). Intervals are defined in terms of a number of measurement units, which leads to a 'measurement rod.' When ranking investment projects on a scale from 0 to 100 interval units, the difference between the scores 2 and 8 is for instance three times more than between 10 and 12.
- *Ratio scale*: which in fact is an interval scale with a 'real', absolute zero (e.g. weight, length, contents or money). Only one object measured can be given the number zero. When using a ratio scale, the relation between two measurement units also has practical meaning. A project with an estimated financial result of US$100 000 not only is worth US$50 000 more than a project with a result of US$50 000, but also has double the value.

6.4   METHODS AND THEIR CHARACTERISTICS

The previous section reviewed the type of methods available for IT investment appraisal and their distinctive characteristics. This section discusses each type of method and number of methods in more detail. These methods serve as examples of the different types of method. The requirements for discussing a method are:

- The method should be well documented and accessible for further analysis.
- The method should have a clearly defined structure. This means that a method consisting of merely heuristic guidelines will not be discussed (see, for example, Clemons and Weber, 1990).
- The method should be characteristic of the type of method reviewed.

Financial Methods

The Payback Period

The payback period is the period between the moment that an IT investment gets funded and the moment that the total sum of the investment is recovered through the net incoming cash flows. If a proposed project, for instance, requires an investment of US$1 million and realizes cost savings of US$500 000 a year, the payback time is two years. The investing organization decides on a time period within which the sum must be recovered; if it is less than or equal to the calculated payback period, then it is justified to invest in the proposed project.

The Average Accounting Rate of Return

When calculating the accounting rate of return, the first step is to estimate the financial return for each year of the projected lifetime of an investment. This is then divided by the lifetime of the project. By then dividing this by the initial investment sum, the remaining ratio is the average rate of return. A related financial indicator, which sometimes is also referred to as the average accounting rate of return, is calculated by deducting the average yearly depreciation from the average yearly net cash flow and dividing by the average investment sum during the investment's lifetime.

The Net Present Value

The starting point in the net present value (NPV) method is the opportunity cost of capital. This rate is used as the discount rate to calculate the NPV. If this value is larger than zero, it is considered to be wise to go ahead with the investment. The higher the NPV, the higher the project priority should be. By using the discounting technique,[4] earnings and expenditures which do not occur at the same moment in time become comparable. To illustrate this: if, for instance, one puts US$100 in a savings account, this will be worth US$105 when receiving an interest of 5%. This also works the other way around; if one has to pay US$105 in a year, this liability is worth US$100 now. By calculating like this, all earnings and expenditures can be made 'today's money.'

The Internal Rate of Return

The internal rate of return (IRR) is the threshold at which, after discounting the incoming and outgoing cash flows, the NPV equals zero. If this threshold exceeds the opportunity cost of capital, it is considered to be worthwhile to launch the project. So instead of using a fixed rate of 5% as in the NPV method, the IRR for earnings and expenditures is calculated and it is checked whether this is higher than 5%. This procedure thus requires substantial calculations.

The latter two methods (often referred to as 'Discounted Cash Flow' (DCF) methods) are, from a financial perspective, considered to be superior to financial methods, as they take into account the time value of money. This means that if the moment of receipt of the cash flow is farther into the future, the value of these cash flows will be less. This is due to the presupposition that decision-makers have an aversion to risk.

Extensions to the Financial Approach

The chapter's review of financial methods focuses on the 'classical' methods of financial investment appraisal. Empirical research studies in capital budgeting and corporate finance have however shown that decision-makers generally do take account of the non-financial impacts of investment proposals (Bower, 1970; Butler *et al.*, 1993). Also for business areas other than IT, for instance organizational design and

---

[4] The appropriate formula for discounting cash flows is:

$$CF_v = \sum CF_n / (1 + d)^n,$$

where:

CF_v = discounted cash flow,
CF_n = cash flow in year n,
d = discount rate, and
n = the specific year.

product innovation, it has become clear that strictly financial methods have many limitations when trying to assess the strategic potential of new investment initiatives. These limitation are well captured in the words of Kaplan (1986): 'Conservative accountants who assign zero values to many intangible benefits prefer being precisely wrong to vaguely right.' In response to this, the financial theory has suggested several additions to the strictly financial approach. Examples of this are the use of sensitivity analysis, adding a risk factor to the discount rate (risk-adjusted discount rates), and the use of so-called certainty equivalents. Sassone (1988), for instance, suggests several of the more advanced financial methods for what he calls 'benefit valuation.' Recently option theory has received increased attention, which tries to evaluate investment using calculation principles from financial option theory (see Dos Santos, 1991; Kambil *et al.*, 1993). For investment projects with a large infrastructure impact this approach seems especially promising. Chapter 9 will discuss this option theory and its limitations for evaluating investments in IT-based infrastructure in more detail. Another proposed alternative is to leave that part of the investment that cannot be financially justified open to management judgment (the 'X gap'; see Wilkes and Samuels, 1991). In the 'strategic cost management' approach, it is tried to systematically link financial effects to the strategic advantages of technological innovation (Shank and Govindarajan, 1992).

Recently the concept of the 'balanced scorecard', as introduced by Kaplan and Norton (1992), has received much attention from business and finance managers. This method can be seen as an extension of the traditional accounting-based financial methods, and has also been applied to IT investment assessment and measurement (Willcocks and Lester, 1994; Zee, 1996). The balanced scorecard has been developed in order to get a broader perspective in management accounting metrics than is available by using strictly financial methods. A division is made between a financial perspective, a customer perspective, an internal perspective and an innovation and learning perspective. In fact, this method uses a multi-criteria approach to performance management, see the next section.

Multi-Criteria Methods

Information Economics

In the field of evaluating IT investment proposals, Parker *et al.* (1988, 1989) have given the multi-criteria approach widespread publicity with their 'Information Economics' method. Quite a lot of firms have already been using this method, and many consulting firms have developed their own variants of it (see, for example, Wiseman, 1992). Although Information Economics has received a lot of attention already, this section will briefly discuss the method.

The first criterion of Information Economics method gives a financial appraisal of a proposed investment. Parker *et al.* call this the 'enhanced' return on investment (ROI). This ROI not only looks at cash flows arising from cost reduction and cost avoidance, but also provides some additional techniques to estimate incoming cash flows:

- Value linking: additional cash flows that accrue to other departments.
- Value acceleration: additional cash flows due to a reduced time-scale for operations.
- Value restructuring: additional cash flows through restructuring work and improved job productivity.
- Innovation valuation: additional cash flows arising from the innovating aspects of the investment (e.g. competitive advantage).

With respect to non-financial impacts and risks, Information Economics makes a distinction between the business domain and the technology domain. The technology domain offers IT opportunities to the business domain, while the business domain focus is on optimal deployment of IT and 'pays' the technology domain for the use of resources. In the two domains several criteria are discerned (see Table 6.3). To summarize, the total appraisal of an IT investments proposal takes place in three steps, covering financial, business and technological criteria, both positive and negative.

SIESTA

The second multi-criteria method that receives a more detailed treatment here was designed in the University of Amsterdam (Van Irsel *et al.*, 1992). The SIESTA method probably is the one of the most extensive multi-criteria methods available to the evaluator. The method is supported by several questionnaires and additional software in order to assess the practical importance of the criteria. The appraisal criteria are deduced from a model in which a distinction is made between the business and the technological domain and three levels of decision-making are discerned. Benefit and risk criteria are deduced from the extent to which the different elements of the model fit the total model (inspired by the 'Strategic Alignment Model', see Chapter 3). Figure 6.1 shows the structure of the model.

Appraisal criteria	Meaning
Business Domain	
Strategic match	The extent to which the investment matches the strategic business goals
Competitive advantage	The extent to which the investment contributes to an improvement of positioning in the market (e.g. changes in industry structure, improvements of competitive positioning in the industry)
Management information	The extent to which the investment will inform management on core activities of the firm
Competitive response	The extent to which not investing implies a risk; a timely investment contributes to strategic advantage
Organizational risk	The extent to which new competencies are required
Technology Domain	
Strategic information systems architecture	The extent to which the investment matches the IT plan and the required integration of IT applications
Definitional uncertainty	The extent to which user requirements can be clearly defined
Technical uncertainty	The extent to which new technical skills, hardware and software are required
Infrastructure risk	The extent to which the investment requires additional infrastructure investments and the IT department is capable of supporting the proposed system

Table 6.3   *The Information Economics Method (from Parker et al., 1988)*

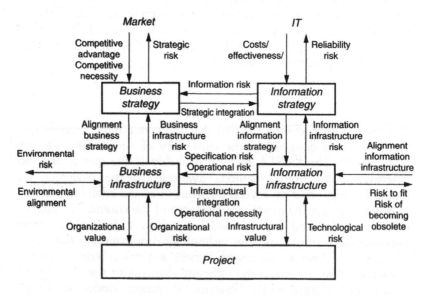

Figure 6.1   *The SIESTA method (after Van Irsel et al., 1992)*

Ratio Methods

The Return on Management Method

A ratio approach that has attracted a lot of attention is the 'Return on Management' (ROM) method of Strassmann (1990); see also Van Nievelt (1992). The method presupposes that in today's information economy management has become the scarce resource, and that the right type of management defines the extent to which business value is derived from IT deployment. In the ROM method the value added by management is related to the costs of management. Analysis with the ROM method is supported by the MPIT database, which contains company data from about 300 companies over several years. This database can be used for complete organizational diagnosis or for analyzing the impacts of specific investments. Unfortunately the database is not for public use, but has a commercial trademark.

The IT Assessment Method

The consulting firm Nolan Norton have designed a method, 'IT Assessment' for the evaluation of information technology effectiveness from a strategic point of view (see Zee and Koot, 1989; Janssen *et al.*, 1993). An important part of the method focuses on the analysis of financial and non-financial ratios. The ratios are subsequently compared with benchmarks, i.e. average values that were collected through research in other organizations. These benchmarks are not for public use. The ratios are also used for an historical analysis of the organization and its use of IT. Used in this way, the ratios can be of help in decision-making on new strategic initiatives.

Portfolio Methods

Bedell's Method

Bedell's portfolio method (Bedell, 1985; Van Reeken, 1992) subsequently answers three questions:

- Should the organization invest in IT applications?
- In which activities should the organization invest?
- Which IT applications should be developed?

The central premise of Bedell's method is that a balance is needed between 'quality' and 'importance.' This is also the basis upon which the answers to the three questions are sought. IT investments are more appropriate if the relation between the perceived quality of the systems and the importance of information systems is worse.

Information systems are more important if they support important activities and if the activities are more important to the organization. Before the three questions can be answered and calculations are made, several assessments have to be performed. These assessments concern:

- The importance of an activity to the organization.
- The importance of IT-based support to the activities.
- The quality of the IT support in terms of effectiveness, efficiency and timing.

In a more detailed investment analysis the three questions are answered by the involved stakeholders: senior management, user management and IT specialists. The prioritization of investment proposals is carried out by calculating the 'contribution' of each IT system and by plotting three portfolios. The contribution of an IT application is defined as the importance of the system multiplied by the improvement in quality after development. To evaluate the business value of the investment, a Project-Return index can be calculated by relating the contribution of the IT system to the development costs. A more detailed review of Bedell's method is provided by Renkema and Berghout (1997).

Investment Portfolio

The 'Investment Portfolio' (Berghout and Meertens, 1992; Berghout, 1997) evaluates IT investment proposals on three criteria simultaneously. The three criteria subsequently evaluate:

- The contribution to the business domain.
- The contribution to the IT domain.
- The financial return, by means of a net present value (NPV) calculation.

The portfolio (see Figure 6.2) serves as a framework to make the preferences of the different stakeholders explicit and debatable. Important stakeholders taken into account are: senior management, IT management and the project management of the development project. These three parties subsequently evaluate the investment proposal on one of the three evaluation criteria.

The size of the Net Present Value (NPV) of an investment proposal is plotted in the portfolio by means of a circle. The larger the circle, the higher the expected NPV. The contribution to the business domain

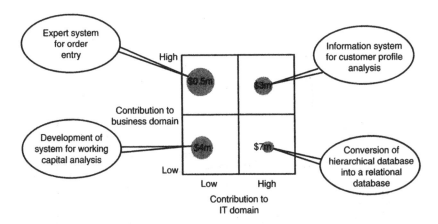

Figure 6.2 *The Investment Portfolio (after Berghout and Meertens, 1992)*

focuses on the long-term benefits, leading to an improvement in the products or services of the organization. The authors suggest that the criteria of the Information Economics method can be used for this. The contribution to the IT domain is assessed by criteria such as conformance to technology standards, market acceptance of the used technologies and continuity of suppliers. In addition to evaluating a single IT investment proposal, the Investment Portfolio can be used to compare and prioritize several investment projects. It also offers a risk and sensitivity analysis by varying the size of the circle and by changing the position of a circle.

Investment Mapping

Peters (1988) designed the 'Investment Map', in which investment proposals are plotted against two main evaluation criteria: the investment orientation and the benefits of the investment. The investment orientation is broken down into infrastructure, business operations and market influence. The benefits are broken down into enhancing productivity, risk minimalization and business expansion. These categories partly overlap. Figure 6.3 gives a visual representation of the Investment Map. The position of an investment proposal on the two axes is determined by a score on the evaluation criteria, which can be input to more detailed evaluation at the individual project level (see Peters, 1990). A portfolio that has been visualized makes the IT investment strategy more explicit and debatable. The Investment Map can also be used to investigate the alignment of the IT investment strategy

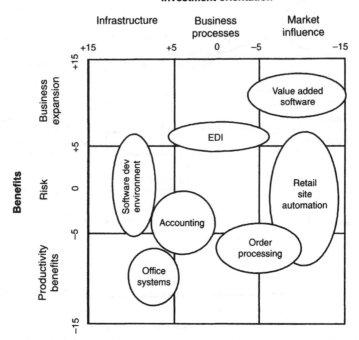

Figure 6.3 *Investment Mapping (from Peters, 1988)*

and the business strategy. To do this, a distinction is made between, for instance, a quality-driven or a cost leadership strategy. Additionally, it is possible to carry out a competitor analysis by plotting the strategies of the main competitors in the portfolio.

Assessment of Appraisal Methods

Section 6.2 discussed how the methods that serve as examples are assessed using a number of assessment criteria. In what follows a summary of this assessment will be given.

Objects of the Method

The methods discussed do not limit themselves much in terms of the objects of the investment.

- *Breadth of the method.* Almost all methods discussed are meant to support the appraisal of specific IT investment projects. The ROM method and Investment Mapping try to measure investment effects on the level of the entire firm. Bedell's methods and IT Assessment additionally look at separate business processes or activities in the organization.

- *Type of application area.* Regarding the type of application area, financial methods differ from non-financial methods. The financial methods are used for all types of business investments. The non-financial methods discussed are all specifically designed for investments in IT. Only the ROM method is also meant for a more generic assessment of organizational value.
- *Financial criteria.* The criteria of the financial methods do not need any further explanation. Almost all non-financial methods take financial criteria into account to some extent, when evaluating investment impacts. Investment Portfolio and Investment Mapping look at cash flows through the NPV and the IRR, respectively. Information Economics calculates the accounting rate of return. Regarding the SIESTA method, it is not clear how financial consequences are accounted for, while ROM uses its own specific financial measure. Bedell's method implicitly uses a financial valuation when evaluating the 'quality' criterion and requires a specification of the investment expenditures.
- *Non-financial criteria.* The non-financial methods take many different criteria into account to evaluate the business contribution of investments. All criteria concern business goals and technology-related aspects. None of the methods explicitly motivates the choice for the set of criteria, or underpins this with a particular theory. Consequently the methods differ much in terms of the number and type of criteria covered.
- *Risks.* The methods look at risks in several ways. Generally risks can be translated into a spread surrounding expectations. A risk analysis can, for instance, be carried by calculating the 'best' and 'worst' cases. Both the financial methods and the Investment Portfolio calculate the most likely outcomes. When using Information Economics, the estimated risk is deducted from the most likely outcomes. The ROM method, IT Assessment and Bedell's method do not consider risks. The SIESTA method uses several criteria with respect to risk but is not clear how these risks should be treated. The Investment Mapping method takes the spread of the possible outcomes into account.
- *Support of the decision-making process.* Strikingly, hardly any methods offer clear practical support for the decision-making process for IT investment. This support is often limited to mentioning the different disciplines to be represented (e.g. management, IT staff and end-users). Issues such as which responsibilities are needed, or how often

an evaluation should be done after an initial appraisal, do not get much attention. A firm and prominent role is given to top management to make the final investment decision. Although the final responsibility for resource allocations lies there of course, it can be doubted whether top managers should be fully informed of the impacts of all investment initiatives.

- *Measurement scale.* Methods that focus on a financial appraisal are, by definition, using a ratio and/or an interval scale. The other methods employ measurement scales rather arbitrarily. Several methods calculate a final score for each investment project using ordinal scores, although an ordinal measurement scale does not allow this (e.g. Information Economics, SIESTA and Bedell's method).

6.5   LIMITATIONS OF EXISTING METHODS

The previous sections have given an overview of existing appraisal methods for IT investments by identifying types of methods and their main characteristics. Taking this into account, this section discusses the main limitations of these appraisal methods for taking adequate investment decisions regarding IT-based infrastructure. This leads to the design of more appropriate management tools for business value assessment of IT-based infrastructure in the remainder of this book. The limitations identified here are in the following areas.

Long-Term and Enabling Nature of Infrastructure Investments

The discussed methods have a clear focus on decisions regarding IT application in an end-user environment. As such, the methods seem to take existing methods for IT system development as a reference. For many of the contemporary infrastructure-oriented IT investments this orientation does not suffice, and in fact can impede a good view on the real business value of infrastructure. To obtain such a view, investment appraisal should focus on the future, long-term advantages of having an IT-based infrastructure. In particular, for the indirect infrastructure, with its enabling and facilitating character, the existing methods have many limitations.

Organizational Collaborations

An implicit starting point of existing appraisal methods is that investment decisions are taken within a clearly identifiable firm or business unit. Consequently, the fact that infrastructure investment crosses the boundaries between individual organizations or organizational units is not reflected in these methods. Also the cooperation structures with organizational entities in the organizational environment are hardly a point of attention. In addition, little attention is given to the integration of an organizational unit within a higher organizational level (e.g. a business unit, division or diversified corporation).

Coherence of Decision-Making Criteria

The evaluation or decision criteria of the existing methods virtually all refer to money, technology and general business goals of profit-oriented firms. There is not much attention given to investment impacts on, for example, organizational culture or work conditions and to the political implications of proposed investments. Contemporary infrastructure-oriented investments do however impact profoundly on such aspects. This limited view on infrastructure impacts may be due to the apparent lack of theoretical grounding and practical validation of methods. Consequently, the decision criteria do not have much cogency and often seem to be based on *ad hoc* choices. A typical example of this is that often no difference is made between earnings/expenditures versus costs/yields. Consequently, with some manipulation, each method can quite easily be translated to another method (Kusters and Renkema, 1996), although individual methods suggest a quite rigid set of criteria. The overall conclusion therefore is that a coherent, structured framework of decision criteria, which can be used to derive appropriate organization-specific value metrics, does not exist.

Integration of 'Hard' and 'Soft' Evaluation Elements

In Chapter 1 it was argued that an important element of business value generation from IT-based infrastructure is the integration of hard, content-related issues with soft elements, focusing on social and political processes. Concerning these softer issues, the available arsenal of appraisal methods does not offer much support for investment decision-making. Virtually all methods focus entirely on the 'hard' side of management decisions by suggesting a set of selection criteria. This is done at the expense of other decision-making elements, such as how and by whom these criteria should be used, and when and in what way these criteria play a role in organizational decision-making. Walsham (1993), in his plea for a more socio-political interpretation of evaluation, puts this as follows:

Much of the literature on evaluation in general, and IS evaluation in particular, takes a formal-rational view of organizations, and sees evaluation as a largely quantitative process of calculating the preferred choice and evaluating the likely cost/benefit on the basis of clearly defined criteria.

On the basis of the organizational change theories of Pettigrew (1985), several researchers working from an interpretative research philosophy have proposed a model for investment evaluation. This consists of the following three elements:

- *Content*: the 'what' of the evaluation. This concerns the criteria covered in decision-making, and the way these are assessed and measured.
- *Process*: the 'how' of the evaluation. This concerns such aspects as mutual understanding, the development of a common language and the use of learning experiences.
- *Context*: the 'who' and 'why' of the evaluation. This refers to the organizational and external environment in which decision-making takes place.

In light of these three elements, it can be concluded that the existing methods for IT investment appraisal pay relatively too much attention to content-related, decision-criteria-oriented aspects of decision-making. A consequence of this is that process- and context-related aspects, which are no less important, do not get sufficient attention.

6.6   CONCLUSIONS

After a discussion of relevant basic terminology, this chapter reviewed and assessed the existing methods for IT investment appraisal. It has become clear that these methods differ in many aspects. In addition to purely financial types of methods, multi-criteria, ratio and portfolio methods can be discerned. Although a plethora of methods can be found, the methods do not offer much support for the infrastructure nature of today's IT investment decisions of organizations. For a more infrastructure-oriented support appropriate attention should be given to the long-term and enabling nature of investments, possible intra- and interorganizational collaborations, the use of a coherent set of decision criteria, and last but not least to a better integration of content-related issues with processual and political appraisal issues.

APPENDIX: OVERVIEW OF METHODS FOR IT INVESTMENT APPRAISAL

This appendix summarizes the survey of existing methods for IT investment appraisal that was conducted in the mid-1990s. Although this research was carried out with the utmost care, the survey cannot be considered exhaustive. Almost daily new methods are published, and consulting firms often use specific well-considered methods which are however not published because of the possible competitive advantage. For some methods the original source is not given, but is referred to articles or books in which the method is mentioned or reviewed. The list of references is not an exhaustive one, but it has been produced to give the best references, preferably from the IT-related literature. Also not all methods are specifically designed for the evaluation of IT investments.

Method	References
Accounting rate of return	Bacon (1992)
Analytic hierarchy process	Saaty (1980); in: Carter (1992)
Application benchmark technique	in: Powell (1992)
Application transfer team	in: Lincoln (1990)
Automatic value points	in: Lincoln (1990)
Balanced scorecard	Kaplan and Norton (1992), in: Douglas and Walsh (1992)
Bayesian analysis	Kleijnen (1980)
Bedell's method	Bedell (1985); in: van Reeken (1992)
Buss's method	Buss (1983)
Benefits–risk portfolio	McFarlan and McKenney (1983); in: van Irsel and Swinkels (1992)
Benefit assessment grid	Huigen and Jansen (1991)
Breakeven analysis	Sassone (1988)
Boundary value	in: Farbey *et al.*, (1992, 1993)
Cost–benefit analysis	King and Schrems (1978); Sassone and Schäfer (1978)
Cost–benefit ratio	Yan Tam (1992)
Cost displacement/avoidance	in: Sassone (1988)
Cost effectiveness analysis	in: Sassone (1988)
Cost–value technique	Joslin (1977)
Cost revenue analysis	in: Farbey *et al.* (1992)
Critical success factors	Rockart (1979)
Customer resource life-cycle	Ives and Learmonth, (1984); in: Hochstrasser and Griffiths, (1990)
Decision analysis	in: Sassone (1988); in: Powell (1992)
Delphi evidence	in Powell (1992)

(*Continued*)

Method	References
Executive Planning for Data Processing	in: Lincoln (1990)
Functional Analysis of Office Requirements	Schäfer (1998)
Gameplaying	in: Farbey *et al.* (1992)
Hedonic wage model	in: Sassone (1988)
Information Economics	Parker *et al.* (1988, 1989)
Investment mapping	Peters (1988, 1989)
Investment portfolio	Berghout and Meertens (1992)
Information systems investment strategies	in: Lincoln (1990)
Knowledge-based system for IS evaluation	Agarwal *et al.* (1992)
MIS utilization technique	in: Powell (1992)
Multi-objective, multi-criteria methods	in: Farbey *et al.* (1992); Vaid-Raizada (1983)
Option theory	Dos Santos (1991); Kambil *et al.* (1993)
Potential problem analysis	in: Powell (1992)
Profitability index	Bacon (1992)
Process quality management	in: Lincoln (1990)
Quality engineering	Hochstrasser (1993)
Return on investment	Brealey and Myers (1988); Farbey *e al.* (1992)
Return on management	Strassmann (1990); van Nievelt (1992)
Requirements–costing technique	Joslin (1977)
Schumann's method	in: van Irsel and Swinkels (1992)
SESAME	Lincoln (1986); Lincoln and Shorrock (1990)
Seven milestone approach	Silk (1990)
Strategic application search	in: Lincoln (1990)
Strategic option generator	Wiseman (1985)
Systems investment methodology	in: Lincoln (1990)
Simulation	Kleijnen (1980); in: Farbey *et al.* (1992); in: Powell (1992)
Socio-technical project selection	Udo and Guimaraes (1992)
Satisfaction and priority survey	in: Lincoln (1990)
Structural models	in: Sassone (1988)
System dynamics analysis	Wolstenholme *et al.* (1992)
Systems measurement	Spraque and Carlson (1982); in: Powell (1992).
Time savings times salary	in: Sassone (1988)
User utility function assessment technique	in: Powell (1992)
Value analysis	Keen (1981)
Value chain analysis	Porter (1985)
Ward's portfolio analysis	Ward (1990)
Wissema's method	Wissema (1983)
Zero based budgeting	in: Zmud (1983)

7
Investment Decisions with the P4 Model

7.1 INTRODUCTION

Following the previous chapter which reviewed the presently available methods for IT investment appraisal, this chapter presents a model for taking and governing investment decisions concerning IT-based infrastructure. The focus of this chapter is on the strategic and organizational dimensions of such infrastructure decisions, and offers a synthesized perspective on how to manage these decisions. First, Section 7.2 discusses a number of important developments in the area of organizational and managerial decision-making, with particular attention to the concept of bounded rationality. Subsequently, Section 7.3 looks at four styles of decision-making, based on a distinction between the product and process dimensions of decision-making and inspired by the way firms take strategic investment decisions. These two sections set the scene for Section 7.4, in which a model is presented—paraphrasing conventional business wisdom in marketing, coined the P4 model—which offers four control options to management investment evaluation and to support organizational decision-making. This chapter's conclusions are given in Section 7.5.

7.2 FOUNDATIONS FOR ORGANIZATIONAL DECISION-MAKING

Decision-making plays an important role in organizational theory, both in a descriptive and a prescriptive way. The decision-making approach can even be considered to be a specific school in organizational theory, and combines several disciplines such as psychology, economics, operations research and statistics. Adequate control of decision-making has become one of the key factors for successfully managing and controlling organizations in strategic, tactical and operational terms. In today's turbulent and often diffuse business environment an important differentiating factor in a firm's ability to innovate and compete is managerial decision-making. As a consequence of ever-faster developments in the environment of organizations, decision-makers need to make the right decisions at the right moment.

Quality of Decision-Making

In line with the increased importance of decision-making in organizations, much decision research effort has been devoted to designing instruments which can increase the quality of organizational and managerial decisions. 'Decision quality' refers to aspects such as (see, for example, Vroom and Jago, 1988, Butler *et al.*, 1993):

- The 'correctness' of a decision, or in other words the extent to which decision-making stakeholders have confidence that the outcome of a decision process will reflect the aspired goals and that all relevant aspects have been adequately addressed.
- The level of organizational commitment and the degree of acceptance of a decision.
- Learning experiences which are gained by taking a decision and by having a learning-oriented decision process.
- The efficiency of the decision-making process: taking a decision with minimal effort, both in financial and organizational terms.

In their study of the behavioral aspects of organizational decision-making, Janis and Mann (1977) extracted the following criteria to judge whether decisions are of a high quality.

- There are clearly defined and well-known goals.
- Decision-makers have clear knowledge of a number of alternative courses of action.
- The projected advantages and disadvantages of a particular choice are carefully evaluated.
- Decision-makers are open to new information, even if they have preliminary ideas regarding a possible solution.
- Even if new information conflicts with preferred choices, there is sufficient room for correct interpretation.

- There is a re-examination of all known alternatives before making the final decision.
- When implementing the final decision, there is a defined implementation plan, which allows for contingency measures to mitigate risks.

The ultimate goal of improving the quality of decision-making should always be to increase the chance of success of the investment considered. As such, a distinction can be made between:

- 'good' decisions, i.e. decisions that have a high degree of quality (e.g. a comprehensive problem diagnosis, complete coverage of all decision alternatives, high organizational acceptance, fast decision-making); and
- 'successful' decisions, i.e. decisions that are successful in terms of their outcomes (e.g. financial results, customer satisfaction or competitive advantage).

Devoting time and resources to improving the quality of organizational decision-making can be considered an important requisite for making successful decisions, and therefore for maximizing the business value gained from IT-based infrastructure. Apart from well-articulated investment goals and valuation criteria this also means process-oriented issues such as management commitment, mutual trust and a common 'language.' Special attention to the quality of decision-making in order to arrive at good (and ultimately successful) decisions becomes more important if, relatively speaking:

- Investments have many (intangible) organizational and strategic impacts.
- Of these impacts many are human and social impacts.
- Investments require much funding and resources.
- There are high expectations and ambitious targets regarding investment results.
- There is much uncertainty concerning the possibility of realizing the results.
- Investment stakeholders have many different interests and power bases.
- Investments have an innovating nature, both in terms of technology and business.

The more projects meet these investments characteristics, the more evaluations and decisions will have to rely on managerial judgment and stakeholder assessment, at the expense of pure financial and analytical techniques. This should not be considered as detrimental for high quality decision-making, but as an opportunity to motivate the use of more qualitative yet relevant methods for decision-making.

The Classical Model of Rational Decision-Making

The classical economic model of the pure rational decision-maker (the *Homo Economicus*) plays an important role in theories of organizational and managerial decision-making. This model can be characterized by three central premises:

- A decision-maker knows exactly what he (or she) wants i.e. he has clear and unambiguous goals in mind. In economic theories this usually means maximization of utility or profits.
- A decision-maker is omniscient, which means that he oversees all possible decision alternatives.
- A decision-maker has unlimited capability to process information.

This rational model is easily recognizable in the support of what have been called 'programmable decisions' (Harrison, 1987) or 'well-structured problems' (Bass, 1983). Often algorithmic, mathematical models from the field of operations research are used. Characteristically the contributions of different decision alternatives are usually projected using historical data. Ackoff (1979) calls this the 'predict and prepare' paradigm, while Rosenhead (1989) speaks of 'colonizing the future.' These kinds of decision-making techniques are abundant within control decisions of operations management for routine, predictable processes (e.g. for inventory management, materials management, sales analysis). This mathematical, statistical approach, however, falls short when supporting non-routine, more strategic management issues. These are characterized by complexity, subjectivity, qualitative effects, uncertainty and possible conflicts between interested parties and stakeholders. Therefore, these kinds of decisions are difficult to structure and to program in advance. Management decisions regarding IT-based infrastructure are typically decisions of the latter category. Advanced mathematical methods and techniques are thus of limited value to support capital-intensive infrastructure investment decisions.

Bounded Rationality as a Decision-Making Paradigm

The central premises of the classical model of rational decision-making have proved to be very unrealistic for organizational decision-making, both in descriptive and prescriptive terms. In fact, rational decision-making can be considered nothing less than a utopian construct. Many empirical studies have made clear that decision-makers generally do not and, more importantly, cannot act according to the rational decision-making model.[1] Apart from evaluations that can more or less be considered 'rational', decision-makers are influenced by, for instance, emotions, self-interest and prejudices. Much of the deviation from the classical rational model can be explained by its 'holistic' view of organizational decision-making: which means that decisions are supposed to be taken by a single entrepreneur and owner of the firm whose main goal is to maximize profits.[2] Employees are assumed to be unfailingly loyal to this profit orientation, and to the organization as a whole.

Practical decisions, however, are generally bound up with the interests and goals of several stakeholder groups, e.g. management, business units or departments, trade unions, and financiers. Also firm goals are not always unambiguous but vague (e.g. 'strategic advantage') or even contradictory (e.g. cost containment and marketing effectiveness). Organizations not only strive for financial returns and maximal profits but also for continuity, power/stature and the realization of a good working environment and climate. Moreover, many firm goals are 'constructed' in the course of a decision-making process, and are therefore not necessarily defined or known in advance (Weick, 1979; Checkland and Scholes, 1990). In addition to this, human decision-making is constrained by cognitive limits: omniscience is nothing less than an illusion; information-processing capabilities are limited.

Nobel laureate Herbert Simon has introduced the more descriptive and realistic view of the 'administrative man' in contrast to the *Homo Economicus*. The decisions of this 'administrative man' are guided by what Simon (1977) refers to as 'bounded rationality', which means that:

- Not all decision alternatives and their consequences are known in advance. In the search process for alternatives every decision-maker constructs a subjective and limited view (or, to use the German noun, a 'Weltanschauung', see Checkland, 1981) of the relevant decision issues, alternatives and possible solutions. This view is highly dependent upon the specific background, knowledge and

---

[1] The classic model of rational decision theoretically is founded within neo-classical economics. Within the academic community of economists many academicians admit that the neo-classical theory is not appropriate for describing or supporting organizational decision-making. Ryan *et al.* (1992) for instance argue: 'Neoclassical theory was developed by economists to predict general patterns of economic behaviour. It was never intended to be an explanation of how individuals do or should behave.'

[2] The holistic model of an organization is also rooted within neo-classical economics, in which a firm is conceptualized as a production function between the supply markets of production factors and the sales markets of products and services.

experiences of the decision-maker. All kinds of heuristics (i.e. rules of thumb) which have proved to be successful in past decision situations are used in the search process

- A decision-maker does not look for all possible decision alternatives in a process of problem resolution, but limits himself to a number of alternatives which are considered to be satisfactory. Subsequently a solution is chosen that best matches his aspiration levels. This is called 'satisficing' instead of 'optimizing' decision behavior. Consequently, decision support should focus on structuring the steps that lead to a satisfactory solution. Simon makes a distinction between three consecutive steps:
  - *intelligence:* situations in the direct operating environment of a decision-maker will prompt the need for taking decisions; a decision-maker can look for these situations himself or can be confronted with them, whether he likes it or not; in all cases the main characteristic is a perceived difference between an actual and an ideal situation;
  - *design:* a more detailed analysis of the perceived problem: decision alternatives are defined, analyzed and evaluated;
  - *choice:* a decision-maker chooses the decision alternative which is judged to be most appropriate for problem resolution.

Following the seminal work of Simon, several applications and extensions of the decision paradigm of bounded rationality can be found in decision-making theory. These generally address the question of how bounded rationality works in an organizational setting, with multiple decision-makers, group interests and goal conflicts. Cyert and March (1963) speak in this respect of 'the behavioral theory of the firm', while Lindblom (1959) introduces the 'the science of muddling through.' An important conclusion of these studies is that organizational decision-making is highly dependent upon all kind of routines and formal procedures in order to foster stability and to prevent conflicts. Consequently, organizational change can only take place incrementally, step by step.

In the 'garbage can' model of Cohen *et al.* (1972) the rationality of organizational decision-making has almost disappeared. Decisions are not necessarily considered to be resolutions of perceived organizational problems. Decisions are more or less unstructured and uncontrolled meetings of problems, solutions, choice situations and persons. At first glance the 'garbage can' model offers little hope for the possibility of designing useful decision support tools. With the publication of the strategic decision model of Mintzberg *et al.* (1976)—with the title 'the structure of unstructured decision processes'—this line of thought goes in a more hopeful direction. From this moment on, decision-making theory pays more attention to finding appropriate methods and techniques to support organizational decision-making.

7.3 THE PRODUCT AND PROCESS DIMENSIONS OF INVESTMENT DECISIONS

Accepting the concept of bounded rationality in organizational decision-making has important consequences for the type of decision support that needs to be given to organizations and managers. Not only the content and goals of decision-making are relevant (see the 'choice' phase in Simon's model as discussed in the previous section), but the focus of managerial support moves to the overall structure of the decision-making process. This has, for instance, been referred to as 'meta decision-making' (Leeuw, 1986), 'the organization of decision-making' (Verzellenberg, 1988), 'decision control' (Aken and Matzinger, 1983), and 'the rationality of control' (Hickson *et al.* 1986). Theories of strategic decision-making make a distinction between a prescriptive, goal-oriented view and a descriptive, process-oriented view (see, for example, Mintzberg, 1994). Idenburg (1992) follows this distinction and speaks in his review of the strategy literature of the 'what' and the 'how' of strategy development. He pictures these dimensions in a 2 × 2 matrix, which results in four views on strategy formation:

- *emergent strategy* (goal dimension weak, process dimension weak);
- *rational planning* (goal dimension strong, process dimension weak);
- *learning process* (goal dimension weak, process dimension strong);
- *incremental logic* (goal dimension strong, process dimension strong).

Four Styles of Decision-Making

Inspired by the four types of strategy formation as defined by Idenburg, this subsection discusses a typology with four styles of investment decisions. Figure 7.1 visualizes the adoption of Idenburg's matrix to investment decisions in the context of IT-based infrastructure. This matrix is one of the basic building blocks for the design of a model for strategic control of IT-based infrastructure investment decisions. The starting point of this model is the division between the product and process dimensions of investment decisions. Every investment decision—essentially a choice to devote resources and funds to a particular course of action—is the 'product' of a decision-

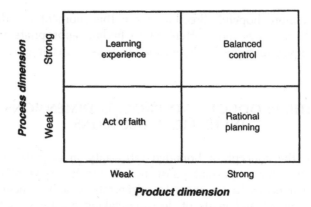

Figure 7.1   *The product and process dimensions of strategic control of investment decisions (adapted from Idenburg, 1992)*

making process (see Figure 7.2). In this decision-making process several
steps are taken, within a certain task division of the participants in this
process and within a political context, resulting from different goals,
priorities and use of power. Depending on the extent and direction of
decision control, several styles of decision-making can be used.

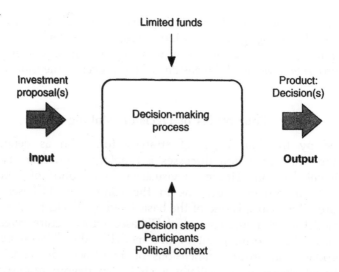

Figure 7.2   *An investment decision as a 'product' of a decision-making process*

Act of Faith

Without any structuring of the product or process dimension, investment decisions will amount to 'act of faith' decisions. This leads to what Shank and Govandarajan (1992) have called a 'technology roulette.' The decision to invest looks like gambling; there are no clear goals or expectations and one can only hope for a successful outcome. After an investment has been made, it is also quite easy to qualify it as a success or as a failure, depending on what someone wants to prove. This situation has become unacceptable in the present IT investment climate, in which not 'acts of faith' but more rigorous analyses are required.

Rational Planning

Too much structuring of the product dimension will lead to 'rational comprehensive planning' (Rosenhead, 1989), i.e. trying to quantify as many aspects as possible, thereby ignoring the much more complex and uncertain organizational reality that decision-makers face. This reflects the classical view of the 'rational' decision-maker. The many finance-based evaluation methods are product-oriented, by concentrating on the consequences of IT investments that can be monetary valued. Also multi-criteria methods, which are applied in mechanistic way, often show the characteristics of rational planning. Logical analyses of investment criteria predominate; these generally take the form of cost–benefit analyses in which there is no room for intuition or emotions.

Learning Experience

An exclusive focus on the process dimension does, wrongly, hardly account for the essence of organizational decision-making: i.e. stating objectives and, given scarce resources, choosing between alternatives to reach these objectives. This implies that an investment decision is merely regarded as a learning experience. The prime purpose of supporting decision-making is to teach involved stakeholders to arrive at a decision (e.g. through building shared 'mental models'; see Senge, 1990; Gregory and Jackson, 1992).[3] Providing them with relevant decision criteria to evaluate and choose between investment alternatives, falls beyond the learning focus.

---

[3] In many respects this variant has similarities with the interpretive school of IT evaluation research discussed earlier (see Chapter 6, Section 6.5).

Balanced Control

The decision-making perspective taken here advocates a more balanced approach towards the evaluation and management of infrastructure investment decisions, what Figure 7.1 refers to as 'balanced control.' It is aimed at structuring investment appraisal through a dynamic alignment of both the product and process dimensions. At the heart of any evaluation lies the establishment of a set of investment arguments to assess the business impacts of investments. This establishment does not, however, take place in isolation from its organizational context. It is the outcome of a communicative process between involved stakeholders.

7.4 THE 'P4' DECISION-MAKING MODEL

As argued in the previous section, the aim of strategic control of investment decisions is to improve and facilitate organizational decision-making on its proposed investments. Therefore an explicit view is needed of IT-based infrastructure investment decision-making as an organizational and largely communicative process. It is not a 'method of pinning numbers on things to prove or disprove a case' (Farbey *et al.*, 1993). Decisions cannot simply be taken by defining a firm's strategic goals and by calculating the optimal investment strategy (see the previously discussed variant of rational planning), although the general opinion in many firms is that this characterizes good decision-making. Investment decisions concerning infrastructure have more to do with eliminating wrong solutions and assessing the risks of project proposals than with a 'numbers game' that uses advanced mathematical scoring techniques. A group of decision-makers, or a management team, is often more successful in this than a single decision-maker or top manager. Making the intuitions and experiences of these decision stakeholders explicit is more important than calculating as much as possible; business impacts should only be translated into financial figures when possible and appropriate.

A decision-making process concerning IT-based infrastructure therefore involves multiple stakeholders who are, through mutual consultation, trying to assess the future value to be gained from a proposed investment. Establishing a common mind-set for change will stimulate a shared investment vision and start a process to commit all involved stakeholders to the final decision and all of its consequences. The product of such a process provides the crucial standards against which the investment's business value can be measured and managed across its life-cycle.

To further develop this view this section introduces a model for strategic balanced control of investment decisions. Four aspects are distinguished which can be used to improve investment appraisal and to manage the underlying decision-making process. Paraphrasing the well-known four P's of conventional business wisdom in marketing (but with a different meaning), the resulting model is referred to as the 'P4' model. The P4 model is grounded in four types of bounded rationality, each leading to a different control option (see Figure 7.3). The distinction between substandard rationality, procedural rationality and structural rationality is made by Kickert (1979) and Leeuw (1986), political rationality can be considered as an additional type of rationality (Renkema, 1998).

The four strategic control options cover the main management issues of decisions concerning IT-based infrastructure (see Figure 7.4). The inner-most circle of Figure 7.4 refers to what in the previous section has been called the product dimension of decision-making, and concerns the content of investment decisions (management of the product). The other three circles refer to the discussed process dimension and are concerned with the structure of the decision process in terms of decision phases and steps (management of the process), involving the right (groups of) people in decision-making (management of the participation), and handling the political elements of decision-making (management of the politics).

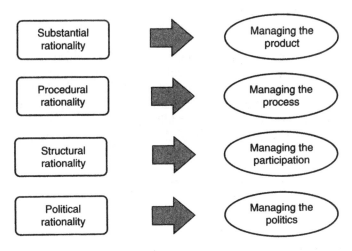

Figure 7.3 *Types of rationality leading to strategic control options*

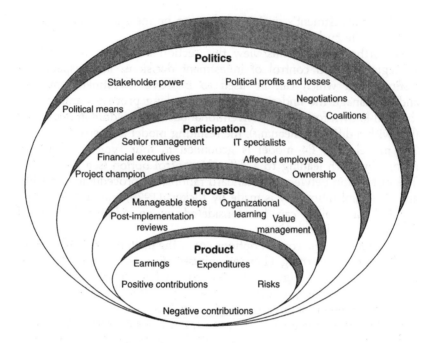

Figure 7.4   *The P4 model of strategic investment control*

Managing the Product

At the heart of the P4 model lies the investment appraisal of the product, i.e. the 'business case' or set of value metrics on the basis of which the decision whether to invest or not is made. Every investment decision is made against the background and judgment of business advantages, disadvantages and risks, which can be both financial and non-financial, see Table 7.1. When making IT infrastructure decisions, these identified impacts should cover both the question of whether a project is justified in terms of its resulting business value, and the question of what the additional value or synergy is if an investment is provided as part of the overall IT-based infrastructure.

Value metrics	Advantages	Disadvantages	Risks
Financial	Earnings	Expenditures	Financial risks
Non-financial	Positive contribution	Negative contribution	Non-financial risks

Table 7.1   *General structure of the business case of an investment*

Although the general structure of value metrics can be given, adequate categorization of all possible and relevant impacts will require local adaptations, reflecting the specific goals and characteristics of the organization in which a decision is made (see Kusters and Renkema, 1996). As such they should be related to the overall investment strategy of a firm (e.g. cost leadership, innovation focus, competitive positioning). In the later stages of an investment, e.g. during realization and use, the defined value metrics in a business case serve as performance indicators to evaluate the realized business contribution of a project.

It is best to make the likely business impacts, and thus the business case, as explicit and debatable as possible, since every evaluation is generally subject to the personal, informal and implicit judgments of the involved stakeholders. By explicating different views on an investment the final decision will, as a rule, have more organizational support and commitment. If not, there is a risk that all involved stakeholders will create their own images concerning the possible impacts and the desirability of these impacts, without talking about them. Good communications amongst involved stakeholders can extract and identify the cause-and-effect relations between IT-based infrastructure, business performance and financial returns, with a focus on organization-specific goals and priorities. What for one organization can be considered 'strategic', does not have to be strategic for another organization, and strategic can mean a lot of different things for different organizations.

Managing the Process

The second control option of the P4 model refers to the process of investment appraisal. This process considers the different phases the evaluation goes through both prior to, and during, project execution and investment management. It is recommended to decompose investment decision-making into manageable steps, analogous to well-known decision-making models (see, for example, Simon, 1977; Harrison, 1987), which make a distinction between:

- formulation of project goals
- evaluation of alternatives
- choice of investment alternative
- implementation of the chosen solution
- follow-up and control of a decision.

Since infrastructure investments provide the long-term foundation for many business-specific applications, decisions should be subject to a thorough preparation. This subdivision of steps is not meant as a sequential and rigid procedure, but more as a pattern of thought, with possible feedback loops (Witte, 1972; Mintzberg *et al.*, 1976). Another important recommendation lies in performing post-implementation reviews of the investment decision in order to monitor and control the investment across its life-cycle. These reviews provide valuable information on whether the investment actually delivers value for money and to what extent there is still room for improvement. The initially defined investment evaluation criteria then serve as performance indicators to assess the actual contribution of an investment to business performance. Unfortunately, most organizations do not take the time to reflect on decisions that were taken in the past. Many reasons are given for this, but often heard are that something which is an historical 'fact' cannot easily be changed, and that project ambitions, scope and conditions have changed too much to be able to make an 'honest' assessment. If reviews of an investment project do take place, these are often used as management audits in order to find 'guilty' employees and to settle-up for a project that is likely to become a failure. This bears the risk of becoming a 'witch hunt', instead of a vehicle for capturing improvement and learning opportunities.

Regular reviews of the investment also minimize the phenomenon of 'investment entrapment' (Dinther, 1993) a situation in which ever-greater resource commitments are made because of too much emotional involvement, without sound evaluations of increased investment. Post-implementation reviews can further be used to establish an investment climate in which—often implicit—knowledge on investment outcomes is well-managed and in which organizational learning is encouraged. Many investment decisions are made by 'jumping from one project to the other.' Explicit knowledge of prior investments and their realized value can contribute greatly to improved decision-making on new investment proposals. In terms of the organizational learning theory of Argyris and Schön (1978), investment control after project implementation means 'single-loop learning', and using prior investment experiences in new decision situations means 'double-loop learning.' Single-loop learning focuses on managing an investment project in such a way that the defined investment goals are met. Double-loop learning, on the other hand, focuses on questioning and critically assessing the way in which an investment project is being managed; investment goals are assessed in terms of their viability and this may mean defining new goals.

Managing the process of investment decision-making ultimately is a process of investment planning and control, which, in order to prevent a too mechanical view, can be conceptualized using the well-known cycle of quality management (see Deming, 1986):

- *Plan:* plan the desired investment outcomes and identify any uncertainties surrounding them.
- *Do:* perform project activities in line with the defined outcomes.
- *Check:* monitor whether actual project behavior and outcomes match the defined outcomes.
- *Act:* perform adequate actions in order to move project outcomes in the desired direction or ensure that the project keeps moving in the current right direction.

Planning and controlling investment projects like these will lead to 'value management' of investments. Value management means managing all the financial and non-financial impacts of an investment (see Table 7.1), ultimately with the goal of finding an adequate balance between cost and risk management (minimizing efforts, expenditures and mitigating risks) versus benefit management (maximizing benefit opportunities and delivery). The 'plan' and 'check' steps are in fact the phases in which investment control is done through decision-making, while the 'do' and 'act' steps are taking place in project reality, guided by the decision taken during investment control. Adjustments of project reality achieved like this are examples of 'single-loop learning', and when the planning phase is subject to a re-assessment of initial goals and preferred outcomes this can be seen as 'double-loop learning.' Figure 7.5 visualizes this process of value management, using the above-mentioned terms and process structure.

The initial stage of investment decision-making, in which project proposals are evaluated and eventually a go/no-go decision is made, is a crucial phase, since in this proposal stage the chance of making the wrong decisions can be minimized. 'Wrong' decisions are decisions in which a likely desirable project is rejected or a likely undesirable project is accepted. Maximizing the quality of decision-making gives a higher chance of making the right decisions (see Section 7.2). In many cases, however, the business value of a project cannot be estimated with much certainty in advance, as external factors (e.g. technology developments, actions of competitors or market trends) may change the basis upon which the decision is based, or because follow-up decisions on controllable project aspects (e.g. organizational scope, ambition level or business process impacts) are made. Managing the process of investment decisions thus goes much further than a one-off formalization of the steps in the proposal and feasibility stages of decision-making. Adequate management of investment processes

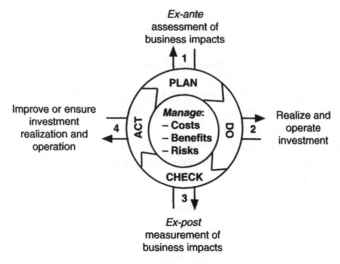

Figure 7.5   Value management of investment projects

requires value management across the full life-cycle of a project, which can be thought of as consisting of several life-cycle stages, e.g. from conceptualization, design, building to managed operations.

Managing the Participation

The third aspect that gets special attention in the P4 model concerns the participation of the different project appraisal and decision-making stakeholders. It is advisable to involve all appropriate (groups of) people in decision-making with respect to the investment. These include senior management, IT specialists, financial executives and the employees whose work is affected by the investment. Organization of the collaboration between involved stakeholder parties and representatives is an important way to increase adherence to and support for a decision. Special attention is needed to ensure senior business management ownership and sponsorship. Infrastructure decisions should be prepared and approved at the highest hierarchical level. It has further been shown that the likelihood of success of investment projects is considerably improved when there are one or more 'project champions' involved (Beath, 1991; Farbey *et al.*, 1993). This championship refers to the special effort that is made by some involved stakeholder to make the investment a success. This stakeholder does not necessarily have a formal role that implies such an effort. The more powerful this champion's position is in the organization the better.

Managing the Politics

The previously discussed control options of the framework merely sketched a homogeneous, rational picture of an organization. This view implies, for instance, that the different stakeholders in the investment appraisal share the same intentions, goals and priorities. A more realistic view is that of an organization in which different stakeholder groups have their own wishes and preferences. In conflict situations the outer political ring of the P4 model may totally overrule the other three rings. Such a view allows for the recognition of conflicting interests and the use of political means to safeguard one's interests (Pfeffer, 1981; Mintzberg, 1983a). The extent to which an organization and key decision stakeholders take behavioral and political issues into account highly depend on the—often implicit—view they have of organizational decision-making. Two contrasting views are the 'rational model' and the 'political model' (Daft, 1986); see Table 7.2. In practice, both models will somehow represent actual decision-making, depending on the political nature of investment issues and the organization in which the decision is made.

Since infrastructure investments are, by definition, for common use and therefore are subject to multi-stakeholder interaction, their evaluation is generally subject to politics. In particular, the division of earnings and expenditures over the different involved stakeholder groups

Organizational characteristics	Rational model	Political model
Goals and preferences	Consistent across participants	Inconsistent, pluralistic within the organization
Power and control	Centralized	Decentralized, shifting coalitions and interest groups
Type of decision process	Orderly, logical, rational	Disorderly, push and pull of interests
Outcome of decision-making	Maximization of choice options	Result of bargaining and interplay among interests
Rules and norms	Optimization of corporate actions	Free play of market forces, conflict is legitimate and expected
Information use	Extensive, systematic and accurate	Ambiguous, information used and withheld strategically
Beliefs about 'cause-effect' relations	Known, at least to a probability estimate	Disagreement about causes and effects
Corporate ideology	Efficiency and effectiveness	Struggle, conflict, winners and losers

Table 7.2   The rational versus the political model (after Daft, 1986)

has an important impact on the political context of investment decisions (see, for example, Goodhue *et al.*, 1992). Managing these politics—the fourth control option of the P4 model—means that, after the initial recognition of the political context of investment decisions, the intentions, wishes and preferences of stakeholders are explicitly taken into account. Experience shows that agreement on the route to follow and a common perspective among evaluation parties gives a greater chance of a successful project (see, for example, Markus, 1983). This should preferably stem from the same motives and a relationship based on equality. In order to reach such an agreement, it may be necessary to use such decision-making strategies as negotiation and coalition building. An investment in IT-based infrastructure can only increase in terms of its outcomes and value if it is done from a shared perspective rather than from individual, diverse or even conflicting perspectives.

Decision support with respect to the politics of the evaluation lies in what has been called 'stakeholder analysis.' Boonstra (1991) suggests the following steps in such an analysis:

- Listing of stakeholders, their estimated power and impacts of the proposed investment.
- Assessment of possible 'winners' and 'losers' and their possible (political) 'profits' and 'losses.'
- Establishment of feasible strategies (e.g. financial compensation) to influence the political account of profits and losses.

The appropriate use of specific decision strategies depends on the specific political context of investment decisions. This can also be conceptualized in terms of degree of agreement amongst involved stakeholders regarding (see Butler *et al.*, 1993; Deitz, 1997):

- The goals of investments: the extent into which there are no different views concerning the purposes of investing in IT-based infrastructure.
- The relation between investment goals and decisions: the extent into which there are no different views concerning the contribution of investment decisions to the defined purposes of investing in IT-based infrastructure.

Different degrees of agreement will lead to different more appropriate decision strategies, such as (see Figure 7.6):

- Relatively greater use of *analytical and measurement techniques* if there is agreement on both goals and the relation between goals and decisions.

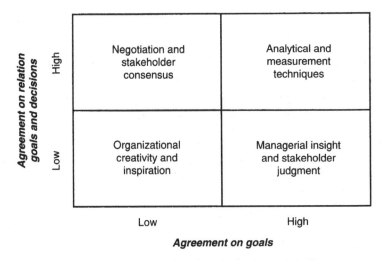

Figure 7.6 *Decision strategies based on the level of stakeholder agreement*

- More reliance on *managerial insight and stakeholder judgment* if there is agreement on goals but little agreement on the relation between goals and decisions.
- Deliberate use of *negotiations and consensus-finding* between stakeholders if there is agreement on the relation between goals and decisions but little agreement on goals.
- Room for *organizational creativity and inspiration* if there is little agreement on both goals and the relation between goals and decisions.

7.5 CONCLUSIONS

This chapter has argued that investment decisions concerning IT-based infrastructure are generally not taken according to the classical, economic model of rational decision-making. It is therefore more realistic to base decision-making support upon the practical consequences of the paradigm of bounded rationality. In correspondence with the distinction between the 'what' and 'how' of strategy formation, a distinction can be made between the product and process dimensions of investment decisions. If both dimensions do not get the attention they deserve, an investment decision will result in an act of faith, the consequences of which are unpredictable and unmanageable. One-dimensional control of decisions on the product or product dimension will respectively lead to pure rational planning or to considering an investment decision merely as a learning experience. Both variants fall short for taking strategic investment decisions on IT-based infrastructure.

In the P4 model, as introduced in this chapter, both dimensions are simultaneously addressed, and are referred to as 'balanced control' of investment decisions. This balanced control captures both the need to arrive at a more sound, rigorous investment appraisal which should focus on assessing business impacts, as well as the organizational decision context in which this appraisal is taking place. This decision context consists of communication-intensive group processes of stakeholder interaction and negotiation, with different steps, many involved parties and political implications. The P4 model integrates four strategic control options which, if managed adequately, will lead to the balanced control of investment decisions. This requires decision support along the following four lines:

- managing the *product*: defining the (evolving) business case through value metrics;
- managing the *process*: following several decision steps to make a final judgment and to manage the evaluation life-cycle;
- managing the *participation*: involving the right (groups) of people in investment decision-making;
- managing the *politics*: finding common interests and managing conflicts of interest.

8
The P4 Model In Practice

8.1 INTRODUCTION

The previous chapter introduced the 'P4 model' as an instrument to diagnose and support investment decisions concerning IT-based infrastructure. This chapter extends the P4 model to a number of practical cases of investment projects, in which actual decisions are analyzed using the model. Section 8.2 elaborates on the type of cases and the case study approach. The Section 8.3 discusses four design-oriented investment cases of InsuraCo, in which attention is also paid to the results of project review sessions that were held concerning these investments. Section 8.4 discusses four additional investment cases of two other organizations: BankCo and InduCo. For reasons of confidentiality not all decision-making considerations and investment issues are discussed in full. The focus of the case study discussions is on the issues that are relevant from the perspective of decision-making support and management control. Subsequently Section 8.5 presents some general case study findings. The conclusions of this chapter are given in Section 8.6.

8.2 CASE STUDY APPROACH

The case studies of the P4 model in practice, as presented in this chapter, have all been carefully chosen to assess the viability, appropriateness and transferability of the model for investment decision-making and control of IT-based infrastructure. The P4 model also originated from and grew in this investment decision practice, which is especially true for the first four investment cases of InsuraCo. The other three cases took place in other organizations referred to as BankCo and InduCo, and were more oriented towards assessing the applicability of the P4 in other decision situations, with new investment issues and new decision stakeholders. Table 8.1 gives an overview and short characterization of the case studies. In order to get a comprehensive view of and feeling for the suitability of the P4 model, an attempt has been made to get a good mix of investments in direct versus indirect infrastructures and of previous decisions and ongoing decision processes.

The case study analysis was foremost action-oriented; where possible the author participated in decision-making meetings and sometimes even acted as a management consultant. In the cases where the initial decision-making and appraisal was already passed, the prior investment decision process was reconstructed using an improvement attitude, thereby focusing on current and future strategic control options. All final case study conclusions were reviewed and commented on by the actual decision stakeholders. In the case of the investment projects of InsuraCo, case study reports also served as input for separate investment review sessions, in which both the actual business value results and the decision-making process were discussed. Participants in these review sessions were key persons in the investment process. As such, these sessions were used to trigger a process of organizational learning and knowledge management concerning IT-based infrastructure investments. The two questions addressed were:

- Was the investment decision, given the present knowledge of the business value achieved, both a 'good' and a 'successful' decision?

Organization and case studies	Type of infrastructure		Decision stage		Case study purpose	
	In-direct	Direct	Decision taken	Decision considered	Design P4 model	Transferability P4 model
1. InsuraCo	•		•		•	
2. InsuraCo	•			•	•	
3. InsuraCo		•	•		•	
4. InsuraCo		•		•	•	
5. BankCo	•		•		•	•
6. BankCo	•		•		•	•
7. BankCo	•	•		•	•	•
8. InduCo	•	•	•		•	•

Table 8.1   *Case studies of the P4 model*

- What have we learnt from investing in this project, and what implications does this have for our decision-making practices?

8.3   INVESTMENT CASES OF InsuraCo

As discussed in the previous section (see also Table 8.1), the P4 model as presented in its final form in Chapter 7 has its roots in the investment appraisal practices of an insurance firm referred to as InsuraCo. This section presents the results of these investment case studies.

Case 1: An Investment in Indirect Infrastructure

This case concerns the investment in infrastructure software which enables on-line telecommunication with mainframe platforms.

Managing the Product

This investment had two main purposes. The first concerned improved security of central data processing and operations in general, formally triggered by a report by the internal auditing department. The second purpose was to increase ease of use, partly through the application of standard software packages. Alternatives were the standard packages from two vendors as well as internal development. The investment evaluation and the choice between the packages and internal development was not made on the basis of explicit investment arguments (financial and non-financial consequences, risks). Valuation and weighting of investment alternatives was not tried. The expenditures were not considered to be a problem or a barrier to management authorization. The wish to conform to IBM standards and the delivery of the needed in functionality were the decisive arguments in the decision to invest in one of the standard software packages.

Managing the Process and Participation

After an explorative phase in which several more general policy reports were written, the project went into the phase in which the decision was prepared and a pilot project was started. A project and steering group with IT employees were in control of this. There was also a formal assignment of management with several management reports. A management steering committee, responsible for successful implementation of the investment, was established. In between the project phases were several gaps, in which nothing really happened.

The total lead-time of the investment, until full implementation, was about 4 to 5 years. There was no formal post-implementation review of the investment decision and no clear project champion. The general feeling is that the project cost much more in terms of human resources and time than was initially expected.

Managing the Politics

During the entire decision-making process, especially when implementation of the investment came into sight, there was political tension between IT staff and user departments. This covered both the individual end-user, who had to learn new log-in procedures, and the system developer in the business who had less 'space' to test new systems. Also the interests of the centralized IT department, i.e. better and firmer control of the supporting infrastructure, sometimes conflicted with the need to 'sell' the system to the business community. Finally, there are, even until now, some political issues because of the lead-time, which is considered much too long by many stakeholders. The different causes of this are also the subject of different opinions.

Case 2: An Investment in Direct Infrastructure

Managing the Product

The first purpose of this investment was to have more consistent and reliable commercial data. The second purpose concerned the fast availability of appropriate commercial management information. There were hardly any explicit investment arguments used, both in terms of financial and non-financial consequences and risks. Explicit valuation and weighting of investment alternatives were also not attempted. Given the then prevailing development practices, the choice for in-house development was quickly made. The option of buying a standard software package was considered too late in the whole decision-making process to be a serious realization alternative. Top management was, in contrast to the wishes of the controlling project committee, unwilling to label the project as 'strategic.' Development costs were estimated using function point analysis and prior experiences. Total costs were justified on the need to solve rather pressing problems in the functioning of the existing infrastructure and on projected (limited) cost savings.

Managing the Process and Participation

The investment was initiated because of perceived inadequacies in the existing infrastructure, which was considered inappropriate for solving the prevailing information needs. This infrastructure originated from a merger in the past of InsuraCo. System development was coordinated by a project committee. The methodology 'System Development Methodology' (SDM) was used, which implied several formal decision points. The project committee worked under the responsibility of a permanent strategic policy committee, responsible for the commercial IT strategy. This latter committee reported to top management. End-users were also regularly consulted. There was a 'project champion' involved. This concerned an employee from the commercial staff. There was no formal post-implementation review of the investment decision. There are, however, regular audits of the functioning of the infrastructure. The general feeling is that the new infrastructure is superior to the old situation.

Managing the Politics

The investment in the direct infrastructure solved several problems that were considered as real problems by many employees of InsuraCo. This led to a decision-making climate in which politics did not play a very prominent role. Some aspects, however, can be traced back to the politics of investment evaluation. In the course of the decision-making process there was a problem of alignment of the interests of IT staff and marketing staff, *vis-à-vis* the interests of the organization as a whole. There were also political tensions between the sales staff and central authorities, arising from increased room for detailed checks and performance evaluations. A final point that raised political concerns was the (often low) priority that was given to infrastructure realization by the several, dispersed business units.

Case 3: An Investment in Indirect Infrastructure

This case concerns an investment in infrastructure to support IT deployment using an advanced client/server architecture.

Managing the Product

The project started as a technology assessment study to investigate the broad issue of client/server architecture. Arguments to invest in client/server architecture were: the wish to keep pace with technological developments; exploiting the strong points of both mainframes, mid-range platforms and personal computers; aligning IT-based infrastructure with the decentralized management philosophy of InsuraCo; and more client-driven IT deployment. Also the estimated rise in expenditure and effort for operations management was addressed. Risk issues that received explicit attention were insufficient business security and a lack of client/server product standardization. The valuation and weighing of investment arguments was merely qualitative and subjective, although the experiences of other firms were taken into account by reading professional business reports. A striking element of this case is that the project mission shifted in the feasibility stage of decision-making from an assessment study with a rather broad character to a policy recommendation. This policy recommendation had the purpose of exploring key developments in the realm of client/server and to propose recommendations for future infrastructure services of the IT department responsible for infrastructure exploitation. As such, there was not really an explicit management decision to invest in client/server architecture, although several ongoing technological developments in fact meant a shift to a client/server architecture.

Managing the Process and Participation

This project was initiated by an issue raised by an employee of the IT department who wanted to know more about the implications of the emerging concept of client/server for the IT-based infrastructure of InsuraCo. To tackle this issue a project group was formed with the mission to write a policy report. The way of working of this project group was not prescribed in advance. Project owners were a specific IT department responsible for exploitation and operations management of the infrastructure, and a staff group for technology research and architecture definition. The project results were also reported to the management of the IT department and the management of the IT strategy staff. A report with preliminary results was presented to the account managers of the IT department who were responsible for client contacts and engagements. After completion of the policy report, the corporate IT manager still had some doubts concerning the projected rise in cost for maintaining and managing IT-based infrastructure due to the introduction of client/server architecture. After an elaboration on this subject by the project manager, the IT manager also accepted the conclusions of the policy report. There was no clearly identifiable project champion in this project.

Managing the Politics

There was no clear evidence of political elements in decision-making concerning this investment project. Within the project group that worked on the preparation of the policy report there were no conflicts of interest or personal differences of option. A striking feature of the project, however, is that no clear initiatives were taken as a consequence of the outcomes of the project. This may be an indication of some political dynamics, although much more overt than covert and not leading to much political action. An explicit management policy to move to a client/server architecture would probably have led to much interaction of a political nature between the several organizational departments, some of which were more conservative in terms of technological innovation and some were more progressive.

Case 4: An Investment in Indirect Infrastructure

This investment case concerns a project to create an application and data infrastructure to administer specific information on the intermediaries of InsuraCo.

Managing the Product

The investment arguments addressed in this case were: improving the flexibility of both IT-based infrastructure and business processes; improving the robustness of infrastructure support for primary processes; better control of maintenance efforts and expenditures; and finally the elimination of several bottlenecks in the existing infrastructure. A separate evaluation took place regarding the level of infrastructure and the resulting synergy of this choice, specifically concerning the corporate versus the business unit level. The investment appraisal also covered the choice between a standard application package and tailor-made software development. Explicit, separate assessments of the financial and non-financial consequences and risks was done to a limited extent. The decision to invest in the project was justified on the basis of the aforementioned qualitative benefits. The decision to invest in an infrastructure at the corporate InsuraCo level was taken after evaluation of central coordination and comparability versus flexibility and more client focus. The choice of a standard application package was motivated in a selection process in which none of the available packages was judged to cover the needed functionality.

Managing the Process and Participation

The move to a more decentralized, unit-based organizational structure, in connection with some apparent problems in the existing infrastructure, triggered the need to define a project proposal. A project group worked on the project and reported to a permanent management committee, responsible for commercial IT decisions and mandated by top management. The project group was accountable for project progress but commissioned a team of system developers to build the infrastructure. This team worked with the SDM method for system development, not as a rigid procedure-driven method but more as a method framework to structure project tasks. After completion of about half of the project tasks, project management was taken over by the line manager of the department who was responsible for offering the proposed infrastructure to user management. There was no clear evidence of one or more project champions in this investment case, although several project stakeholders were mentioned by interviewees.

Managing the Politics

Several project elements of a political nature influenced the decision and appraisal processes of this investment case. Political tensions emanated from the relationship between the central support organization, responsible for providing the infrastructure, and the various business units that were expected to use the resulting infrastructure. Although the business units were involved in and even participated in investment decision-making, they did not really commit themselves to creating a solid, corporate-wide infrastructure. The main motivation for this seemed that they gave priority to building their own business-unit-specific infrastructure, necessitated by the recently introduced decentralized organizational model. Decision-making in this project was also influenced by personal conflicts regarding competencies, which also impacted on the role that business units played, i.e. participation in decision-making versus first creating the infrastructure and then 'selling' it to the units.

Results of the Review and Improvement Sessions

As discussed in Section 8.2, all four investment cases within InsuraCo were subject to separate project review sessions. The main objectives of these sessions were to make a diagnosis of decision-making practice and to identify a number of learning experiences in order to capture improvement opportunities. The sessions were not meant as formal project audits, which are generally meant to assess management performances in terms of their accountabilities, but as learning sessions which take place in an open atmosphere to exchange personal opinions and judgments. As such, the risk of seeking individuals settlements for disappointing results, which may eventually deteriorate into a 'witch hunt', was minimized.

The overall conclusion that emerged from these review sessions was that the P4 model provides adequate starting points for a diagnosis of investment decisions. The decision-making stakeholders generally were of the opinion that the appropriate use of the P4 model, with allowance for organization-specific adaptations, was bound to increase decision-make quality and would improve the extent of management control of major investments. In all cases, a process of informal and personal evaluations had already started, but any formal post-implementation audit was not planned. The review sessions were thus seen as useful additions to the present ways of working.

The review of investment arguments showed that an assessment of current (technical) quality and user satisfaction of IT-based infrastructure generally gives sufficient justification for taking investment decisions. An appraisal in terms of expected efforts and projected benefits was not done regularly, although a cost–benefit analysis and calculation of financial returns is formally required. When considering the question of whether the initially defined business goals were achieved, it proved to be quite easy to come to a common view and to shared conclusions. The flexibility deployed is striking; several times the initial investment purposes were reformulated or the ambition level redefined. Also several times it was argued that the final investment effort and expenditures were much more and higher, respectively, than initially expected. This cannot, however, be supported by clear measurement data.

Much attention in the reviews was devoted to the 'softer' , socio-political aspects of decision-making. A recurring issue is the alignment between the corporate interests of InsuraCo and the business interests of the several business units, including the role of IT strategy staff and of the IT department. Adequate management of the politics emanating from this is seen as a prerequisite for capturing the full business value of investments which impact on communication amongst business units and the corporate level and which directly impact on the market positions and choice of the distribution channel.

Themes which are frequently mentioned are 'communication' and 'commitment.' The project review participants are of the opinion that many improvement opportunities can be captured if investment stakeholders communicate better, especially with respect to communication among individual business units. Sometimes this relates to and becomes bound up with the 'public relations' of the central IT departments, which should take a more 'signaling' role instead of a 'regulating' role in the overall investment process. Business unit commitment to investing in and creating a solid, shared IT-based infrastructure is considered to be vital for achieving maximum business value. Ultimately their adequate use and the profitable exploitation of this infrastructure will, to a large extent, make the difference between success and failure of investments. Also senior management commitment, both at the corporate and business unit levels, is considered to be crucial for success. The loyalty of all investment stakeholders to the final decision is seen to be highly dependent on this management commitment.

8.4   INVESTMENT CASES OF BankCo and InduCo

After the initial design and validation of the P4 model within InsuraCo, the model was also used within BankCo and InduCo to assess the applicability and transferability of the model in other decision contexts (see Section 8.2). This section presents the results of the investment analysis in these two organizations. The cases cover both direct and indirect infrastructure.

Cases 5–7: Investment Cases of BankCo

The investment cases of BankCo concern a new infrastructure to support communications between head offices and subsidiaries of banks (case 5), a new database management system and operating system for centralized computing (case 6), and infrastructure support for a new type of customer support, enabling more autonomy of banks (case 7).

Managing the Product

In all investment cases of BankCo a number of investment purposes or advantages were identified which led to a definition of the business case. In cases 5 and 6 these referred to arguments such as controllability, availability and capacity of the IT-based infrastructure, as well as to possible savings within the existing infrastructure. In case 7 arguments concerned improving the customer-orientation of business operations. There was little use of explicit and complete evaluations of business benefits, effort and risk. Project expenditures were addressed, although rather roughly. Regarding cases 5 and 6, the investment was more or less justified within the context of a larger, overarching investment program in order to innovate the indirect infrastructure. Regarding case 7, the investment was abandoned for commercial reasons, although the purpose of a follow-up project was to install the planned infrastructure, but with a more technology-oriented mission. Relatively speaking, much time was devoted to identifying and evaluating products and supplier selection. Predefined criteria and scoring procedures were used for this (e.g. prices, market position, complexity).

Managing the Process and Participation

In cases 5 and 6 the investment process was initiated by an assessment of the existing indirect infrastructure. The reason to start case 7 was a commercial program to increase customer focus. In all cases project plans and milestone plans were used, together with deliverable planning, decision points and project guidelines concerning architecture and ways of working. These were however not used as rigid planning procedures, but more as overall 'roadmaps' to structure the planning process. In all three infrastructure projects a feasibility field study was performed through pilot evaluations in order to assess the scalability of the chosen solution and to decide the roll-out policy. For a good understanding, it should be noted that all local banking offices of BankCo remain responsible for the choice of using the planned infrastructure. The basic starting point will always be organization-wide use and local banks are generally involved in the decision-making process, e.g. through reference boards. In all cases the projects were managed by project teams and steering committees. A striking element of case 5 is that end-user and user management were not much involved in decision-making. In case 6 there was much involvement of external consultants, and a dedicated team was installed to negotiate with potential suppliers. In case 7 there was dominant business management ownership, since line management of a specific business department actively monitored project progress and intervened intensively. There are several opinions concerning the role of project champions; sometimes there is no clear evidence of championship, and sometimes certain managers act like champions. In all cases, however, the very aspect of project championship is seen as relevant and important.

Managing the Politics

In all investment cases of BankCo political elements have influenced investment decision-making. The general feeling is that there were not many personal conflicts between project stakeholders, although some examples can be found. For instance, the choice to redefine the project scope in case 7 probably had to do with the different interests of the initially accountable manager and his successor. There were several conflicts of interest and interactions of a political nature between the different organizational departments, many of which related to the role of external suppliers and consultants. In case 5 project management changed after it became clear that there were 'political' motivations to favor a certain supplier and this had pushed business arguments too much to the background. In this case the project stakeholders felt that an external consultant was playing a 'double role', since he had an interest in supplying several products. Consequently his advice played only a minor role in actual decision-making. Several stakeholders pointed out that in this case conflicts of interests were deliberately used to assess decision alternatives from several perspectives. In case 7 there was a contradiction between business needs and technological capabilities, which influenced the evaluation of investment feasibility.

Case 8: An Investment in Direct and Indirect Infrastructure within InduCo

This case concerns an investment in an infrastructure for engineering data management in a large, multinational manufacturing firm which produces and sells professional equipment, referred to as InduCo.

Managing the Product

This engineering data management (EDM) investment project was justified on the need to improve the product development process in order to meet increased competitive demands. An improvement in this respect would mean delivering a more complex product in a shorter timescale with lower costs. The more efficient management of product and process data was regarded as an important prerequisite for this. One of the important 'selling points' of the EDM project was that it would enable an improved development process, where improvement was particularly visible in the estimated cost savings. EDM was considered an infrastructure product that would facilitate the redesign of the development process. The estimated cost savings were projected in the report of a large industrial consulting firm, commissioned to assess the feasibility of implementing the EDM system. These consultants organized a workshop with several developers, which investigated current practice and identified the core problems with the development process. Estimates were made of the cost savings possible from the removal of these problems by EDM, and these cost savings outweighed the financial expenditures considerably. As such, the report sketched a picture of an investment with only limited risks. The more qualitative, strategic benefits emerged later on in the investment evaluation. There was also the choice of the standard software package in order to be able to implement the proposed EDM system. A 'buyer's guide' of available EDM software packages (which was commercially available) was used to get an initial idea of the available packages. The choices between the three final candidates (two external packages, one package developed by a subsidiary company) was made on the basis of functional and technical requirements and intuitions concerning the packages.

Managing the Process and Participation

The initial EDM investment idea was initiated by the IT department. The department foresaw major advantages in the use of a uniform EDM software tool. Internal triggers within the IT department were the limited capacity of the existing data-management tools and their lack of uniformity. Several years earlier, a comparable investment initiative had been proposed by the IT department. This project was far from successful, and finally abandoned. Perceived causes for this lie in technological and organizational immaturity, and the fact that the then proposed system was installed on a mainframe computing environment. This centralized structure contrasted markedly with the professional, autonomous working environment of the product developers. The IT department put great effort into 'selling' the investment idea to development and management. The projected improvements in the development process gradually turned their efforts into a success. The management team established an investment budget and decided to install a 'study committee' to investigate the possibilities of EDM implementation. After an analysis by a consulting firm, the committee proposed to invest in the system and management decided to go ahead with the EDM investment. A project team was installed to guide the implementation of the system. It was also decided to implement the system gradually, through pilot projects. One member of this team put a lot of personal effort into the success of the EDM project. He is seen as a good candidate for the title 'project champion.'

Managing the Politics

Several issues can be mentioned that relate to the politics of the investment evaluation. The political atmosphere was greatly influenced by the different backgrounds and perceptions of the IT department versus the product developers. This can be regarded as a typical example of the classical conflict between 'IT' and 'users.' Political issues resulted from the rather long distance between the management of the IT department and the business management team. Communications mainly took place via separate hierarchical channels. A final point worth mentioning is that the focus on the justification through cost savings can be traced back to the politically motivated cost consciousness of the Engineering Department representatives in the 'study committee.'

8.5   GENERAL CASE STUDY FINDINGS

The case study application of the P4 model made clear that the model has the potential to be a helpful tool for the diagnosis and support of investment appraisal practices. The main advantages mentioned by investment stakeholders are:

- insight into strategic control options as visualized by the four P's;
- comprehensive estimation of efforts and expenditures to install infrastructure;
- categorization of business impacts and business value metrics of planned infrastructure;
- identification of investment risks and initiation of risk management;
- making political and interpersonal conflicts elements more manageable;
- fostering organizational learning by capturing learning opportunities.

Explicit, multi-dimensional metrics to appraise the business impacts of an investment are hardly used, although all decisions are subject to a formal cost–benefit appraisal. Generally there is little evidence of a clearly defined business case. In many of the cases, solving some 'problems' in the existing infrastructure gives sufficient justification for a proposed investment. The actual influence of financial arguments is therefore unclear. This supports the observation that (financial) calculations often play a 'ritualistic' role (Currie, 1989; Symons, 1990). In our opinion, for many stakeholders the advantage of this approach is that they cannot easily be held accountable for project outcomes, since there are no performance measures that are commonly agreed upon. This, however, makes investment management and performance control very difficult.

The decision process and stakeholder participation are the most important factors that are used to control investment appraisal and decision-making. The general approach seems to be that a number of knowledgeable evaluation stakeholders suggest investment arguments deemed relevant, which leads to a categorization of the main business impacts. Structuring this process with formal phases and regular reports, milestones, etc.—elements of what is seen as 'good' project management—offers options for control. After a decision is made, evaluation activities are generally not an integral part of project control. There are no regular post-implementation reviews performed. Although this can be partly explained by the 'ritualistic' role of investment arguments, and the wish to avoid 'witch hunts', this also seems to be caused by the competitive pressure to focus management attention on decisions about new investments instead of reviews of previous decisions.

Politics is very important in the decision-making process, ensuing from different interests of the organizational stakeholders. An important cause of politics regarding infrastructure investment evaluation is the tension between central control and local autonomy. The politics of decision-making is an aspect that is considered relevant by all stakeholders, but is discussed more covertly that overtly. This often inhibits an open discussion to improve and learn from investment decisions and project outcomes. Generally, great importance is placed on good communications between the involved stakeholders and a commitment to the decision and resulting infrastructure by users and senior management.

8.6 CONCLUSIONS

This chapter has been devoted to the practical applications of the P4 model for investment decision-making and control. The investment cases of three large multinational firms, InsuraCo, BankCo and InduCo, show that the P4 model provides a comprehensive tool to support and diagnose decisions concerning IT-based infrastructure, and management control of infrastructure projects. A diagnosis can be used to foster organizational learning, which in turn is a prelude to an improvement of decision-making practice. The use of the model as a decision-making tool usually requires adaptations to organizational characteristics and preferences, but the involved practitioners concluded that it is bound to increase decision-making quality.

Part IV
The Business Case for Investment

9
Assessing Infrastructure Projects

9.1 INTRODUCTION

In Chapter 7 it was argued that defining the expected business impacts of a proposed infrastructure project lies at the heart of investment control, and that together these constitute the business case for investment in IT-based infrastructure. Part IV of this book is devoted to the issue of defining these business impacts, which, if managed well, will lead to the formation of a set of organization- and investment-specific value metrics to assess the positive, negative and possibly risky outcomes of an investment. This chapter addresses value metrics which can be used to evaluate the discrete business value added of infrastructure projects, and will be of help in making the investment decision. First, Section 9.2 looks in more detail at the role and purposes of defining value metrics. Subsequently Section 9.3 presents the results of case study research concerning the appropriate value metrics for assessing infrastructure investments. Then Section 9.4 pays attention to the management questions, which should be addressed when justifying investments, and to the general structure of business impacts. In Sections 9.5 and 9.6 a review is given of appropriate value metrics for business value assessment of investment in both direct and indirect IT-based infrastructure. The following three sections then examine the management processes of financial assessment (Section 9.7), non-financial assessment (Section 9.8) and risk assessment in financial and non-financial terms (Section 9.9). The conclusions of this chapter are given in Section 9.10.

9.2 THE ROLE AND PURPOSE OF VALUE METRICS

Essentially every investment is a particular choice from different optional patterns of corporate behavior, given limited organizational funds and other scarce resources. The motivation and justification for this choice will always take place by defining value metrics, be they implicit or explicit. Or, in the words of King and Schrems (1978), in one of the seminal papers on the economics of business computing:

> Major decisions concerning computer-based information systems are always made in light of some specific criteria, whether explicit or not. These criteria may range from the subjective preferences of top decision-makers to more rigorous criteria of decision analysis.

Purposes of Value Metrics

In order to be able to make high-quality management decisions on IT-based infrastructure, and to maximize the chance of successful decisions, it is important to make value metrics as explicit as possible. Well-articulated value metrics serve several purposes (see Figure 9.1).

Appraisal Criteria and Priority Measures

Appropriate use of value metrics makes the difference between investment projects that are worthwhile and investment projects that do not deliver value for money, against the background of limited funding. A high-quality investment selection process will, on the one hand, not have as output projects those that only have a limited chance of being successful and, on the other hand, ignore projects that have a high chance of being successful. Value metrics serve as appraisal and prioritization criteria and 'they determine whether the "right" projects are selected' (Bacon, 1992). Since decisions will never be made in a purely rational way (see Chapter 7), value metrics in this sense also serve to

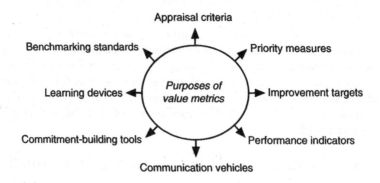

Figure 9.1   *Purposes of value metrics*

increase knowledge and to decrease uncertainty regarding the likely business impacts of investments.

Improvement Targets and Performance Indicators

In principle, value metrics also serve as business targets for improvement that should be reached and as performance measures to measure investment progress and outcomes and, if deemed necessary, to take corrective or improvement actions (see also Chapter 7 where 'value management' was discussed). As such, value metrics can also be used to define project deliverables, which reflect business targets, and to identify certain 'value owners' who are accountable for delivering the business targets. Having clearly defined value metrics prevents projects being judged as a success or a failure, depending on one's personal interests, and thus enables a more robust comparison between intended and realized business impacts.

Communication Vehicles and Commitment-Building Tools

Apart from being instruments for managerial decision-making and control, value metrics can be valuable in the process of communicating the business impacts of an IT-based infrastructure investment to all involved stakeholders. This offers a 'language' to create a shared mind-set, to establish commitment to a decision, and to enforce and foster loyalty in project execution. Without a shared investment vision, which allows for the different interests of investment stakeholders, the risk of unproductive conflicts and too diverse views becomes apparent.

Learning Devices and Benchmarking Standards

Clearly defined value metrics are the first step in mobilizing the learning abilities of a firm, and to capturing learning opportunities. Through a systematic comparison of intended and realized value profiles a valuable knowledge base can be created which captures the collective experiences and intuitions of many project stakeholders. Unfortunately, many of these experiences and intuitions generally remain implicit, and few organizations have a learning-focused knowledge management process in place. Measuring and articulating the full business impacts of an investment in IT-based infrastructure also enables benchmarking with best practices, across projects, internal business units or other organizations, or with investment outcomes which are qualified as being 'world class.'

The Need for Multi-Dimensional Value Metrics

It has become clear that today's quest for new and better value metrics should not be in the direction of constantly refining financial methods or optimization models. There is no 'magic formula', i.e. a universal measure or one best method for business value assessment of IT-based infrastructure. In a review study of IT business value research, Banker *et al.* (1993) conclude that researchers have too much been looking for the 'holy grail' of IT business value:

> The 'holy grail' of IT value research is to find a single, unified method or metric that will produce useful information under many circumstances of investment.

In line with their conclusion, at least two important reasons can be given for having a multi-dimensional perspective on value metrics for IT-based infrastructure:

- Many different stakeholders, who can be persons or parties, are involved in an investment in IT-based infrastructure. It can be expected that these stakeholders will also have different perspectives and personal judgments concerning the business impacts of such an investment.
- The possible business impacts of an investment in IT-based infrastructure are very diverse in nature. This diverse nature of business impacts requires that the possible consequences of an investment are reviewed and assessed from different perspectives.

This explains why this chapter pays attention to value metrics from a multi-dimensional perspective. Financial calculations will always be an important element of investment appraisal, but financial calculations alone are insufficient to arrive at a complete picture of the business impacts of proposed investments, which generally go beyond clear efficiency or cost containment. Although financial results are the bottom-line yardstick of many profit-oriented firms, the final financial result itself will be the result of different direct and indirect investment effects. As such, non-financial impacts can be seen as secondary value drivers of financial investment results, which finally are the prime measure of business value, but which in many cases cannot be estimated in isolation from its driving forces (see Kaplan and Norton, 1996).

Formulation of Value Metrics

Defining a comprehensive set of value metrics is an essential step in creating a managerial 'dashboard' for value management of IT-based infrastructure. This does not mean, however, that this should be a stringent, normative, quantitative set of approval criteria which investment proposals should meet in order to be justified. The definition of appropriate value metrics is more a process of organizational inquiry to extract existing and preferred value propositions from all involved stakeholders, who as a collective have valuable knowledge and many implicit experiences and relevant intuitions. No quantitative analyses, be they as rigorous as can be, can stand in the place of good human and managerial judgment, and nothing can be a greater hindrance to rigorous investment analysis than unspoken or conflicting human judgments. Value metrics thus set the agenda for an open discussion and make motivations arguable, debatable and able to stand up to keen questioning, which will ultimately make the business value of infrastructure projects more predictable and manageable.

Defining value metrics involves more than organizational communication and negotiation to arrive at a set of shared indicators that set improvement targets and measures of control. Introducing, managing and maintaining value metrics themselves is a vital organizational task that can easily be ignored, suffer from a lack of senior management ownership or devolve into a 'numbers game.' Adequate management of value metrics satisfies both the requirements of practical usefulness on the one hand and rigorous design on the other. It is virtually impossible to define an 'absolute' set of value metrics that would work in many investment situations and for many organizations. Every organization needs to define its own specific set of measures, reflecting its characteristics, ambitions, and investment purposes. A well-known set of criteria that, focusing on business benefits, gives a clear review of what are called 'SMART' value metrics is:

- Simple: they are easy to understand and reflect operational performance measures.
- Measurable: they can in one way or another be judged against some standard for comparison (e.g. a rate, ratio or degree).
- Achievable: they inspire all involved stakeholders to achieve the defined value propositions.
- Realistic: the targets set can be reached, given the starting conditions and the experience with previous projects.
- Time-specific: the value metrics reflect the ambitions with respect to the time-scale of defined business targets.

Case Study Experience

A case study that was conducted in the context of this book in a public sector, governmental organization (referred to as GovOrg) made clear that taking specific local circumstances into account is essential for successfully introducing and using value metrics for project appraisal (Kusters and Renkema, 1996). In GovOrg a choice was made for a localized variant of the Information Economics method as defined by Parker *et al.* (1988), see Chapter 6, to suit the value metrics needs of this particular firm. Major conclusions are:

- There is a major risk of failure when the fit between value metrics and organizational context is absent. Consequently, value metrics should reflect locally accepted definitions, terminology, or even jargon, and agreed upon measures of performance.
- Given the intangible nature of many benefits, value metrics should not be based solely on financial arguments, but be based upon the organizational ambitions and goals of the organization. In GovOrg, this was for instance secured by introducing 'political information' and 'political pressure.'
- Organizational conditions for the successful implementation and maintenance of value metrics lie in the softer areas of organizational change, e.g. communication, cooperation, consensus between and commitment of all involved stakeholders.
- The number of value metrics should be limited, and if required possible higher-level categorizations should be made to reduce the number of metrics. This will enable senior management overview and the presentation of clear criteria for investment appraisal and project prioritization.
- Value metric definitions will never be finished. During practical use many organizational changes are likely to occur, with all kind of new business impacts. By keeping the options for change explicitly open, value metrics will evolve together with the organization and a future mismatch can be avoided.

9.3 PRACTITIONER VIEWS ON VALUE METRICS

In the context of the research study that underpins this book, several case study investigations were done in order to identify appropriate value metrics for infrastructure assessment from a practitioner point of view. The results of these investigations are presented in this section.

Results of Brainstorming Sessions

This section discusses the findings of a number of brainstorming sessions that were held in each of the business units of the case study organization InsuraCo. These brainstorming sessions had a very open character, and focused on exchanging ideas, wishes, and preferences surrounding the theme of investing in IT-based infrastructure. The author of this book acted as a moderator and process facilitator in a discussion between all employees of the IT organization of business units. The main objective was to extract the implicit practical views of the most important value metrics for assessing business impacts. The results of the brainstorming sessions differ much in terms of both content and business implications. In what follows, a review will be given of the general characteristics of the different reactions by addressing the different types of reactions and value metrics mentioned. In addition to this, examples of the statements made are given in Table 9.1.

Financial Metrics

The overall conclusion is that brainstorming session participants have a strong preference for financial value metrics. In several cases the general opinion was that solely financial criteria could give a valid motivation for an investment. Non-financial investment impacts then need to be translated into clear and measurable indicators for financial results.

Strategic Advantage

A considerable part of participants' reactions refer to the 'strategic' importance of investment in IT-based infrastructure. The label 'strategic', however, seemed to suffer from a lack of common understanding; a more detailed discussion revealed that InsuraCo's market position *vis-à-vis* its direct competitors was what was meant. An important element of this positioning was the time-to-market, i.e. the evaluation of being a leader with the risk of innovation versus being a follower, with the risk of running behind the main competitors.

Market and Customer Focus

A large group of reactions, which is closely related to the previous category, refers to a more market and customer focused IT-based infrastructure deployment. The general feeling is that many past investments were 'pushed' by technology, while now there is an urgent need for an explicit orientation towards business goals.

Quality Standards

Different reactions refer to the quality standards that were deemed necessary for appropriate quality assurance of infrastructure development. Examples of quality standards are:

Type of reaction and value metrics	Examples of statements made
Financial metrics	• 'Ultimately, every investment, also in IT-based infrastructure, is about money. An investment project therefore has to deliver cash flow, in order to increase shareholder value'
	• 'Financial techniques such as Return On Investment are important but questionable. It is not easy to estimate business benefits in strictly financial terms, although this forces you to make a very thorough investment analysis'
Strategic advantage	• 'A very important aspect of investment evaluation is the advantage you can get at the expense of competitors'
	• 'The "time to market" of infrastructure is essential: an investment can be too early or too late'
Market and customer focus	• 'Fast and customer-driven business operations in insurance can be a very important motivation to allocate funds to an investment'
	• 'A good starting point is to focus on market-oriented thinking instead of focusing on your own internal infrastructure'
	• 'Value metrics should reflect the business goals, for instance in terms of turnover or customer values'
	• 'Investment justification is in many cases based on commercial motives'
Quality standards	• 'Relevant "second-order" metrics are the responsiveness and availability of infrastructure'
	• 'Regarding investment in technical infrastructure components, metrics such as maintainability and future flexibility are important'
Situation-specific and personal preferences	• 'The precise ranking of value metrics differs from person to person and very often depends on intuition'
	• 'Investment appraisals are not stable across time, but are dependent on the present needs of a firm'
	• 'If someone wants a project to be authorized by management, it is important to know the personal motivations of a manager'

Table 9.1   Sample practitioner views on project value

• infrastructure coverage or automation degree;
• availability and responsiveness of infrastructure;
• continuity and maintainability of infrastructure components;
• flexibility for future use.

Situation-Specific and Personal Preferences

Several reactions from brainstorming participants referred to their observation that the use of appropriate value metrics is highly dependent on the characteristics of a specific decision-situation and on the personal preferences of decision stakeholders. There are doubts concerning the possibility of defining a comprehensive set of value criteria which can be used for the assessment of different infrastructure investments, apart from financial value metrics. It is however also realized that without a clearly defined set of metrics, investment appraisal will be much more subject to manipulation and disruptive political maneuvers.

Case Study Findings

In Chapter 3 (see Section 3.2) the results of a survey of empirical views of the notion of IT-based infrastructure were presented. A second theme of this survey was the use of value metrics to assess investments in IT-based infrastructure. This section presents the findings concerning this second theme. Survey data were collected by interviewing employees from the case study organizations. All interviewees were responsible for a specific part of IT-based infrastructure. The survey results were verified and feedback was received by sending a report to all personnel involved.

All interviewees were of the opinion that it is impossible to combine all relevant value metrics for IT-based infrastructure into one comprehensive measure of (financial) value. On the other hand, sticking to solely financial measures was also considered to be inappropriate, and would certainly not sketch a complete picture of the business case for investments in IT-based infrastructure. According to the interviewees, relevant value metrics should:

- Meet the demand for infrastructure coverage of end-users, with a focus on functional coverage (i.e. automated support for all business tasks which can potentially be supported).
- Increase efficiency through improved price/performance ratios, and through exploiting scale effects when purchasing and operating infrastructure components.
- Ensure technical conformance, due to the fact that an infrastructure component is outdated in technological terms, or because a supplier no longer supports the components.
- Anticipate future infrastructure needs or possibly interesting technological developments, which implies that investments now are meant to secure future flexibility.
- Enable interconnectivity with internal (e.g. across business units or management levels) and external (e.g. with customers or supply chain partners) IT-based systems.

- Increase the level of standardization and consistency within the total IT-based infrastructure.
- Secure continuity, maintainability and business security of IT-based infrastructure.

Conclusions Regarding the Views from Business Practice

The practical investigations of this section show that business professionals have a strong preference for using finance-based value metrics for assessing investments in IT-based infrastructure. This can also be explained by the fact that the case study organizations have a strong strategic orientation towards profit-making, and thus have a relatively stringent financial discipline. However, the general opinion also is that non-financial value metrics do play an essential role in investment appraisal and decision-making, and in many cases are decisive for final management approval. The brainstorming discussions held also show that respondents somehow shy away from using explicit and well-articulated non-financial value metrics. A general feeling is that too situation-specific and too personalized factors stand in the way of this. An emerging conclusion is therefore that decision-makers do not like the idea of losing the flexibility inherent in existing assessment practices. Value metrics that are considered appropriate to get a good view of the business impacts of infrastructure investments predominantly lie in the areas of competitive strategy, market- and customer-focused infrastructure use, and quality assurance (e.g. regarding responsiveness and maintainability) of IT-based infrastructure deployment. The interviews with infrastructure managers make clear that a recurring—and possibly the prime—element of investments in IT-based infrastructure is the interaction between the supply of and demand for infrastructure components. In contrast to the participants in the brainstorming sessions, to a lesser extent these managers do consider financial value metrics as essential to investment evaluation. Although they do regard efficiency benefits to be relevant, more important value metrics are found in the enabling nature of IT-based infrastructure and in the manageability of infrastructure (e.g. visible at the levels of continuity and standardization).

9.4 FROM BUSINESS IMPACTS TO BUSINESS VALUE

Every investment in IT-based infrastructure should be evaluated against the background of the long-term benefits it delivers, the efforts needed to install and maintain the infrastructure across its entire expected life time, and the risks associated with the investment. This long-term, strategic perspective is needed since the infrastructure consists of standardized components that will be shared across the company and will enable business-specific IT deployment now and in the future.[1] A structured way to do this is to answer the following consecutive questions:

1. What are the expected *business impacts* and overall value metrics of an investment?
2. To what extent can these metrics be translated into *financial* terms; in other words, what are the potential expenditures (cash outlays) and earnings (cash proceeds)?
3. What are the remaining *non-financial metrics* and are these judged to be positive or negative by involved stakeholders?
4. What are the uncertainties of the different assessments; in other words, what are the *risks* involved?
5. In light of these assessments, what is the *final judgment* with respect to business value and thus the justification for the investment?

Answering these five questions will result in a business case for the investment, which links business impacts with business value through defined value metrics (see Figure 9.2). The following section will, in addition to the practical findings discussed in the previous section, discuss in more detail the business impacts of infrastructure and the translation of these impacts into value metrics using the distinction between direct and indirect infrastructure. The generic structure of both types of business impacts is presented in Table 9.2. In addition to the impacts given in Table 9.2, the possible business impacts and resulting value metrics result from the total life-cycle efforts needed to initiate and operate a planned investment (commonly referred to as the 'total cost of ownership'). Relevant efforts are:

- *Realization efforts:* designing, developing and purchasing infrastructure components.

---

[1] It is important to note that the approach advocated here does not match the practical viewpoint of many managers, who argue that infrastructure investments should be justified solely on the back of business-specific applications (see Ward *et al.*, 1996a; Fitzgerald, 1998). While it is recommended to identify a number (e.g. two to three) committed business-specific projects that will benefit from the proposed IT-based infrastructure, separate and well-articulated business value assessment of infrastructure should have explicit management attention.

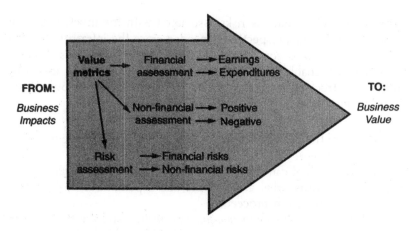

***Figure* 9.2**   *From business impacts to business value*

Direct infrastructure	Indirect infrastructure
• Organizational learning • Business process structure • Strategic positioning • Decision-making and management control • Organizational structure • Individual roles and organizational culture	• Organizational learning • Business orientation and partnership of IT function • Supply of capabilities and capacities • Quality of basic services • Robustness of facilities

***Table* 9.2**   *Business impacts of IT-based infrastructure*

- *Maintenance and operating efforts:* using infrastructure components and securing defined quality standards (e.g. functional maintenance, availability, responsiveness, security).
- *Organizational change efforts:* introducing the infrastructure component and integrating it into existing ways of working.

9.5 VALUE METRICS FOR DIRECT INFRASTRUCTURE

In line with the business implications of what has been defined as direct infrastructure (see Chapter 4), this section will give a more detailed review of suitable value metrics for assessing investment in IT-based infrastructure. For several value metrics, typical ratios are known to be used by more advanced organizations for performance management; if appropriate, these too will be mentioned.

Organizational Learning

In some cases the main purpose of an investment in direct infrastructure is not so much the direct improvement of business processes, products, or services, but to learn from investment impacts. Often, these investments are typified as pilot or research investments in which the likely impacts of a new type of infrastructure are assessed.

Business Process Structure

Direct infrastructure investments, by definition, impact on the business processes of an organization. Many of the business improvements enabled by advanced infrastructure support materialize in terms of process performance, e.g. costs, speed, structure, and quality:

- Process speed (e.g. order fulfillment and acceptance rates), cycle times (e.g. for quotations and invoices, development times).
- Regulation of business controls (e.g. inspections, checks and authorizations).
- Incorporation of expertise and 'tacit' knowledge into processes.
- Monitoring of product and service operations.
- Standardization and parallelization of process steps.
- Degree of process structure and quality (e.g. slippage levels, completeness of deliverance).
- Level of accuracy and fault tolerance (e.g. conformance to specifications, waste and defects levels, product return ratios).
- Extent of duplication of information processing.
- Inventory levels of intermediate and final products.
- Required scarce capacities and limited resources (e.g. process productivity, capacity load factors).

Strategic Positioning

Direct infrastructure investments have an important impact on the long-term profitability of a firm and on the ability to compete. Relevant value metrics relate to:

- Overall strategic course and long-term strategic goals (e.g. market growth, industrial performance, international expansion).
- Competitive positioning and customer satisfaction (e.g. sales ratios, hit rates, order intake level, customer acquisition and retention rates).
- Technology capacity building.

- Supply chain positioning towards supply chain partners (e.g. suppliers, customers).
- Corporate (public) image and branding (e.g. customer loyalty and reorder level, retention rate, market preference position).
- Turnover and profit perspective (e.g. revenue growth, capital ratios, asset ratios, liquidity ratios).
- Number of markets and distribution channels covered (new market ratios, channel coverage and performance).
- Product and service scope/range of product features.
- Responsiveness towards new business development (e.g. number of new products, contribution to market innovation).
- Time to market new products and services.
- Type and quality of customer interaction (e.g. degree of electronic commerce).
- Capture of customer data and knowledge.
- Customer service quality (e.g. response times to service calls, repair and solution times).

Decision-Making and Management Control

Investments in direct infrastructure may change the way in which decisions are taken and management control is effectuated. Relevant value metrics concern:

- Accuracy of business plans and performance projections (e.g. degree of estimate accuracy).
- Timeliness of decision and control signals (e.g. number of required exception reports).
- Speed and timing of decision-making (e.g. number of people involved, use of resources, decision throughput time).
- Quality and diversity of information covered (e.g. degree of un-reliable decision information, number of new data sources).
- Standardization of decision reports (e.g. level of conformance to corporate or audit standards).
- Ability to analyze key figures.
- Objectivity of decision-making and control measures (e.g. degree of stakeholder acceptance).

Organizational Structure

Direct infrastructure investment may have consequences for the way in which an organization is structured. Relevant value metrics refer to:

- Managerial span of control (e.g. number of processes, functions or employees managed).
- Orientation on functions versus processes (e.g. ratio of functional versus process ownership).
- Fragmentation of task division (e.g. number of different departments or employees required for task completion).
- Number of hierarchical layers.
- Number and type of functions.
- Degree of (de)centralization.
- Degree of departmental/functional specialization.
- Level of task delegation and empowerment.
- Governance approach and accountability structure (e.g. degree of local or unit autonomy).
- Location and time (in)dependence of business activities.
- Alliance and networking with external business partners (e.g. number of key suppliers, quality level of partnership contracts).

Individual Employees and Organizational Culture

Investments in direct infrastructure may impact on work activities and possibly employee behavior. This in turn may have consequences for the organizational culture, which shapes the norms and values underlying organizational cooperation (see Schein, 1988). Relevant value metrics can be found in the following impacts:

- Spread and retention of employee knowledge.
- Extent to which employees use IT innovatively.
- Professionalism and task content of employee activities (e.g. education level, professional association membership).
- Employee motivation and satisfaction (e.g. personnel retention rate, absenteeism level, new talent attraction).
- Mental and physical workload.
- Work flexibility in terms of place and time.
- Degree to which new knowledge is gained (e.g. training levels, dependence on external consultants).
- Employee privacy.
- Degree to which inexperienced or handicapped employees are hired.
- Type and intensity of employee communication (e.g. degree or formal/informal/electronic communication).

9.6 VALUE METRICS FOR INDIRECT INFRASTRUCTURE

Similar to the previous section, this section will give a more detailed review of suitable value metrics for assessing investment in indirect infrastructure. As argued in Chapter 4, the main rationale behind these types of infrastructure investments is to create a shared, standardized set of technological and organizational facilities, which are manifest in essential indirect infrastructure capacities and capabilities. For different value metrics, typical ratios are known to be used in the context of more advanced performance management; if appropriate, these will be mentioned as well.

Organizational Learning

Just as for investments in direct infrastructure, the main value of an investment in indirect infrastructure may be not so much the direct improvement of infrastructure capacities and capabilities, but to learn from (emerging) investment impacts. This can be assessed, for example, through basic research or pilot projects covering new technological or supplier developments.

Business Orientation and Partnership of IT Function

As discussed in Chapter 4, the indirect infrastructure can be conceptualized as the capacities and capabilities that are generally organized and managed from within an IT function (or IT department). As such, indirect infrastructure investment impacts on the way in which these functions are organized and managed. This may lead to an IT organization that has more business-like organizational characteristics. From this respect it is important to assess the degree to which the IT function positions and transforms itself into a business partner. Relevant value metrics can be found in the following areas:

- Managing IT as a business; see, for example, the relevant impact areas of direct infrastructure: process structure (e.g. systems development, managed operations), decision-making (e.g. regarding outsourcing, package and product selections), organizational structure (e.g. departmental structure, IT task division) and culture (e.g. regarding developers or operators).
- Business partnership (e.g. degree of understanding and anticipation of business issues, level of mutual trust between IT and business, degree of being an obvious partner and 'first choice' supplier in strategic business renewal).

- Business planning of IT (e.g. alignment of IT versus business strategies and priorities, degree of planning maturity and actuality).
- Innovation abilities (e.g. degree of proven versus new technology deployment, implementation speed of new technologies, level of legacy/obsolete technology components, deployment of high caliber IT specialists).

Supply of Capabilities and Capacities

Indirect infrastructure capacities and capabilities are essentially supplied in order to support and enable successful IT deployment in business processes, products, and services. Therefore, appropriate value metrics for assessing the business value of indirect infrastructure investment can be found in the effects it has on the supply of capacities and capabilities (e.g. for system development, managed operations, and telecommunications). Relevant value metrics concern:

- Availability level of supply facilities for support of current business needs (e.g. down times, level of honored requests).
- Ability to respond to changes in current business needs (e.g. unexpected peak loads, *ad hoc* infrastructure requests, growth in business volume, product or services mix, new product features).
- Build up of supply facilities for innovative use of IT in business processes, products and services.
- Creation of flexibility options for presently unknown supply needs (e.g. resulting from new types of business IT deployment).

Quality of Basic Services

Many indirect infrastructure investments lead to building a set of standard capacities and capabilities, which can be thought of as delivering basic infrastructure services that have to meet certain quality levels. Increasingly, these quality levels are defined and managed through service level agreements. Service quality of basic infrastructure services thus becomes a relevant business impact of investment in indirect infrastructure. Appropriate value metrics can be found in the following impacts:

- Required scarce capacities and limited resources (e.g. system development productivity, operations and networking resource requirements).

- Speed of service fulfillment (e.g. system development and maintenance throughput times, implementation time, conversion speed, processing and communication times).
- Responsiveness of services (e.g. accessibility of information and knowledge, processing response and throughput times, network performance, helpdesk response time).
- Reliability of services (e.g. development defect rate, repair requirements rates, level of processing correctness and print/output accuracy, network integrity degree).

Robustness of Facilities

Since the capacities and capabilities of indirect infrastructure will be used by many different users, and enable more business-specific IT deployment for a longer period of time, it is essential that these infrastructure facilities have an adequate degree of robustness. Relevant value metrics are in the following areas:

- Stability (e.g. number of required changes, degree of proven technological ability, level of conformance to market or supplier standards, durability and continuity of components).
- Scalability (e.g. ability to increase user level, ability to extend to other technological environments or networking standards, or user communities).
- Maintainability (e.g. conformance to structured methods, required maintenance efforts, ability to secure defined quality levels and to install upgrades, level of component uniformity across user community, complexity of overall structure).
- Interconnectivity (e.g. degree of reuse of software, portability to other technical environments, efforts to migrate to new versions or releases, ability to interface to legacy or new components, ability to connect with internal or external partners).
- Security (e.g. prevention of unauthorized access, securing back-up and recovery, level of integrity and confidentiality of processing or output).

9.7 FINANCIAL ASSESSMENT

After getting adequate insight into the likely business impacts and relevant value metrics of investments in IT-based infrastructure, an assessment can be made as to the extent these can be translated into financial figures. As such, a financial assessment of investment impacts is only one part of a comprehensive assessment through financial and non-financial value metrics. Investment impacts do not have to be translated into financial terms *per se*, but only when there are sufficient opportunities for sound financial analyses. Financial value metrics should cover both the negative and positive sides of business impacts, i.e. the expenditures that are needed to realize and operate the investment, and the possible earnings from the investment. Earnings and expenditures generally follow certain patterns, where in a financially justified situation total investment earnings exceed expenditures (see Figure 9.3). Expenditures are high when an infrastructure is installed and tend to rise after a certain period when maintenance (e.g. from functional or technical adjustments) efforts increase rapidly. Earnings come later than expenditures and tend to decrease after a period of time since it will be increasingly harder to deliver these (e.g. breakdown of initial benefits opportunities, other organizational requirements, new competitive conditions). When the total financial results become zero or even negative, an infrastructure component has reached its financial end-of-life.

Investment Expenditures

Investment expenditures can be determined by a financial assessment of value metrics (see the previous section) which cover the efforts needed to build and operate infrastructure components. This refers to the efforts required to realize an investment, to use and maintain it, and to the organizational changes that accompany the investment. These latter expenditures for organizational change are often not taken into account, although these may account for up to 30% to 50% of total investment expenditures (Hochstrasser, 1990). Table 9.3 gives a

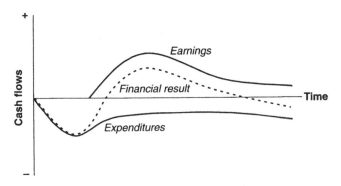

Figure 9.3 *Patterns of investment earnings and expenditures*

Direct infrastructure	Indirect infrastructure
Realization	
• Personnel and tools for strategy and planning (including cost estimation, quality management, risk management) • Identical for system analysis and design • Identical for software development • Identical for package selection and acquisition • Identical for conversion and implementation	• Specialist hiring and consulting • Resource acquisition (equipment, tools, systems software, telecommunications, etc.) • Development of new procedures (methods, ways of working, etc.)
Use and exploitation	
• Personnel and tools for system maintenance • Identical for IT operations • Identical for IT managed operations • Identical for telecommunications • Identical for user training and support	• Maintaining specialist knowledge and expertise • Tools maintenance • Keeping procedures (methods, ways of working, etc.) up to date
Organizational change	
• Personnel and tools for training and education • Identical for transition from old to new ways of working • Identical for reorganization efforts (e.g. managing resistance to change, securing user commitment) • Earnings reduction because of temporary productivity loss	• Introducing personnel, tools, and procedures into the IT function • Reorganization efforts for IT function (e.g. managing resistance to change, securing user commitment) • Earnings reduction because of temporary productivity loss • Side effect for user organizations

Table 9.3   Investment expenditures on IT-based infrastructure

summary of the most important expenditures concerning investments in IT-based infrastructure.

Investment Earnings

The first step in assessing investment earnings is to evaluate present earnings that would be forgone if an investment would not have been approved of ('what-if-not analyses'). Any estimation of to-be-received cash flows should not be done from a status quo perspective ('before' versus 'after') but from an appraisal of business performance with or without the investment (Kaplan, 1986). In many cases, financial justifications for investments in indirect infrastructure will be based upon what-if-not analyses, since an essential motivation of these investments is that without them vital enabling capabilities and capacities would be unavailable. Consequently, the final earnings of successful IT deployment in business processes, products, and services can to some extent be attributed to investment in indirect infrastructure capabilities and capacities. In conjunction with what-if-not analyses, possible additional earnings through infrastructure support need to be assessed. There are two engines of additional earnings: improved efficiency and increased earnings (see Table 9.4).

Improving Efficiency

An important source of efficiency improvements can be found in replacing purely manual or mechanical tasks with IT-based infrastructure support. Regarding the direct infrastructure this is true for paper-intensive administrative back office processes (e.g. payroll or inventory accounting, invoice handling, or purchase order management) and for primary processes (e.g. robots in manufacturing processes, workflow management in service processes). Similarly, the efficiency of many processes of indirect infrastructure can be improved by substituting laborious manual tasks with IT-enabled infrastructure support (e.g. through using computer-aided development or maintenance tools, or tools for system management). Reducing the need for working capital can capture further efficiency improvements. Appropriate deployment

Direct infrastructure	Indirect infrastructure
Improving efficiency	
• Replacing manual and mechanical tasks	• Replacing manual and mechanical tasks
• Reduced working capital and space	• Reduced working capital and space
• Time savings	• Time savings
• Fewer inaccuracies	• Fewer inaccuracies
• More efficient organizational structure	• More efficient organizational structure
Increasing earnings	
• Direct earnings increase	• Related profitable IT deployment in business processes and products
• Improved market and competitive positioning	• Options on future IT deployment in business processes and products
• Faster cash flow receipt	

Table 9.4 *Sources of additional earnings from IT-based infrastructure*

of IT-based infrastructure generally reduces the need for inventories, storage, and warehousing (e.g. of raw materials, intermediate, or final products). Within paper-intensive processes, using fewer documents, less printing and less copying can reduce spending. Infrastructure investment may also reduce expenditures on required, factory, office, and computing space. An additional source of efficiency improvements can be found in faster and more accurate process executions. The latter will generally lead to less waste, fewer defects, and fewer corrective actions within business processes. Consequently, less redundant capacity is needed to repair inaccuracies and faults. Opportunities for more accurate processes and ways of working also lie within the indirect infrastructure (e.g. automated test procedures or dedicated system management tools), which may reduce the need for infrastructure facilities (e.g. test platforms or system management resources). Efficiency gains can further be captured by the cost-effective management of business impacts on the organizational structure (e.g. fewer managerial levels, fewer support functions, and improved communications among departments or units.)

Increasing Earnings

Apart from efficiency improvements, investments in IT-based infrastructure may cause a direct increase in earnings. Such an increase sometimes emanates from an increase in turnover, e.g. in the case of investments in product, process, or service innovation. Additional earnings, which can be less directly traced back to increases in turnover generally result from an improved position in the market. For a firm operating in competitive markets this generally means gaining and sustaining a comparative advantage through advanced IT-based infrastructure exploitation, at the expense of direct or new competitors. Possible competitive strategies are for instance:

- Creating entry barriers for new competitors through innovative, capital intensive investments.
- Integrating the infrastructure with the infrastructure of suppliers or customers (e.g. through electronic commerce or dedicated networks).
- Adding new features to products (e.g. putting functionality into 'embedded software' in cars).
- Introducing new services (e.g. telebanking, teleshopping).
- Entering new markets and distribution channels (e.g. electronic publishing by 'traditional' publishers, cellular telephony by 'traditional' electronics manufacturers).

- Strengthening client bonds (e.g. through data-based marketing or client cards).

Next to increasing absolute earnings, an investment in IT-based infrastructure also has the potential to speed up the timeframe within which the cash flows are received. This generally leads to a higher valuation of cash flows, not only because of interest advantages, but also because decision-makers have an aversion to risk.

Many investments in IT-based infrastructure get management approval and are justified without a detailed estimation of additional earnings generated by the investment. The prime motivation generally given for this is that future options generated by the planned infrastructure provide sufficient justification and thus make an investment worthwhile. However, it proves to be very difficult, and often highly contentious, to define all future options enabled by an infrastructure investment in terms of projected earnings. Regarding investments in indirect infrastructure, in some cases a quite direct relation with a very profitable investment in direct infrastructure can be identified. It then may be necessary to base the projected earnings of an investment in indirect infrastructure partly on the earnings that result from expected investment with high financial returns.

Possibilities and Limitations of Option Theory

Recently, it has been suggested to use so called 'option theory' for evaluating future earnings of investments in IT-based infrastructure, and several (quite theoretical) applications of option theory in the context of IT investments can be found (see, for example, Kambil *et al.*, 1993; Dos Santos, 1994). Option theory is considered to be very promising within finance-based investment planning and capital budgeting theories, mainly because of the attached uncertainty elements (Dixit and Pindyck, 1995; Luehrman, 1998). Option theory addresses operational flexibility (e.g. postponing investment steps, changing project scope) and strategic flexibility (follow-up investments or growth options) of an investment project. Regarding investment in IT-based infrastructure, this strategic flexibility is most important for assessing the desirability and business value of a proposed project. Option theory proposed in the context of IT-based infrastructure investments and other capital investments addresses the valuation of real options in contrast to financial options, which are traded on financial markets (see, for example, Brealey and Myers, 1988). Rather like a financial call option, it is assumed that an organization by executing an investment project 'buys' the possibility of executing follow-up projects with high financial returns. It is therefore allowed to approve of a project with a negative financial valuation in terms of net present value (NPV), if this is sufficiently compensated by profitable follow-up projects. Investment uncertainty then becomes an element of investment control, since an option will only be executed if follow-up values are positive and not if these are negative.

Several conceptual and practical issues emerge when trying to use in business practice option theory as proposed in the current literature. An important barrier to the successful implementation is a general inability to reliably estimate cash flows that are enabled by infrastructure investment. It is virtually impossible to define potential future projects in their entirety, and even more difficult to give a realistic estimation of the cash inflows resulting from these projects. Existing models for option valuation assume a certain distribution of the resulting cash flows, based on an efficient market or another appropriate indicator of expected returns. However, this is only rarely the case in the context of investments in IT-based infrastructure, which are known for their uncertain, and unpredictable, business impacts. It has been further shown that finance-oriented option valuation models are too complex for managerial decision-making practice (Sharp, 1991). It can therefore be concluded that option theory in its present state does provide a conceptual decision framework to evaluate the pros and cons of an investment in general terms, but cannot yet be considered an operational tool for management. In many cases it is much more feasible, simpler and faster to apply what could be called 'option thinking' in the form of decision tree analysis. This means that alternative investment options (i.e. follow-up investments) are systematically defined and categorized. Subsequently, the chance of occurrence based on decision evaluations and the probability distribution of expected earnings are defined (see, for example, Hares and Royle, 1994).

9.8 NON-FINANCIAL ASSESSMENT

Relatively speaking, it is quite simple to assign a positive or negative judgment to cash flow estimations of proposed investments in IT-based infrastructure. Earnings are 'good' and expenditures are 'bad.' Such a trivial judgment does not, unfortunately, exist for the many non-financial business impacts of an investment. For example, a direct infrastructure investment may lead to more structured business processes and procedures (which is judged to be positive) and consequently also include a competitive disadvantage, since flexibility and speed to respond to important business changes have been lost (which is judged to be negative). Similarly, an investment in direct infrastructure may have as a positively judged impact that the response and reliability of processing increases, but have as a negatively valued impact that infrastructure capabilities for new, innovative local applications cannot sufficiently be guaranteed.

The tradeoffs between positively and negatively valued business impacts, both of which may be legitimate value metrics, thus complicates an unambiguous non-financial assessment. Ultimately, the value judgments of key decision stakeholders, and most importantly senior management judgments, intuitions and articulated value propositions, should have the last word in assessing the contribution of investment proposals to business performance. A complicating factor in this is that what is deemed to be beneficial to the organization as a whole does not necessarily have to be experienced as such by all persons or parties involved. The aforementioned example, for instance, discussed the positive valuation of more structured processes and procedures. However, not all individual end-users have to appreciate this as solely positive. For some, increased structuring may also mean increased opportunities for control or a violation of privacy expectations. Similar examples can be given for other business impacts. If this is not recognized and actively managed, the risk of obstruction because of conflicts of interest becomes apparent.

Possible different visions and mind-sets, and conflicts of interest with respect to investment impacts necessitate a process of intensive mutual consultation regarding which business impacts are considered to be advantageous and which disadvantageous. Each business value assessment and investment appraisal of a proposed project should be the outcome of a communication and negotiation process, where management attention needs to focus on establishing an open atmosphere with no hidden agendas. If managed well, individual, informal and implicit assessments will be translated into collectively shared and clearly defined value metrics.

After assessing the overall advantages and disadvantages of a proposed investment it in principle becomes possible to give a final judgment regarding the business value and thus desirability of a project. However, such a final judgment also depends on the relative importance of defined value metrics. This prioritization of value metrics will not be the same for each organization and for each decision situation. Important situational aspects are general and business-specific experience with a particular type of investment and technology, the strategic ambitions and long-term business priorities of an organization, and the possible synergy emanating from defining an investment as being infrastructure (see the following chapter for the latter issue). The situational aspects of business value assessment and investment appraisal also will be discussed further in Chapter 11.

9.9 RISK IDENTIFICATION AND MANAGEMENT

Investment risks emanate from the uncertainty surrounding any assessment of business impacts through value metrics. Although risks are generally addressed in the context of system development, they are surprisingly undermanaged or even ignored or suffer from lack of management attention in the context of capital-intensive investments in IT-based infrastructure (Clemons, 1991; Willcocks and Margretts, 1994). Risks are not necessarily uncontrollable. After comprehensively identifying relevant risk factors, a separate management assessment is required as to whether risks can be mitigated and managed, and which measures are needed for this (Kepner and Tregoe, 1981; Drummond, 1996). As with other assessments of business impact through value metrics, this should be the result of intensive communication and debate among involved stakeholders. Potential risks should be defined in terms of their:

- *investment impacts*—the harmful effect if the risk actualizes;
- *chance of occurrence*—the possibility that the risks actualizes;
- *likely moment of occurrence*—the investment stage at which the risk may actualize.

After recognizing and clearly identifying potential risks, decision-makers have a number of alternatives, which can be used in a preventative and corrective manner:

- *acceptance* (e.g. do nothing, build in margins, define contingency plans);
- *reduction* (e.g. redefine scope and ambitions, design alternative realizations);
- *transfer* (e.g. project insurance, define third-party accountabilities, risk-sharing);
- *rejection* (e.g. reassess project desirability, abandon risky project elements).

For a good assessment of the acceptable risk exposure of a project it is required to evaluate (manageable and unmanageable) risks against the background of the overall business value gained. As such, the overall investment portfolio should be balanced in terms of 'risks' and 'rewards.' High risk/low reward projects are generally not desirable; however, projects with low risks/high rewards are particularly desirable, but these types of projects are often rare (see Figure 9.4). Projects with low risk/low reward profiles are generally easily approved of, but might bring limited business value, i.e. below expectations and the required competitive level. Too many high risk/high reward projects may however be too demanding for adequate risk management.

Although risks may impact on both the advantageous and disadvantageous effects of an investment, a general distinction can be made between uncertainty of investment efforts (e.g. for realization or organizational change), versus uncertainty of investment benefits. Consequently, the focus on the types of risk to be managed, and the risk management ambition level will also differ in accordance with this. Figure 9.5 gives an illustration of this, identifying four risk management scenarios:

- *Zero-defect ambition*—uncertainties regarding investment efforts and benefits are limited. Risks are manageable, making a 'zero-defect' investment outcome, i.e. without much deviation from the defined business case, viable and realizable.
- *Full value management*—uncertainties regarding investment efforts and benefits are substantial. Risks are a complicating factor in invest-

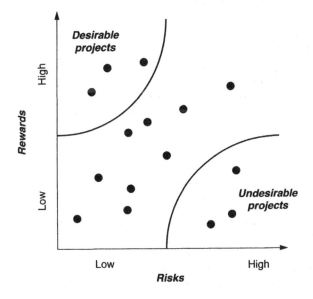

Figure 9.4 *Investment portfolio in terms of risk and reward*

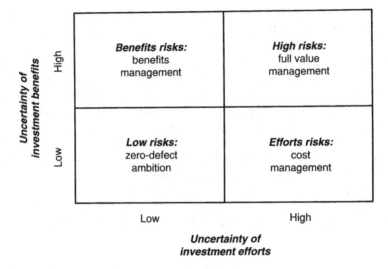

Figure 9.5   *Risk management scenarios*

ment management, thus prompting the need for full-scale value management.

- *Cost management*—uncertainties regarding investment efforts are substantial, but regarding benefits limited. Since a disappointing investment result will generally be caused by too high investment efforts, managing this risk in terms of its cost effects should be the focus of investment risk management.

- *Benefit management*—uncertainties regarding investment benefits are substantial, but regarding costs limited. Since a disappointing investment result will generally be caused by insufficient benefit delivery, managing this risk in terms of its effects on benefits should be the focus of investment risk management.

Financial Risks

All estimations of expected earnings and risks will generally move between certain margins. In the worst case, real earnings are much lower than projected, and real expenditures are much higher than initially expected. Much of this uncertainty is a consequence of the *a priori* unknown expected life-time of an investment project. The existence of financial risks implies that expectations of earnings and expenditures should not be considered as 'hard' figures and as point estimates. It is much more important to explicitly analyze expectations and the factors that determine the final outcomes. Financial risks can be assessed and analyzed in more detail by performing:

- *sensitivity analyses*, in which pessimistic, optimistic and realistic projections of all discrete cash flows are analyzed in order to assess their impact on overall results;
- *scenario analyses*, in which the effects of different future developments and optional decisions are analyzed in order to assess their effects on cash flow projections.

As argued in Chapter 6, from a theoretical capital budgeting perspective, discounted cash flow methods (e.g. net present value (NPV) and internal rate of return (IRR)) should be preferred for a financial appraisal of investment impacts. These methods make 'dollars of tomorrow' comparable with 'dollars of today.' According to more advanced financial theories the actual opportunity cost of capital used in these calculations should reflect the specific risks of a particular investment project which is subject to investment decision-making. Since each project will generally have a different risk exposure, the actual risk needs to be redefined each time, based upon previous or other investment projects with a comparable expected financial return. This may be the correct approach in terms of theoretical robustness, but does not really work in investment practice (see, for example, Pike and Ho, 1991). Also, firms often use too high discounting rates in order to neutralize investment risks (Kaplan, 1986).

Non-Financial Risks

In addition to financial risks, the final outcomes and business contribution of an investment in IT-based infrastructure also depends on the effects of non-financial risks. Table 9.5 gives a summary of the most important non-financial risks, with a distinction between investments in direct and indirect infrastructure. With respect to indirect infrastructure, non-financial risks mainly have to do with factors that impact on direct infrastructure.

External Risks

External risks are risks which are a consequence of uncertainty that emanates from the unpredictable behavior of actors in the external environment of organizations, for instance of competitors, governments, trade unions, customers and suppliers. Additional external risks ensue from macro-economic developments in both domestic and international markets. Competitors can engage in defensive or

Direct infrastructure	Indirect infrastructure
External risks	
• Competitor behavior • Government behavior • Trade union behavior • Customer and supplier behavior • Macro-economic developments	• Impact of external risks on direct infrastructure • Lack of key supplier support and continuity
Realization risks	
• Required functionality cannot be delivered • Unstable and ambiguous information needs • Investment too large and too complex	• Impact of realization risks of direct infrastructure • Requirement needs cannot be satisfied • Investment too large and too complex
Organizational risks	
• Resistance to change • Lack of cooperation and communication • Lack of senior business management commitment and ownership • Interdepartmental and interpersonal political conflicts	• Impact of organizational risks of direct infrastructure • Lack of cooperation and and communication • Lack of senior business management commitment and ownership • Interdepartmental and interpersonal political conflicts
Technological risks	
• New type of application, data and knowledge • Unproven tools from indirect infrastructure • Too new skills and knowledge requirements from indirect infrastructure	• Impact of technological risks of direct infrastructure • Required experience and skill level cannot be delivered • Too advanced tools

Table 9.5   *Non-financial investment risks*

offensive strategic actions and investment programs, which can make initially assessed business advantages less realistic. Political decisions and administrative policies by governmental bodies may lead to all kinds of legal and/or fiscal regulations which an organization may have to comply with in the context of an investment in IT-based infrastructure. Trade unions may impose all kinds of restrictions with respect to investment consequences for individual employees and to projected labor savings. The reactions of customers or suppliers concerning infrastructure investments which try to influence their buying or selling behavior are, to a large extent, unpredictable. A more specific point of attention regarding external risks of indirect infrastructure investment is the expected continuity of external suppliers of key hardware and software infrastructure products. Since this infrastructure should provide solid, basic technological facilities for an extended period of time, lack of supplier support can be disastrous.

Realization Risks

Realization risks refer to the uncertainty of whether the defined deliverables of a project can really be realized. As regards direct infrastructure, it is uncertain whether the required software functionality for business process support can be built, and whether information needs are stable and unambiguous enough to be clearly specified. Realization risks are further determined by the size and complexity of a project (e.g. the number of users, total project duration, process coverage, geographical scope, interdependencies with other direct infrastructure projects). With respect to investments in indirect infrastructure, realization risks refer to the uncertainty of whether the basic facilities to be created satisfy current and future capacity and capability requirements, and will be sufficiently used to cover up-front efforts. Again, this is closely related to the demand for these infrastructure capacities and capabilities from within business processes, products, and services. Concerning investments in human resources, this means satisfying requirements in terms of knowledge and skills. Concerning investments in basic infrastructure tools, this means delivering sufficient capabilities and capacities with the required quality level. Similar to direct infrastructure, the size and complexity of an investment also determines the realization risks of investments in indirect infrastructure. Important risk factors are: the number of IT specialists and departments involved, the project throughput time, the number of interdependent indirect infrastructure projects, the required scalability of infrastructure solutions, and the interconnectivity requirements with other infrastructure components.

Organizational Risks

When investing in direct infrastructure it usually is required that intended users of this infrastructure familiarize themselves with new ways of working. This also entails an amount of risk with respect to project and investment success. The more end-users who are loyal and committed to an investment, the higher the chance of success. If, however, individual users fear that their current functioning, freedom of action and business routines may be threatened, they are prone to develop defensive routines. Organizational risks further emanate from the extent to which cooperation amongst key stakeholders is well-structured and there are high-quality communications in place. Particularly for investments in IT-based infrastructure, senior management commitment and business management ownership are vital. The fact that many organizational units or departments participate in project decision-making and execution makes an investment open to institutional conflicts of a socio-political nature, although these may also be at an interpersonal level between key executives. Again, organizational risks of direct infrastructure influence investments in indirect infrastructure. In addition to this, investments in indirect infrastructure involve organizational risks in the areas of resistance to change, poorly managed cooperation and insufficient communication, lack of senior management support and project ownership, and political conflicts amongst involved actors and parties.

Technological Risks

Deploying a new type of application, database, or knowledge base entails a risk for the likelihood of success of an investment in direct infrastructure. This success is, to a considerable degree, dependent upon tools from the indirect infrastructure, especially if these are not yet proven technology. Technological risks also have to do with the required knowledge and skills of the specialist who has to develop and build infrastructure components. Hiring or recruiting new specialist employees involves technological risks, since it cannot be guaranteed that they are available, and have the required experience and skill-levels. In addition to this, tools of the indirect infrastructure can be too advanced, both from the IT market maturity and organizational maturity perspectives.

9.10 CONCLUSIONS

Using explicit and well-articulated value metrics is vital to be able to perform business value assessments of IT-based infrastructure. In this respect, value metrics serve the purposes of: appraisal and prioritization criteria, improvement targets and performance indicators, communication tools, and vehicles for organizational learning and benchmarking. The diverse nature of business impacts of infrastructure investment, and the many different stakeholders involved in the assessment, have made clear that multi-dimensional value metrics are more appropriate in assessment activities than solely financial metrics. If considered appropriate, financial calculations should be used with great care. This is confirmed by practitioner views on value metrics for project evaluation, although great emphasis is being placed on financial metrics. This chapter has reviewed the most important business impacts of investment in IT-based infrastructure, amended with appropriate value metrics. A distinction has been made between metrics for direct infrastructure and indirect infrastructure. These can be used for defining expected business impacts, financial impacts, positive or negative impacts, financial and non-financial risks, and the overall assessment of an investment. The process of identifying and establishing appropriate value metrics will always be organization-specific, where value metrics reflect the goals and strategic priorities of a particular organization. This in itself is a communication and negotiation process, in which implicit business value propositions, informal evaluations and intuitions are articulated and exchanged in order to make them debatable, and ultimately make investment results manageable and more predictable. Initiating and managing this process should have senior management attention and ownership, otherwise value metrics might suffer from lack of relevance, rigor, or both.

10
Assessing Infrastructure Synergy

10.1 INTRODUCTION

The previous chapter addressed value metrics for assessing the business impacts of investments in IT-based infrastructure. This chapter examines additional value metrics in order to assess the possible synergy leverage resulting from defining an investment as being an infrastructure investment. First, Section 10.2 presents practitioner views on appropriate value metrics for the assessment of infrastructure synergies. Subsequently, Section 10.3 looks at the type of evaluation questions that should be addressed when assessing infrastructure synergy, and the types of insights relevant for identifying suitable value metrics. Section 10.4 discusses sources of investment synergy in the context of IT-based infrastructure. Building on these synergy sources, the focus moves to value metrics regarding the additional advantages of infrastructure (Section 10.5), the additional disadvantages of infrastructure (Section 10.6), and additional risks (Section 10.7). With respect to infrastructure advantages and disadvantages in the context of synergy, direct and indirect infrastructures are discussed separately. The conclusions of this chapter are given in Section 10.8.

10.2 PRACTIONER VIEWS ON VALUE METRICS

In the previous chapter (see Section 9.2) the results of a number of brainstorming sessions were discussed in which appropriate value metrics for assessing investments in IT-based infrastructure were identified. In these sessions, also the additional question of synergy value of shared infrastructure was discussed. The results of these discussions will be presented in this section, where the presentation order reflects the order of importance. First the different types of reactions and value metrics will be reviewed, and Table 10.1 gives some sample statements made within the brainstorming sessions. A more general conclusion of these sessions is that participants in these brainstorming sessions were of the opinion that infrastructure synergy is difficult to translate into financial terms. Nonetheless, it was argued that financial evaluations should be the main investment and decision-making criteria, and that non-financial value metrics are 'second-order' arguments.

- *Result-driven business unit strategy.* The majority of reactions referred to the general opinion that the IT-based infrastructure should match, support and preferably enable decentralized, result-driven unit strategies. In many cases, respondents said: define infrastructure capacities and capabilities at the lowest possible organizational level, i.e. as much as possible at the business unit level.
- *Shared knowledge exchange and competence building.* Appropriate value metrics suggested for creating infrastructure capacities and capabilities often relate to the need to have a shared platform for knowledge exchange and competence building regarding IT-based infrastructure.
- *Common needs for IT deployment.* Many value metrics also address the issue of having an IT-based infrastructure that covers common needs for IT deployment, also typified as 'roof systems.' Several times the advantage of generating opportunities for cross-selling was mentioned.
- *Information exchange and communication standards.* Several respondents raised the importance of having clear standards for information exchange and communication. This was deemed to be essential both internally (between units or between units and the corporate level) and externally (e.g. with customers, suppliers, or business partners).
- *Faster decisions and less coordination effort.* A value metric that was put forward several times in favor of a corporate infrastructure with a limited scope is the advantage of being able to speed up managerial decision-making, and to have less coordination effort. The latter aspect relates to a reduced need for all kinds of project controls (e.g. meetings) and to a limited need for change in conflicts and political tensions.

To summarize, respondents convey a strong preference for defining infrastructure at the lowest possible level, i.e. to deploy and exploit IT as much as possible at the level of the individual business unit. A important driver of this preference seems to be the prevailing decentralized management control philosophy of the case study organization. At the same time, respondents acknowledge that decentralized control may be ineffective if there are no rules and regulations at the higher corporate level. Opinions as to how a reasonable compromise can be found between the extremes of absolute centralized and purely decentralized control, however, differ greatly. Potential candidate components of a shared and standardized IT-based infrastructure on a corporate level are:

- A platform for knowledge exchange and specialized expertise.
- Common systems covering external parties and financial consolidations.
- Standards for information exchange and communications.

Type of reaction and value metrics	Examples of statements made
Result-driven business unit strategy	• 'Maximum effectiveness of business units should be secured, also for IT investments' • 'Infrastructure building shapes the specific identity of business units' • 'Maximum power and autonomy on a business unit level should also be visible in the IT strategy' • 'Flexible marketing campaigns and sales programs require a large degree of autonomy regarding IT-based infrastructure support'
Shared knowledge exchange and competence building	• 'Knowledge sharing and exchanging infrastructure experience is of great value' • 'An important advantage of having infrastructure facilities is to be able to use shared know how
Common needs for IT deployment	• 'Common client data' • 'Common system for general ledger and financial consolidations' • 'Common system for messaging and communications'
Organizational culture of cooperation	• 'Identifying and capturing common interests is highly dependent upon the ruling organizational culture. Sometimes certain legacies have to be ruined in order to clearly see what can be shared' • 'The trust in, and the commitment of the different parties involved are essential for an infrastructure investment'

Table 10.1   Sample practitioner views on infrastructure value

10.3 VALUE METRICS FOR ASSESSING INFRASTRUCTURE SYNERGY

Given a certain organizational level (e.g. department, business unit or division), the question of synergy in the context of IT-based infrastructure relates to the issue of whether providing an investment as infrastructure will have a positive or negative impact on the business case which was defined when assessing the business impacts of the investment. For managers and decision-makers at this particular level, the synergy question means deciding whether an investment project will have an individual (and thus local) or shared (and thus infrastructure) nature. Generally speaking, the higher an organizational level, the more difficult it will be to realize synergy, since both coordination efforts and the complexity of this infrastructure will increase.[1] This results in a tradeoff between infrastructure size and infrastructure level, which can be visualized through an indifference curve, discerning viable infrastructure from non-viable infrastructure (Ribbers, 1996); see Figure 10.1.

The IT-based infrastructure of an organization generally will be created incrementally and get its final shape by consecutively answer-

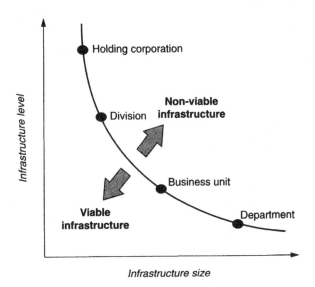

Figure 10.1 *Viable and non-viable infrastructure (adapted from Ribbers, 1996)*

---

[1] In economic terms this is a consequence of the laws of increasing marginal costs and decreasing marginal returns.

ing the following questions for several related investment projects (see the governance approach discussed in Chapter 5). Assessing the synergy of infrastructure projects means answering the following questions at a particular organizational level:

- What are the additional *advantages* (i.e. business benefits) of providing a project as infrastructure?
- What are the additional *disadvantages* (i.e. efforts, expenditures and disbenefits) of providing a project as infrastructure?
- What are the additional *risks* of providing a project as infrastructure?

Individual Control Versus Shared Control

Assessing infrastructure synergy to some extent resembles, and easily becomes bound up with, the classical debate of 'centralization versus decentralization.' Essentially, this assessment is a matter of evaluating individual versus shared control of people/skills, tools and procedures in the area of IT. This is succinctly argued by King (1983): 'control is the major factor in centralization/decentralization issues, and other aspects of the debate must be seen in light of this fact.' In all cases, the central issue is the assessment of centralized coordination through IT-based infrastructure versus decentralized autonomy through local applications.[2] Creating an IT-based infrastructure should however not be mixed with historical pleas for increased centralization of IT. Infrastructure creation should repeatedly, for each candidate project, be subject to business value assessment based on clearly defined and motivated value metrics. In turn, these value metrics should reflect business impacts which center around establishing and securing the required control and coordination across the different users of a proposed infrastructure.

Modern styles of management and organizational design, wherein the maximum autonomy of the constituent organizational parts is paramount, have as a binding element that organizational control is focused on coordinating the activities and levering the business relations which (potentially) exist between autonomous units (Galbraith, 1995; Nolan and Croson, 1995). Within flat, networked organizations information exchange and shared knowledge are crucial (Rockart and

---

[2] As argued, the concept pair centralization/decentralization has to do with individual versus shared control. The concept pair concentration/deconcentration is a separate distinction, which has to do with the physical location of resources. Experience shows, however, that decentralization often correlates with deconcentration (Ahutiv *et al.*, 1989).

Short, 1991). The central coordination which is enabled and supported by IT-based infrastructure should never be a goal in itself, however; the synergy of infrastructure will only become clear after identifying common, shared IT capabilities and after assessing the business value of these capabilities.

Streams of Thought for Identifying Value Metrics

Appropriate value metrics to support the infrastructure decisions are for the most part of a non-financial nature. The principal advantage of defining an IT-based investment as being an infrastructure investment is that it enables innovating things which could not have been achieved by the individual infrastructure users on their own. The value metrics discussed in this chapter are based upon three, partly overlapping, streams of thought with respect the added value of co-ordination and control in corporate activities.

Centralization and Decentralization of IT

The issue of centralization and decentralization regarding IT concerns the classical question of dividing and coordinating decision rights for IT acquisition, deployment and use. Important views used here are from the works of Zmud (1984), Edwards *et al.* (1989), Bacon (1990), and Allen and Boynton (1991).

Organizational Coordination

Organizational coordination covers the issue of how to coordinate different, often dispersed, business activities in order to achieve and secure overall corporate goals, e.g. in terms of structure, strategy, operational efficiency and innovation (Galbraith, 1973; Mintzberg, 1983b). Recently, it has become clear that insight from (business) economics, transaction cost theory and principal agency theory can contribute to solving coordination issues (Beath and Straub, 1989; Gurbaxani and Kemerer, 1990). These theories analyze how transaction costs among parties, and contracting costs between principles (who commission a certain task) and agents (who perform this task), change as a consequence of different types of organization. Several authors have also addressed coordination issues separately from an IT management perspective (see, for example, Goodhue *et al.*, 1992; DeSanctis and Jackson, 1994; Malone and Crowston, 1994).

Synergy Creation

Synergy creation has been examined from several theoretical perspectives. The common element in all of these is to analyze why and how autonomous organizations, i.e. business units covering their own product/market combinations, can leverage the business benefits of cooperation. This view has also been addressed in the realm of IT management (Andreu *et al.*, 1994; Brown, 1994; Oosterhaven, 1994).

10.4 SOURCES OF INVESTMENT SYNERGY

The notion of synergy is one of the most frequently used, almost 'magical', terms with respect to evaluating, justifying and approving an investment in infrastructure, be it IT-based or not. Synergy used in this context refers to the fact or assumption that shared provision of an investment will lever the returns or deliver more value than the sum of all individual investments by users, in the case of not investing in infrastructure. However, not all infrastructure investment will, by definition, lead to synergy; infrastructure investments may also lead to dissynergy (also referred to as 'antagony'). Two investment characteristics have the strongest influence on the synergetic nature of investment in IT-based infrastructure. The first characteristic is, relatively speaking, most important for direct infrastructure, the second for indirect infrastructure:

- *Network externalities*: the added value of providing an investment as infrastructure depends to a large degree on the final number of users who will actually use an infrastructure component. This is, for instance, very clear in the case of creating a communications infrastructure for electronic mail or for building a corporate Intranet, which will potentially deliver more value if more users use this facility.
- *Scale effects*: investment expenditures and the cost of ownership will be lower per user if capacities and capabilities are shared ('economies of scale'), cover scarce knowledge and skills ('economies of specialization') or are exploited in several directions ('economies of scope')

Strategic and Operational Synergy

It is easier to identify and operationalize synergy, and to turn it into something more than corporate magic, when keeping the aforementioned two investment characteristics in mind. Again, the distinction between direct and indirect infrastructure is a key differentiating factor. Direct infrastructure is aimed at capturing investment synergies through common and standardized IT deployment in business processes and products or services. Indirect infrastructure is aimed at capturing synergy through sharing basic IT facilities. The former type of infrastructure synergy focuses on *strategic synergy*, which means that via common provisions, strategic business targets can more easily be achieved or be even improved. As such, it can be typified as being benefit synergy. The latter type of infrastructure synergy concerns *operational synergy*, which centers around the exploitation of scale effects within the IT function (cost synergy). Table 10.2 summarizes the main differences made.

Investment synergy in the context of IT-based infrastructure is a relative notion, and should always be seen from the perspective of shared versus individual control. This implies, for instance, that the disadvantages of defining and providing an investment as infrastructure also include the benefits that would have been captured when the investment was of an individual nature, e.g. leading to local business unit-specific deployment instead of deployment at the corporate level. Consequently, the issue of creating an infrastructure from a business value perspective is foremost an issue of balance: taking management decisions which leverage the business advantages of having shared and standardized provisions, without losing too many of the business advantages of having local applications. In order to realize this, many firms choose an investment strategy that will lead to the creation of hybrid structures, in which an 'optimal' mixture of infrastructure provisions and local applications is sought. In terms of corporate control, these organization try to capture both the value of autonomy and interdependence.

Direct infrastructure	Indirect infrastructure
Main investment characteristic: Network externalities	*Main investment characteristic:* Scale effects
Type of synergy: Strategic	*Type of synergy:* Operational
Purpose: Achieving and improving business targets through commonalities and standardization	*Purpose:* Capturing scale effects through commonalities and standardization
Realization: Through business processes, products and services	*Realization:* Through basic IT facilities of the IT function

Table 10.2 *Synergy characteristics of direct and indirect infrastructure*

Vertical and Horizontal Synergy

Delivering investment synergy and leveraging common business elements generally are most controversial in organizations consisting of clusters or units with a relatively large degree of autonomy. Communication between and coordination across different units are in fact the managerial control issues that remain at the overall corporate level. This ultimately is the level where IT-based infrastructure should prove its existence. In order to be able to do so, with respect to the previously introduced strategic synergy a useful distinction is between vertical and horizontal synergy (Wijers, 1994); see Figure 10.2:

- *Vertical synergy* concerns the added value of cooperation between the corporate level and individual business units.
- *Horizontal synergy* refers to the added value of cooperation across individual business units.

Vertical synergy can be achieved, for instance, by defining a shared applications and data infrastructure for planning and control, or for standardizing business results. This particularly is the case for controlling processes such as strategy formation and review, finance and accounting, human resource management, and legal and fiscal compliance. Regarding horizontal synergy, infrastructure capabilities for standardizing knowledge and skills are most important, in addition to mutual transactions, leverage of product and customer data, and

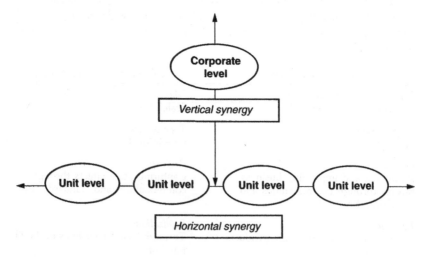

Figure 10.2 *Vertical and horizontal synergy (after Wijers, 1994)*

systems that enable close cooperation with third parties (e.g. customers, suppliers, or industry partners). Adequate exploitation of scale
effects is most important with respect to indirect infrastructure.
Important candidate components of indirect infrastructure are:

- Strategic IT management with respect to standardizing and planning
  infrastructure-type applications and data or knowledge bases.
- System development and maintenance of direct infrastructure.
- Managed operations of infrastructure components with substantial
  scale effects (e.g. mainframes), telecommunications (including
  Intranets, key applications or electronic commerce), and of security,
  back-up and recovery.
- User training and support, for non-business-unit-specific IT deployment.

10.5 ADVANTAGES OF INFRASTRUCTURE

Before examining additional value metrics for assessing infrastructure
synergy in more detail, Table 10.3 summarizes the generic advantages
and disadvantages of defining an IT investment as being an infrastructure investment. In Chapter 9 is was argued that whether business
impacts in a specific situation are considered to be positive or negative
value metrics depends upon the value judgments of informed stakeholders, and amongst others, on the direction in which an organization
wishes to go. Similarly, the same is true for business impacts and
resulting value metrics in the context of infrastructure synergy.
However, for reasons of readability and practical usefulness, this and
the following section give a review of value metrics which generally
are considered to be advantageous and which disadvantageous.

Direct Infrastructure

Apart from financial gains which can be realized by avoiding duplica-
tions, strategic synergy concerning direct infrastructure can be
captured through an integrated deployment of applications, data and
knowledge bases. More and more the conviction has raised ground
that this area might well accommodate the most significant business
benefits of IT-based infrastructure (see, for example, Bradley and
Nolan, 1998). Successful and sustainable innovations are increasingly
based upon intensive cooperation across several business processes
(e.g. product creation, manufacturing, distribution and sales), where
modern IT plays an enabling and coordinating role. This is well

Direct infrastructure	Indirect infrastructure
Advantages	
• Avoiding duplication of efforts	• Avoiding duplications of capacities and capabilities
• Less control efforts and suboptimal solutions	• Reaching a critical mass of facilities
• Reaching a critical mass of IT needs	• Increasing stability of facilities
• Increasing integrity and consistency of IT deployment	• Less efforts for creating a coherent and learning-oriented IT function
• Increasing stability of IT deployment	• Less control efforts and suboptimal solutions within IT function
• Improved IT use for strategic and commercial goals	• Bundling of scarce expertise/less scattered specialist competencies
• Increasing management commitment and ownership	• Avoiding incompatibilities amongst components
• Improving stakeholder dialogue and learning abilities	• Improved security and continuity of IT deployment
• Reduced efforts for external transactions	• More efficient acquisition of supplier products and services
Disadvantages	
• Fewer recognizable business processes and user identity	• IT employees less open to user needs
• Fewer motivated and learning oriented end-users	• Threatened learning abilities and business partnership of IT employees
• Lower speed of implementing IT into business processes	• Less IT-minded end-users
• Less innovative and competitive IT deployment	• Limited flexibility when using capacities and capabilities
• More communication efforts and formalization	• More communication efforts and formalization
• More vulnerable business processes	

Table 10.3 *Generic advantages and disadvantages of IT-based infrastructure provision*

illustrated by the words of Simson (1990, p. 85): 'information technology is the glue of these integrated business activities.' Relevant value metrics which can be used to justify the shared and standardized use of applications, databases and knowledge bases can be found in the following business impacts.

Avoiding Duplication of Efforts

Efficiency improvements can be achieved by reducing duplicate efforts regarding infrastructure capabilities for system development and maintenance, software package acquisitions, and by transferring previous solutions to new situations which will lead to increased standardization.

Less Management Control Effort and Avoiding Suboptimal IT Solutions

By having common direct infrastructure capabilities less management control effort will be needed to ensure that infrastructure users act in the interests of the organization as a whole (also known as 'agency costs'). A related metric is avoiding suboptimal IT solutions, caused by a too localized IT deployment to fit business-specific conditions, which is done at the expense of overall organizational interests.

Reaching a Critical Mass of IT Needs

If investing in localized IT deployment is likely to deliver insufficient financial returns, it can be argued that there is a need to provide the IT capabilities as part of the corporate infrastructure. For instance, acquiring a capital-intensive, integrated package for building a data warehouse may be financially justified if several local implementations can build on this investment.

Increasing Integrity and Consistency of IT Deployment

Unambiguous interpretation of information and messages is essential when communicating across different organizational units. This also ameliorates management control of the organization as a whole, e.g. through standard reporting. In addition to this, standardized direct infrastructure enables enforcement of consistent ways of working in similar but dispersed business processes (e.g. invoicing or order management).

Increasing Stability of IT Deployment

Since shared and standardized IT capabilities generally refer to IT needs which do not change fast in comparison with localized IT deployment, IT-based infrastructure components will generally be more stable. This in turn enables IT-based infrastructure to be exploited as a business lever, which secures long-term reliance on basic capacities and capabilities.

Improved IT Use for Strategic and Commercial Goals

Individual users, be it institutional (e.g. business units) or personal (e.g. end-users) have a clear interest in markets needs with a high business priority and operational necessity. Consequently, they generally pay less attention to the needs and goals of overarching organizational levels (e.g. the corporate level) although it may be needed to cross the borders of individual autonomies in order to initiate organization-wide strategic renewal (e.g. penetrating new markets, adding a distribution channel, broadening the scope of operations). Strategic goals and commercial value propositions can also be highly dependent on exploiting the commonalities in IT deployment to the maximum (e.g. by establishing 'one face to the customer', a shared corporate image, optimal use of cross-selling opportunities). This latter value metric has clearly gained in importance since the introduction of Web-based electronic commerce.

Increasing Top Management Commitment and Business Management Ownership

Appraising the business contributions and priorities of shared and standardized applications, databases and knowledge ultimately is the final responsibility of top management. As such, this will lead to increased top management commitment, compared with the situation with mere local autonomy and thus little need for top management control, except perhaps for escalation purposes. If IT-based infrastructure is adequately governed and managed, infrastructure decisions will be the prime decision-making issue facing senior business managers, and therefore lead to clearer project and infrastructure ownership.

Improving Stakeholder Dialogue and Learning Abilities

Since components of IT-based infrastructure will, by definition, be shared, infrastructure stakeholders are more or less 'forced' to engage in a process of communication and negotiation. This will in most cases lead to the stakeholder dialogue underlying this process being amended. A related value metric, at least in terms of 'soft' orientation, is that individual units and users are able to learn from similar and standardized solutions. This may lead, as an important byproduct, to more equal distribution of key knowledge, both in terms of technology impacts and business alignment of these impacts.

Reduced Efforts for External Transactions

Typically, transactions with external parties can be executed more efficiently if shared infrastructure provisions are in place ('transaction cost savings'). Examples are shared funding, hiring of personnel, purchasing, or distribution.

Indirect Infrastructure

The main vehicle to achieve and lever functional or operational synergy of indirect infrastructure is to exploit scale effects. Appropriate value metrics for standardized and shared use of basic technological and organizational facilities can be found in the following.

Avoiding Duplication of Capacities and Capabilities

Indirect infrastructure investment is targeted at installed basic capacities and capabilities to be shared across different organizational units. Appropriate exploitation of intrinsic scale effects of these infrastructure components can deliver substantial efficiency gains (e.g. economies of scale for mainframe operations). Also, using scarce capacities and capabilities for different purposes is likely to lower investment expenditures and costs of ownership (e.g. shared network management, re-use of software components).

Reaching a Critical Mass of Infrastructure Facilities

Some capacities and capabilities of indirect infrastructure do not give sufficient financial returns if they are used on a, relatively speaking, small scale. An advanced business process simulation environment or new type of database standard may, for instance, give only an adequate return on investment if these are shared across several divisions or business units.

Increasing Stability of Facilities

Shared and standardized use of basic facilities of indirect infrastructure will generally lead to a relative longer investment life-cycle than localized exploitation of capacities and capabilities.

Less Efforts for Creating a Coherent and Learning-Oriented IT Function

Since specialist-type IT employees with similar competencies and interests will meet each other more often, this will lead to an IT function with a coherent business culture and consistent ways of working. Consequently, IT employees generally capture more learning opportunities, without much communication effort.

Less Management Control and Avoiding Suboptimal Solutions Within the IT Function

IT managers will have to put less management control effort into ensuring that IT employees act in the interest and spirit of the long-term strategy and defined policy principles of the IT function.

Bundling of Scarce Expertise/Fewer Scattered Specialist Competencies

Especially with respect to innovative technologies, of which users and local experts have limited knowledge, it may be advantageous to bundle scarce expertise in shared, facilitative units. This provides opportunities for indirect infrastructure users to learn and profit from competencies of a specialist nature and which are offered to them from within the IT function.

Avoiding Incompatibilities Among Infrastructure Components

Securing compatibility (also referred to as 'interoperatibility' or 'inter-connectivity') across different infrastructure components is essential for a robust and sound indirect infrastructure. This has recently become more important as a result of the emergence of network-based IT applications, Intranets and Internets, and the business exploitation of these technologies through electronic commerce. Standardized communication protocols, interface standards and common middleware solutions are typical examples of infrastructure elements that guarantee compatibility.

Improved Security and Continuity of IT Deployment

Having a total and integral overview of all infrastructure components enables improved signaling and identification of possible threats for infrastructure security and continuity. Also it is easier and more economic to manage solutions or protection tools and procedures (e.g. for viruses, contingencies, back-up and recovery).

More Efficient Acquisition of Supplier Products and Services

When providing investments as part of the overall indirect infrastructure it is, in many cases, possible to purchase external supplier products and services on a larger scale. This may often lead to a lower volume or item price, e.g. with respect to licenses, tools, or specialist services.

10.6 DISADVANTAGES OF INFRASTRUCTURE

The disadvantages of defining an IT investment as being infrastructure, visualized as dissynergies, can to a large extent be found in lost benefits that would have been apparent if infrastructure users had individual autonomy over their investments.

Direct Infrastructure

Lack of Business Process Specificities and Less Recognizable User Identity

Possibly one of the prime disadvantages of proving applications, databases and knowledge bases as part of the direct infrastructure, is that the business-process-specific features will not all be captured in the final infrastructure capacities and capabilities. This is caused by the fact that these infrastructure components will always be a compromise between the different, dispersed local IT needs (e.g. concerning customers, supplies, products, markets and distribution channels) in order to enable shared and standardized use.

Fewer Motivated and Learning-Oriented End-Users

A disadvantage of shared and standardized infrastructure is that it matches the individual identities of users to a lesser degree than in the case of purely localized IT deployment. Consequently, users of this infrastructure will generally be less motivated to apply (new) IT opportunities and to learn from their impacts.

Lower Speed of Implementing IT into Business Processes

When investing in direct infrastructure capacities and capabilities for business process support, the implementation result will depend on the cooperation and the commitment of the planned infrastructure users. Since user numbers will be higher than for local applications it will, in relative terms, take longer to finalize infrastructure implementation.

Less Innovative and Competitive IT Deployment

The innovative use of IT within the direct business environment of individual users generally leads to the most competitive advantages from IT. Providing IT capacities and capabilities as part of the overall direct infrastructure thus has less chance of achieving competitive success.

More Communication Efforts and Formalization

Identifying, evaluating, building or acquiring, and implementing a shared or standardized provision requires relatively much more communication among important stakeholders. This also accommodates the risk of needing more formal procedures to guide and control stakeholder interaction.

More Vulnerable Business Processes

If something goes wrong when using a direct infrastructure component for business process support, the impact may be much higher than when using relatively autonomous IT applications across business processes. Although adequate contingency planning will contribute to managing this risk, the vulnerability of the business is likely to increase.

Indirect Infrastructure

Similarly to direct infrastructure, the disadvantages of providing an IT investment as part of the indirect infrastructure are primarily determined by the lost benefits of individual control over capacities and capabilities. These disadvantages lie in the following areas.

IT Employees Less Open to User Needs

Specialist-type IT employees will generally be placed within an infrastructure-based IT unit, which means that they have less direct contact with business processes and with employees working in these processes. Consequently they are less open to the needs of infrastructure users, which may lead to a more introvert culture and, partly because of fewer satisfied users, less motivated IT employees.

Threatened Learning Abilities and Business Partnership of IT Employees

The larger distance between IT employees, business processes, and eventually users, ensures that these employees are acquainted with fewer (new) business situations. As such, they might also learn less quickly, and adopt a limited repertoire of skills.

Less IT Minded End-Users

If individual end-users have less direct contact with IT employees, they will also be less receptive towards technology in general. In addition, they might not consider IT-based infrastructure-enabled innovation as a serious option in their improvement strategies.

Limited Flexibility when Using Capacities and Capabilities

When acquiring or developing indirect infrastructure capacities and capabilities, the need for a common use requires that these match different and possibly differing user needs. Consequently, indirect infrastructure supply will be less dedicated to specific demands of localized business applications, databases, or knowledge bases. Many components of indirect infrastructure only deliver adequate returns and business value if all individual units or users agree to use this particular component (e.g. a database management system, a middleware component or a development tool).

Identifying, evaluating, building or acquiring, and implementing a shared or standardized provision requires relatively much more communication. This also bears the risk of needing more formal procedures to guide and control stakeholder interaction.

More Communication Effort and Formalization

Similarly to direct infrastructure, installing and providing an indirect infrastructure in a shared and standard way requires greater communication among important stakeholders, especially between business management and IT management. Again, this bears the risk of more formal procedures for management control of their interactions. In addition, top management will have to take intensified actions to control and monitor the IT function.

10.7 ADDITIONAL RISKS

In Chapter 9, a review was given of investment risks in the context of IT-based infrastructure. When assessing the potential synergy of investments in IT-based infrastructure it is important to evaluate to what extent:

- The spread of earnings and expenditures will change as a consequence of defining an investment as being infrastructure. As such, this determines the total *financial risk exposure* of an infrastructure investment.
- External risks, realization risks, organizational and technological risks will change because of the infrastructure nature of the proposed investment. As such, this determines the total *non-financial risk exposure* of an infrastructure investment.

It has become clear that it is difficult, and in the light on the synergy discussions surrounding IT-based infrastructure, also contentious, to make very definite statements regarding the risk effects of defining an investment as being an infrastructure investment. This reinforces the relevance and importance of adequate risk management procedures and risk control. The ultimate effects of infrastructure risks are difficult to predict in advance, and can to a large degree be managed in order to (re-)direct the course an investment is taking or to mitigate risks.

Concerning financial risks, again it is required to apply sensitivity analyses and scenario analyses as much as possible. Opportunities for leveraging shared and standardized infrastructure and for capturing synergy can be assessed if this is considered to be a separate decision-making option, with its own specific risk exposure. Investment exposure of non-financial risks may change in different directions when executing an investment as part of an infrastructure program, which can be judged as being either positive or negative. All investment risks of IT-based infrastructure discussed in Chapter 9, Section 9.9, should be re-assessed when considering the question of infrastructure leverage and synergy creation. The following generic risk impacts are relevant in this respect.

External Risks

If an investment is approved of and executed by several relevant stakeholder units or user groups, this may increase the overall vulnerability to threats in the external environment of an organization. If possible external risks do materialize, they will have a large-scale impact and effect more stakeholders, business processes, end-users, or infrastructure components. In contrast to this, in some cases the final external risk will be lower, since investing on a larger scale offers the opportunity of combining offensive or defensive strategies towards external actors (e.g. suppliers, competitors, or potential entrants to the market).

Realization Risks

The larger the size and the more complex an investment project (e.g. more end-users, longer project duration, larger process and organizational scope, more interdependencies), the more persons, units or divisions will generally be involved in project decision-making. These will often have different, and possibly conflicting, requirements regarding the deliverables of a project. Consequently, realization risks generally increase if an investment is defined as infrastructure.

Organizational Risks

With respect to organizational risks, the general tendency is that project risks increase if an investment impacts on more stakeholders in the business or IT domain. A more positive effect, however, is that it may be easier to introduce and implement an innovation organization-wide, chiefly since top management should be very much involved in decision-making, and deploy project ownership.

Technological Risks

Project exposure to technological risks depends on the extent to which an investment uses state of the art knowledge and skills, and technology proven products. These characteristics will usually not change much when an investment is defined as infrastructure and evaluated and managed as such. This requires extra management attention, given the large number of people and organizational units involved, and the detrimental risk of taking the wrong technology decisions.

10.8 CONCLUSIONS

In order to get a comprehensive assessment of the business value of proposed investments in IT-based infrastructure, it is necessary to pay explicit attention to the potential business leverage of investments, resulting in infrastructure synergy. Value metrics can be found in additional advantages, disadvantages and risks of defining an IT investment as being an infrastructure investment. Practitioner views suggest a preference for having as much local autonomy as possible (e.g. at the business unit level), although several candidates for an overarching infrastructure at a higher organizational level (e.g. corporate) are considered beneficial. An essential synergy distinction is between strategic synergy, delivered through direct infrastructure, and operational synergy, delivered through indirect infrastructure. Strategic synergy refers to improved or easier achievement of business targets through common provisions, which can be of a horizontal (across autonomous units) or vertical (between corporate and units level) nature. Operational synergy refers to the exploitation of scale effects.

Part V
Concluding Management Perspectives

11
An Investment Methodology for IT-Based Infrastructure

11.1 INTRODUCTION

After an introductory Part I, which focused on the management challenges and investment issues surrounding IT-based infrastructure, Part II clarified the business role and implications of this infrastructure as a strategic capital asset. Subsequently, Part III examined investment governance and control of IT-based infrastructure, with an emphasis on investment appraisal and managerial decision-making to maximize decision quality and business value deliverance. Part IV looked in more detail at appropriate value metrics for investment business value assessment and prioritization, both in terms of project value and possible infrastructure synergies. The purpose of this chapter is to bring the investment and business value concepts discussed in the previous chapters together, and to synthesize them into an investment methodology for IT-based infrastructure. As such, it summarizes which design issues an organization should address, and which management options are available for defining an adequate investment methodology for IT-based infrastructure. First, Section 11.2 discusses the characteristics and role of a proposed investment methodology. Next, Section 11.3 gives an overview of this methodology in the form of a generic framework, based upon the life-cycle of an investment in IT-based infrastructure. Section 11.4 addresses some essential situational aspects of investment strategy and decision-making. Conclusions are presented in Section 11.5.

11.2 ROLE AND CHARACTERISTICS OF AN INVESTMENT METHODOLOGY

The title of this chapter speaks of an 'investment methodology', a term that was chosen deliberately. The reason for this can be found in the observation that the existing methods and accompanying techniques for business value assessment of IT-based infrastructure generally are of a rather rigid, mechanistic, almost 'cookbook-like' nature (see Chapter 6). Many methods seem to suggest that their particular approach can be applied straightforwardly in virtually every situation and in all organizational settings. However, the context-bound nature and clear managerial degrees of freedom with respect to infrastructure investment appraisal and decision-making make this claim very questionable. Hardly ever do existing methods take specific organizational conditions and preferences into account, such being for instance:

- The extent to which IT-based infrastructure is a vital business enabler, and how this can be translated into an appropriate procedure for identifying potentially valuable investment opportunities.
- The steps which should be taken in investment decision-making, and the type of managers who should participate and be held accountable for the investment results.
- The value metrics which are best suited to serve as business case components and measures of performance, given an organization's strategic goals and individual circumstances.
- The specific political context of investment decision-making, reflected in, for instance, the extent to which there is room for decision strategies such as negotiations, collective judgment, coalition building, and compensation and reward procedures.

Assessing Investments in their Organizational Context

The term 'investment methodology' used here is meant to be a comprehensive set of generic guidelines for the organizational-specific design of an investment method. In line with this view, an 'investment method' is seen to be a systematic process of identifying, appraising, selecting and controlling investments in a specific organization. An investment methodology defines in general terms which conditions should be met to be able to speak of methodically sound organizational decision procedures and management controls regarding IT-based infrastructure. An investment method should be considered a specific, localized implementation of this generic investment methodology, tailored to the needs of a particular decision-making situation and organizational context. Regarding this distinction between investment methodology and method, Checkland (1989) is followed when he argues:

> It is the essence of a methodology, as opposed to a method or technique, that it offers a set of guidelines or principles which in any specific instance can be tailored both to the characteristics of the situation in which it is to be applied and to the people using the approach.

As argued when presenting the design-oriented approach of this book (see Chapter 1), there is no 'one best way' of assessing and managing investments in IT-based infrastructure. In light of this conclusion, the investment methodology presented in this chapter gives a synthesized perspective and synopsis of the methodical visions, concepts, and practical recommendations introduced in previous chapters. When discussing these results, attention was paid to the situational characteristics of many of them in order to suit the organizational characteristics and purposes, e.g.:

- The specific capabilities and contents of IT-based infrastructure, and the way in which infrastructure investments are proposed, differ from organization to organization (see Chapters 4 and 5).
- The P4 model, introduced for strategic investment control, offers several control options for managing decisions concerning individual investment projects in the most adequate way (see Chapters 7 and 8).
- The formulation of value metrics, as input to the business case for investment, depends on the specific goals and priorities of a particular organization (see Chapters 9 and 10).

Design Principles for Investment Value Management

Summarizing the design knowledge discussed in this book in the form of an investment methodology means that applying the generic result in business practice requires some rather fundamental thinking and possibly some re-working to suit purposes that are more organization-specific. The way in which infrastructure assessments take place, and investments are appraised and monitored to manage business value—which constitutes the investment method—is shaped by the design choices made by key stakeholders, especially senior business management. These choices should reflect the needs and preferences of the final users of a method, and the ambitions of senior decision-makers towards business value assessment of IT-based infrastructure. In turn, these needs, preferences and ambitions originate from what investment stakeholders consider to be the characteristics of their 'own' organization and their 'own' style of decision-making. Every investment method should be considered a 'facilitative device' (Eden, 1989), in order to make investment decisions in a structured manner, to manage benefits and control investment value, and to maximally exploit the learning abilities of the organization. An investment method is, above all, a communication device, with the purpose to increase consensus amongst stakeholders, to build stakeholder commitment, and to create a decision atmosphere and shared mind-set in which an investment will get full organizational support.

11.3 A FRAMEWORK FOR INVESTMENT ASSESSMENT AND MANAGEMENT

The previous section argued that every organization has to make its own choices regarding the way in which it wants to assess and manage investments in an IT-based infrastructure. Although appreciating these situational characteristics, this section will give an integrative overview of relevant design aspects. This overview of the investment methodology should be seen as an ideal-typical framework, assuming that the available investment budget has been determined (within certain margins). Figure 11.1 gives a graphical representation of this framework. The framework builds on and extends the three interlinked basic processes of infrastructure governance, which were presented in Chapter 5. This figure should not be considered as a sequential and rigid planning structure of phases that an organization should necessarily go through. It more represents a pattern of thought; a synthesis of the aspects one should think of when taking investment decisions, and when managing the project benefits and business value resulting from these decisions.

Identifying Potential Investments

The first step in the investment framework concerns the comprehensive identification of potential investments. A checklist of infrastructure components can be of great value in this process (see Chapter 4 and its Appendix). Such a checklist provides support in two types of investment identification:

- *Top-down generation* of investments proposals, by systematically evaluating the present and future infrastructure ('AS-IS' versus

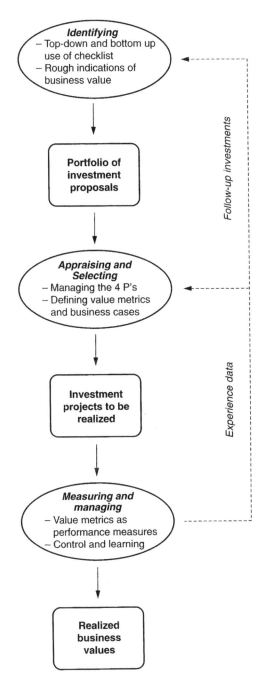

Figure 11.1   A framework for investment assessment and management

'TO-BE') in the light of present and future business processes, and taking into account technological developments.

● *Bottom-up canalization* of investment proposals, by assessing where and how these proposals influence the existing infrastructure, what the possible impacts of these investments are, and what the business value of these impacts is.

The terminology of this checklist should match as closely as possible the local language and terminology of the organization in which it is applied. Only then will sufficient guarantees be created for establishing a shared vision of the actual and preferred infrastructure, and for exchanging prevailing stakeholder preferences, which are often implicit judgments that have not been articulated before. If an organization has prior experiences with using explicit, well-articulated value metrics and performance indicators, a post-implementation review of this in the context of benefits management may already suggest new investments (see the dotted arrows in Figure 11.1). If this is not the case, it is endorsable to develop or use other managerial devices for the top-down generation of investment proposals (e.g. checklists, question-naires, or graphical tools). An easy to use and quite straightforward method is to assess for each present infrastructure component:

● What the *infrastructure coverage* is, i.e. to what extent does it cover all potential opportunities for infrastructure-enabled support?
● What the *strategic importance* is, both in terms of alignment with current business strategies and enabling future business strategies.
● What the *functional quality* is, i.e. to what extent does it deliver the functionality for adequate business deployment?
● What the *technical quality* is, i.e. to what extent does it conform to technological standards, is maintainable, and meets defined service levels (e.g. regarding availability, responsiveness, connectivity, stability and support)?

Whether the accent of investment identification will be on top-down or bottom-up identification depends to a large degree on the prevalent style of decision-making and management of an organization. Although identification procedures should not conflict too much with existing practices, it is vital to find a good balance between top-down and bottom-up procedures. On the one hand, it is important to give clear guidance to the strategic course an organization intends to follow from a top-down perspective. On the other hand, sufficient room should be created (and fostered) for everyone to propose invest-ments in a free and open manner, whenever there are improvement opportunities identified. Not only is this favorable from the perspective of encouraging and exploiting organizational creativity, but also generally it will have a stimulating impact on securing stakeholder commitment to a decision made. Therefore, comprehensive identification of potentially beneficial and valuable investment proposals should be considered a responsibility of all employees. A practical method is to assign responsibility to senior IT management for guiding and facilitating investment identification, with clear accountability, ownership and a formal mandate for senior business management. Planning of investment identification may be in line with the prevailing business planning and budgeting cycle of an organization (generally a yearly process with milestone planning). This guarantees that IT investments as much as possible have a 'normal' place, in conjunction with other business investments. Within this identification process it is essential to keep an eye open for new intermediate developments across the year in order to prevent stringent planning cycle procedures standing in the way of considering promising investment proposals.

The outcome from the identification of potential investments is a portfolio of investment proposals, each representing a claim on limited capital funding. Therefore, it is desirable to accompany each project proposal with an initial estimate of the expected business value, in terms of generic financial and non-financial value metrics (advantages, disadvantages, and risks). This enables the realization of a rather rough indication of the possible business impact and potential business value of each investment proposal. Organizations may decide to use classifications of investments and budgets, e.g.

- *Strategic innovations*, i.e. introducing substantial business improvements in terms of efficiency, effectiveness or competitiveness.
- *Going concern activities*, i.e. implementing appropriate new infrastructure solutions in line with the current operational needs of the business.
- *Maintenance projects*, i.e. ensuring that the business can be operated free from problems and disturbances within the context of the existing infrastructure.
- *Stimulus projects*, i.e. encouraging and sponsoring new infrastructure opportunities.

Such a categorization also has the advantage of being able to give a first, quick impression of investment proposals which seem most relevant in terms of their business value added. In order to get a good overview of all possible infrastructure impacts of proposed IT investments, it is wise to make a distinction between investments in direct and indirect infrastructure (see Chapter 4) at this stage of the investment process. A single project proposal may however impact on both types of infrastructure. This subdivision into types of infrastructure offers the opportunity to define and assess separate value metrics, targeted at the different business purposes and synergies of the two types of investment, and to appraise both types of investments separately.

Appraising and Selecting Investments

The portfolio of investment proposals should be treated as the starting point for evaluating and selecting investment projects that will get management approval and will be executed. The way in which appraisal and selection activities will be carried out in a particular organization depends on how the P4 model of strategic investment control (see Chapter 7) will be implemented. This means that clear design choices will have to be made regarding:

- Which value metrics serve as appraisal and selection criteria, and how these will be presented in terms of a business case to facilitate management approval or rejection (*'managing the product'*).
- Which steps will be taken in the appraisal and selection processes and to manage the evaluation life-cycle (*'managing the process'*).
- Who will be involved and has which responsibility when appraising and selecting investment proposals (*'managing the participation'*).
- How will the different interests of stakeholders be taken into account and how will political issues be addressed (*'managing the politics'*).

For management of the product (see Chapters 9 and 10) it is important to assess both financial value metrics (expenditures, earnings, financial risks) and non-financial metrics (positive contributions, negative contributions and non-financial risks). In addition, it is important to pay attention to value metrics which are of help in assessing infrastructure synergy.[1] In both cases this implies a (re-)evaluation of life-cycle efforts, business benefits, and risks. Together, the assessment of project value and infrastructure synergy will lead to a comprehensive business case. Value metrics should be translated into decision criteria, which are

---

[1] These synergy propositions may already emanate from an overall governance approach towards IT-based infrastructure, in which predefined choices have been made regarding certain infrastructure capacities and capabilities (e.g. regarding customer or product data, or shared telecommunications provisions). It may still be worthwhile to perform a (re-)assessment of infrastructure synergy in order to confirm earlier value expectations and to identify additional options for delivering synergy.

relevant in the organizational context used, unambiguous and easy to communicate to all involved stakeholders.

Several choices can be made with respect to the way in which value metrics are presented (see Chapter 6). Regarding financial impacts, primarily a choice will have to be made between 'simple' techniques (e.g. accounting return, payback time) or discounted cash flow techniques (net present value (NPV), internal rate of return (IRR)). Financial risks should be expressed in estimate ranges, since point estimates ignore the financial risk exposure of investment projects. Multidimensional metrics are most appropriate, whereas choices can be made between several types of presentations (e.g. tables, scoring sheets, portfolios, etc.). Presentations should not be too complex, since this may lead to disproportionate attention to mere calculation issues at the expense of attention to managerial approval and issues of business value. Generally it is more sensible to work with a limited number of evaluation criteria on a nominal scale than to make calculations with many criteria and a high level of detail. This will only suggest a degree of precision and rigor, which simply is not justified in the context of investments in IT-based infrastructure. In addition, the number of criteria taken into account and the presentation style should be in line with the experience and knowledge level of the organization in which investment decision-making takes place. It is to be expected that the more experience an organization has with investment evaluations, the more criteria and advanced presentation styles will be used.

In addition to establishing a comprehensive and meaningful set of value metrics, an organization will have to make design decisions with respect to the steps to be taken when evaluating and selecting investment projects. The systematic use of learning experiences gained in previous investments can be very beneficial when making high-quality investment decisions. Since infrastructure investments provide the long-term foundation for many business-specific applications, decisions should be subject to a thorough preparation. It is therefore recommended to decompose investment evaluation into manageable steps. Investment decisions have an impact on many stakeholders and the risk of making the wrong decisions is substantial. This also makes clear the importance of involving the right (groups of) people in decision-making. In addition to assigning responsibilities from a financial, technological, social or end-user perspective, senior management project ownership and investment commitment is vital for securing the likely success of an investment project. Accountabilities for the process of investment evaluation and selection should therefore be assigned at the highest hierarchical business management level.

The participation of all involved stakeholders also is an important means to increase support for and adherence to a decision made. Not all stakeholders share the same goals, wishes, and preferences. It is important not to ignore this, but to manage the politics of decision-making as much as possible. The chance of a successful project increases considerably if shared motives are found and contradicting interests are brought together, preferably from an attitude of equality. Depending on the extent to which there is sufficient agreement on investment purposes, and on the route to follow, it may be necessary to use such decision strategies as negotiation and coalition building. This always has to take place against the background of a common interest and of establishing the synergy in the organization. If this is not, or insufficiently, the case, then top management intervention may be needed to enforce the route to be followed.

Measuring and Managing Investment Results

The result of the appraisal and selection of investment proposals is a collection of investment projects that will be executed. The right execution of a project eventually determines whether the defined value metrics and business case have been realistic, and whether an investment is really delivering value for money. In order to be able to find evidence of this, it is necessary to measure project benefits and business value on a regular basis, and perhaps to take adequate control measures. Without any knowledge regarding the real value impacts of investments it is simply not possible to manage investment results ('if you can't measure it, you can't manage it'). Measuring investment results means that previously defined appraisal and selection criteria serve as performance measures. Assessing what the actual efforts and benefits of an investment are, also prevents the psychological phenomenon of devoting ever more funds and resources to a project, without sound evaluations of the additional value delivered ('investment entrapment').

Organizations generally do not devote much time to investment evaluations after the proposal and management approval stages, although deliverance targets in terms of time and budget are usually set. Therefore, in addition to assigning appraisal responsibilities from the perspective of selecting the most valuable projects, responsibilities for evaluations after the initial investment decision stage should explicitly be assigned. It is crucial to establish a climate and cultural setting in which post-implementation evaluations are used as control and learning devices, and not as a vehicle to identify individuals who can be held accountable for disappointing value expectations.

Regular re-evaluations and measurements of benefits and realized values provide an excellent source of experience which can be used in the evaluation and selection of new investments (see the dotted arrows in Figure 11.1). As discussed before, well-articulated knowledge regarding realized business value propositions should be closely related to the identification of potentially worthwhile new investments.

11.4 SITUATIONAL ASPECTS OF INVESTMENT ASSESSMENT

The previous section summarized the investment methodology proposed in this book in the form of an ideal-typical investment assessment framework. This framework gives a synopsis of relevant aspects for the design of an investment method in a specific organization. How an investment method finally looks will be influenced by and reflect situational characteristics ('contingencies'), which themselves should reflect the preferences and design choices of decision-makers and key stakeholders. To discuss the broad spectrum of all possible and potentially relevant situational aspects falls beyond the scope of this book.[2] A limitation will thus be made to two situational aspects, covering the decision-making style of an organization and the relative importance of value metrics.

Decision-Making Style

It obviously is wise to take the prevailing overall decision-making style of an organization into account when assessing the business value of an IT-based infrastructure. A review of empirical research shows that the two main distinctive features of decision-making styles across organizations are the extent of formalization and the extent of centralization (Koopman and Pool, 1992). It can be expected that the chance of a successful design of an investment method is highest when the consequences of these differentiations are explicitly taken into account. Depending on where the decision-making emphasis is placed, Koopman and Pool make a distinction between four decision-making configurations (see Figure 11.2):

---

[2] These types of discussions also easily become rather abstract and academic exercises, which would not meet the design-oriented approach of this book. It has also become clear that organizations are very capable of designing an approach that meets their own expectations and purposes, once they have access to the right generic concepts.

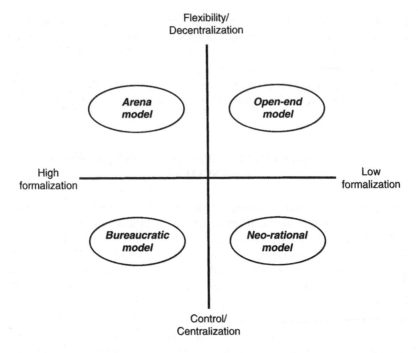

Figure 11.2   *Decision-making configurations (after Koopman and Pool, 1992)*

- the arena model
- the open-end model
- the bureaucratic model
- the neo-rational model.

In light of the four strategic control options introduced within the P4 model (see Chapter 7), it can be deduced that in each different model relatively much attention is paid to one of the four P's. The downside of this is that one control option will be used 'by default', and thus dominate decision-making. This bears the risk of producing a rather unbalanced style of decision-making, since there is little room for the other control options.

Within the *arena model*, decision-making has a very political nature. Decision-making is dominated by negotiations between several stake-holders, with only little differences in relative power. This means that management of the politics is the main instrument in managing investment decisions. Senior managers and other important investment stakeholders will mainly use this control option to gain control of investment decision-making. Although in this model the different interests of involved stakeholders do get ample attention, it is important to ensure also that management of the product, the process and the participation get the attention they deserve.

Within the *open-end* model, investment purposes, decision goals, and the route to follow are not clearly defined and managed. Accidental and unpredictable circumstances impede any predefined decision approach. The only alternative to gaining control of decision-making is to encourage decision participants to pay sufficient and combined attention to a perceived problem by exchanging their knowledge and expertise. Management of the participation thus comparatively is an important element of decision-making. Although decision-makers may pay attention to involving the right people in decision-making, it is essential to safeguard appropriate attention to the management of the product, the process and the politics.

Within the *bureaucratic model*, decision-making is 'constrained' by rules and regulations; there are only limited degrees of freedom in the decision-making process. Several individual and stakeholder groups are held accountable for formally contributing to a decision. The main control option in the bureaucratic model is management of the process of decision-making. Although undoubtedly clear attention will be paid to the different steps in decision-making, it is important to build in guarantees that management of the product, of participation and of the politics will not be forgotten.

Within the *neo-rational model*, decision-making is characterized by the dominant role of evaluating decision alternatives and options by business executives. Much attention is paid to evaluating the likely contribution of decision-making to predefined business goals. Consequently, management of the product of decision-making is a particularly important element of decision-making. There is much attention to underpinning investment choices with clear metrics and calculations, but it should be explicitly ensured also that management of the process, of participation and the politics is taken into account.

The Relative Importance of Value Metrics

Chapter 9 has already touched upon the issue of the relative importance of value metrics when assessing the business value of IT-based infrastructure investment. This relative importance will, to a large degree, be conditioned by the business experience with a particular type of investment and by the strategic course an organization aims to follow. Ultimately, the relative importance of value metrics determines which business impacts of infrastructure investments will, given a certain investment situation and decision context, be judged as being positive and which negative. When there is only limited experience with a particular type of investment, stringent use of finance-based value metrics will be detrimental to innovation. In the early stages of technology assimilation, it is important to encourage and capture learning experiences. Financial and more competitively motivated metrics are appropriate only when it is sufficiently clear what the potential business value added is of new types of investment.

The relative importance of value metrics also greatly depends upon the strategic priorities of an organization. Theories of strategic management have made clear that organizations continuously interact with their external business environment. In order to be able to cope with, and preferably anticipate, the demands of an increasingly dynamic external business environment, organizations have to innovate and grow. There is no 'absolute' way of organizing which will work always, and in every possible situation. Organizations therefore adapt to new business demands, e.g. in terms of their structure, style of management, culture, markets, and products. The interdependencies and match between likely business impacts of an investment and the overall strategic priorities of an organization may give important guidance to assessing the relative importance of value metrics.

Many ideas, visions and concepts concerning the (preferred) strategic priorities of organizations have been put forward, both in the context of academic research and by consulting firms. These will not be repeated or reviewed here, but reference is made to the work of Hardjono (1995), who presents a 'four phase model' with strategic reference points (see Figure 11.3). He builds on and extends several other models, including the model of Koopman and Pool discussed previously. These reference points are based upon two basic strategic orientations: the strive for external versus internal focus, and control versus change. Hardjono argues that it is simply not possible to pay equal attention to all reference points simultaneously, although these may seem very attractive and rewarding. It is more plausible to give priority to one particular strategic reference point, depending on the preferred organizational course at a given period of time and evolutionary state. This book has made clear that the likely business impacts of IT-based infrastructure, and thus its business value proposition, may cover many different business aspects (see Chapters 9 and 10). The model of Hardjono can be considered a point of departure with respect to the role financial value metrics will play and regarding the relative importance of more qualitative, non-financial metrics. The discerned reference points and their implications for the relative importance of value metrics are:

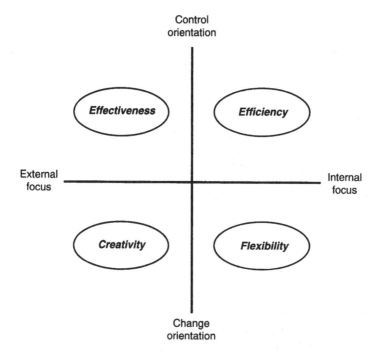

Figure 11.3 *Strategic reference points (after Hardjono, 1995)*

- *Efficiency*: metrics to assess cost savings and cost displacements.
- *Effectiveness*: metrics to assess business and IT process improvements.
- *Creativity*: metrics to assess process, market and product innovations.
- *Flexibility*: metrics to assess responsiveness to market, competitive and technology changes.

A recent contribution to the issue of relative importance of infrastructure value metrics has been made by Weill and Broadbent (1998), who add important insights, particularly with respect to infrastructure synergy. They identify a model with four different approaches, or what they define as 'strategic views', towards investments in IT-based infrastructure. Their model is in line with the situational perspective of the aforementioned model of Hardjono, since they argue that none of the views is best for all organizations, but one is more appropriate for a particular firm, according to its strategic context and ambitions at a particular period of time. Next to different benefit and synergy profiles, and thus the different relative importance of value metrics, the four views also represent different levels of increasing infrastructure investment and top management attention. The four strategic views are:[3]

- *None* view: no organization-wide infrastructure, synergies are forgone.
- *Utility* view: infrastructure is administrative expense, capturing costs savings from economies of scale.
- *Dependent* view: infrastructure is business expense, created to support current strategies.
- *Enabling* view: infrastructure is core competence, generating options for new strategies.

11.5 CONCLUSIONS

The investment method of a specific organization should be the result of clear design choices by this organization and of its investment stakeholders. Appropriate design choices reflect organizational characteristics and senior management decisions concerning the way in which IT-based infrastructure investments will be appraised, selected, measured, and managed. The investment methodology presented in this chapter represents an ideal-typical investment assessment framework, giving an overview of generic concepts which can guide the final design choices of a specific organization. As such, this assessment framework gives a synthesized perspective on the results of this book, as presented in the previous chapters. The framework is built around a life-cycle model of investment in IT-based infrastructure, in which a distinction is made between the identification of potential investments, the appraisal and selection of investment projects, and the measurement and management of investment results. The final appearance of an investment methodology should be guided by the situational characteristics of investment decision-making in a particular organization. Important situational characteristics discussed here are the overall style of decision-making of an organization and the relative importance of value metrics. Concerning the latter, important aspects are prior experiences with a type of investment, and the prevailing strategic priorities of an organization.

---

[3] Weill and Broadbent (1998) mention several organizations as being typical of a particular view, e.g. Ralston Purina Company (none view), Carlton & United Breweries (utility view), Maybank (dependent view), and the Commonwealth Bank of Australia (enabling view).

12
Managing IT-Based Infrastructure for Business Value

12.1 INTRODUCTION

The previous chapters of this book have proposed a range of ideas and instruments for assessing and managing IT-based infrastructure investments successfully. The perspective taken has been a managerial one, focusing on the investment issues that senior business managers are likely to address when trying to find optimal strategies for business value generation and to be an equal sparring partner to their technology specialists and suppliers. This final chapter reviews the key concepts, messages and recommendations conveyed in this book. First, Section 12.2 gives a short summary of the main managerial implications for getting control over IT-based infrastructure and investments in this infrastructure. Subsequently, some concluding thoughts are given in Section 12.3.

12.2 KEY IMPLICATIONS FOR SENIOR MANAGEMENT

This section summarizes the main results of this book for senior management. Several key themes will be discussed, all of which have been the recurring subject of the previous chapters. The order in which the themes will be presented follows the line of reasoning of the previous chapters. An overarching theme is the basic recognition by senior business managers that IT-based infrastructure investments are simply too important, and too expensive, to be ignored, ill-managed or left to specialists. If organizations really want to exploit the business potential of modern IT, infrastructure decisions and investment assessment should be at the top of the management agenda. Despite the continuing debate surrounding the IT 'productivity paradox', it still is very well possible to deliver business value from IT-based infrastructure. However, this can only be delivered if business value propositions and ambitions are well-articulated, communicated and managed. Given the business issues and the spending levels at stake, no organization or senior business manager can allow itself anything less than that.

IT-Based Infrastructure: a Strategic Business Asset

It has become clear that the notion of infrastructure, although still used in a variety of meanings, has undergone a shift in both content and tenor. Until recently, the notion of infrastructure had a rather narrow, technological connotation, generally referring to centralized computing equipment and facilities for telecommunications. In accordance with increased usage of the term infrastructure in the context of the 'electronic superhighway', IT-based infrastructure now refers to all IT that is in common use in an organization for a longer period of time. As such, IT-based infrastructure is a business asset and reflects the increasingly shared and coordinated nature of today's IT investments. The infrastructure provides the IT base foundation with organizational commitment and top management ownership that enables subsequent local application of IT, tailored to more business-specific characteristics and preferences.

'Direct' and 'Indirect' Infrastructure

What in a specific case can be called infrastructure, depends on the organizational level under consideration. An IT-based infrastructure is a layered notion, therefore one can speak of infrastructures on several levels, e.g. of the infrastructure of a department, of a business unit infrastructure, of a corporation-wide infrastructure, of an industry infrastructure, and of an (inter)national infrastructure. Two main types of infrastructure are important from an investment perspective:

1. *Direct infrastructure*, consisting of IT capacities and capabilities which are to a large extent integrated with the business processes, product and services of an organization. This infrastructure manifests itself in the application infrastructure and the infrastructures of data and knowledge bases. Therefore it makes a more direct

business contribution, e.g. in terms of efficiency, speed, and quality of business deliverables.

2. *Indirect infrastructure*, consisting of IT capacities and capabilities that enable the use of IT in the business processes and product and services of an organization. The indirect infrastructure manifests itself in the infrastructures of technological and organizational facilities, which make a more indirect contribution to business performance, e.g. in terms of speed, availability, responsiveness, and maintainability of infrastructure facilities.

'Controlled Dynamics' as an Infrastructure Governance Approach

The actual infrastructure of an organizations will behave in a dynamic way, since management decisions on proposed investments (or divestments) to change the infrastructure will be made continually. Consequently, the well-known 'blueprint' methods for strategic IT planning do not adequately meet the planning and control needs of modern organizations. The prime planning question today is how to decide on investment projects that incrementally change the existing IT-based infrastructure, instead of planning all IT in a top-down manner. The governance approach underlying IT-based infrastructure management can be typified as 'controlled dynamics'. This means that only the basics of IT capacities and capabilities are fixed (the 'substructure'), while local, business-specific IT deployments (the 'superstructure') build on these 'pillars' with substantial degrees of freedom. Three interlinked processes are important for investment governance of the IT-based infrastructure:

1. Top-down or bottom-up identification of potential investments ('conceptualization').
2. Decision-making on investment proposals ('calculation').
3. Measurement and management of investment results ('control').

Important elements of the latter are 'single-loop learning' (to monitor and control the investment across its life-cycle) and 'double-loop learning' (to use the results achieved to learn from the investment and to use this knowledge in new investment appraisals).

Infrastructure Decisions as a Communicative Process

Decisions on infrastructure investments are not taken according to the classical idealized picture of the 'rational decision-maker'. It is more realistic to base decision-making support upon the practical consequences of the paradigm of 'bounded rationality'. As a consequence, investment evaluation should, above all, be looked upon as a communicative process that does not take place in isolation from its organizational context. Although top management accountability is crucial, this process involves multiple stakeholders who, through mutual consultation, are trying to assess the business value to be gained from a proposed investment. The product of such a process provides the crucial value metrics against which the investment's business value can be assessed, measured and managed across its life-cycle.

The P4 Model for Strategic Investment Control

The decision-making perspective taken in this book captures both the goal and process dimensions of strategic decision-making, thus leading to a more 'balanced control' of investment decisions. Building on practical experiences in several organizations, four important control options are discerned, coming together in the 'P4 model' for strategic investment control:

1. Management of the *product*: defining the business case and related value metrics to justify and prioritize investments.
2. Management of the *process*: taking appropriate evaluation steps in order to decide on, monitor and control investments across their entire life-cycle.
3. Management of *participation*: involving the right stakeholders in investment decisions, thereby securing management ownership and organizational commitment.
4. Management of the *politics*: managing conflicts of interest and political dynamics (e.g. through negotiations and coalition building).

Defining Business Cases through Value Metrics

Business cases for investment, based on well-articulated value metrics, are needed to be able to justify investments, to assess the likely impacts of investments, to communicate investment consequences, and to be able to measure, manage and learn from investment results. Financial calculations should be used with great care, and only when possible and appropriate financial metrics serve a role within a set of multi-dimensional value metrics. Option theory, although conceptually strong, still has too many theoretical and practical drawbacks to be prominent in the business case definition. Non-financial assessment in terms of what is considered positive and what negative is less trivial than that of financial impacts. It is not always clear which consequences should be qualified as positive and which as negative owing to the interactions between consequences and different value-judgments of involved stakeholders. The final business case should resolve such interactions and differences through agreed-upon and committed value metrics. Since investment impacts move between certain margins, a business case should also cover investment risks, which are input to establishing a risk management process. Infrastructure synergy—essentially an evaluation of shared versus individual control—influences the business case through additional advantages, disadvantages and risk effects.

Organization-Specific Design of an Investment Method

Organizations face several choices when designing a method to identify, evaluate, measure and manage its IT-based infrastructure investments. The final choices are the result of the tailoring of the method to organizational characteristics and the preferences of the people using the method. Many of the existing methods for IT appraisals do not allow for such choices, which turns them into rather mechanistic, cookbook-like approaches. Two important contingencies should be taken into account: the decision-making culture of the organization and the relative importance of the value metrics. Organizations tend to give one of the four P's of strategic investment control more attention by default. In order to prevent decision-making from becoming too unbalanced in character, special attention is needed to appropriate inclusion of the other control options. The investment priorities and synergies of an organization will not always be the same, but will be influenced by its strategic direction and evolution, which should be reflected in the set of value metrics used.

12.3 CONCLUDING THOUGHTS

From a management perspective it often seems as if there are 'three worlds of IT deployment' (Luitjens and Tas, 1995). Two extreme perspectives can be discerned. In the first perspective, which can mainly be found with IT specialists and suppliers, IT seems to be a panacea for an ever-increasing range of organizational problems. In the second perspective, which can mainly be found with business managers with IT accountabilities, skepticism or even a high degree of pessimism regarding the business value and benefits of IT prevail. The 'dark side' of things is the focal point of attention in this latter perspective. A more realistic, pragmatic perspective, which can be seen as a compromise between the two extremes, is that investing in IT is complex and delicate, and will only lead to the desired outcomes if investment governance and management get sufficient attention. It is thus a 'normal' management issue, where all issues of structure, culture, strategy and technology will play their respective part and interact. Regarding investments in IT-based infrastructure, skepticism and even pessimism abound with respect to the likely success of investments and the business benefits to be gained from them. The debate concerning the IT productivity paradox is not yet resolved, and offers, at least for the time being, fertile soil for skepticism and pessimism. Success stories concerning seemingly ground-breaking and extremely profitable IT deployment will also remain, with or without a new type of promising technology or new innovative ways of organizing. Investment in an IT-based infrastructure will never, however, be a universal remedy, but it is just as naive to expect that all projects will almost by definition fail to deliver business value. Every organization and every accountable manager should at least be able to make careful judgments regarding benefits, investment efforts and risks, and to install clear business procedures concerning the way in which investment decisions are taken, communicated and monitored. Only then will it become possible to speak of successes and failures, and to be able to learn from these experiences. Reviewing the results of this book it becomes clear that an important part of managing IT-based infrastructure and infrastructure investment decisions is balancing several elements (see Figure 12.1):

- Well-balanced IT deployment necessitates a balance between *infrastructure* capacities and capabilities and *local, business-specific* applications. Too much infrastructure will lead to a rigid, inflexible type of IT deployment and will inhibit profitable localized IT deployment at the level of the users of the infrastructure. Too little infrastructure, however, will lead to inconsistent, too expensive IT deployment which does not capture business leverages of scale, scope and co-operation.
- Well-directed identification of potential investments requires a balance between *top-down* and *bottom-up* identification. On the one hand, it is important to define the overall strategic course of organization in a top-down manner. On the other hand, there should be enough room for everyone to propose improvement on their own initiative.
- Good management of decisions regarding infrastructure projects requires a balance between the '*product*' and the '*process*' dimensions

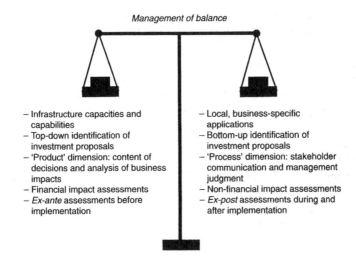

Figure 12.1 *Balancing elements of IT-based infrastructure management*

of decision-making. The analytical content of decision-making and the value metrics used are very much dependent upon the steps in the decision-making process, the involvement of the right people, and sufficient attention to the politics of decision-making. An exclusive focus on the way in which decisions should be made in terms of stakeholder communications and managerial judgment is only of limited usefulness if there is no well-articulated analysis of the business impacts of an investment.

- A complete picture of the possible business impacts of an investment can only be given if a balance is made between *financial* and *non-financial* impact assessments. If only financial arguments are taken into account, essential consequences that cannot easily be translated into financial terms are likely to be ignored. Financial impacts are however fundamental for investment justification and resource allocation and therefore should not be ignored.

- In order to manage and learn from investments across their entire life-cycle, a balance should be found between evaluations *before* and *after* the initial investment decision (*ex ante* and *ex post* assessments). Initial investment evaluations have much more meaning if information concerning the outcomes of prior investments is incorporated. Evaluations after the initial investment decision are only possible if there are committed value metrics that can be used as performance drivers and improvement targets.

Concerning the latter balancing issue, it has been argued in this book that few organizations deliberately devote time and resources to reflect on investment decisions made earlier. Managers generally favor looking forward, to new strategies and new investment opportunities. The review sessions which were held proved that it can be very valuable to evaluate what the real outcomes and business contributions of an investment are. As discussed, such reviews should be considered as an opportunity to manage and learn from investment results, and not as an audit device to 'settle up' with employees regarding their failing contributions or to find managers who can be held accountable for disappointing results and supposed mismanagement. Finding strategies to create and foster an investment climate that embraces the use of business value assessments as genuine, collective tools of management provides a unique challenge to all of us.

References

Ackoff, R.L. (1979), The future of operational research is past, *Journal of the Operational Research Society*, **30**, 93–104.

Agarwal, R., Tanniru, M.R. and Dacruz, M. (1992), Knowledge-based support for combining qualitative and quantitative judgments in resource allocation decisions, *Journal of Management Information Systems*, **8**, no. 1, 165–184.

Ahituv, N., Neumann, S. and Zviran, M. (1989), Factors affecting the policy of distributing computing resources, *MIS Quarterly*, December, 389–401.

Aken, J.E. van (1994a), Management studies as design science: the regulative and reflective cycle (in Dutch), *Bedrijfskunde*, **66**, no. 1, 16–26.

Aken, J.E. van (1994b), *Strategy Formation and Organizational Structuration: Organization Science from a Design Perspective*, Kluwer Bedrijfswetenschappen, Deventer, The Netherlands.

Aken, J.E. van and Matzinger, B. (1983), A neo-rational model of decision-making: decision preparation between intuition and logic (in Dutch), *M&O Tijdschrift voor organisatiekunde en sociaal beleid*, no. 6, 478–493.

Allen, B.R. and Boynton, A.C. (1991), Information architecture: in search of efficient flexibility, *MIS Quarterly*, December, 435–445.

Andreu, R., Ricart, J. and Valor, J. (1994), Information systems planning at the corporate level, in: Ciborra, C. and Jelassi, T. (eds), *Strategic Information Systems: A European Perspective*, Wiley, Chichester.

Ansoff, H.I. (1971), *Corporate Strategy: An Analytic Approach to Business Policy for Growth and Expansion*, McGraw-Hill, London.

Anthony, R.N. (1965), *Planning and Control Systems: A Framework for Analysis*, Harvard University Press, Boston.

Applegate, L.M. (1994), Managing in an information age: transforming the organization for the 1990's, in: Baskerville, R., Smithson, S., Ngwenyama, O. and DeGross, J.I. (eds), *Transforming Organizations with Information Technology*, Elsevier Science, Amsterdam.

Argyris, C. and Schön, D.A. (1978), *Organizational Learning: A Theory of Action Perspective*, Addison-Wesley, Amsterdam.

Bacon, C.J. (1990), Organizational principles of systems decentralization, *Journal of Information Technology*, **5**, 84–93.

Bacon, C.J. (1992), The use of decision criteria in selecting information systems/ technology investments, *MIS Quarterly*, September, 335–353.

Bakos, J.Y. and Kemerer, C.F. (1992), Recent applications of economic theory in information technology research, *Decision Support Systems*, **8**, 365–383.

Ballantine, J.A., Galliers, R.D. and Stray, S.J. (1994), Information systems/technology investment decisions: the use of capital investment appraisal techniques in organizations, in: *Proceedings of the First European Conference on IT Investment Evaluation*, Henley.

Ballantine, J.A., Galliers, R.D. and Powell, P.L. (1995), Daring to be different: capital appraisal and technology investments, in: *Proceedings of the Third European Conference on Information Systems*, Athens.

Banker, R.D., Kauffman, R.J. and Mahmood, M.D. (1993), *Strategic Information Technology Management: Perspectives on Organizational Growth and Competitive Advantage*, Idea Group Publishing, Harrisburg.

Baskerville, R., Smithson, S., Ngwenyama, O. and DeGross, J.I. (eds) (1994), *Transforming Organizations with Information Technology*, Elsevier Science, Amsterdam.

Bass, B.M. (1983), *Organizational Decision-Making*, Dow-Jones Irwin, Homewood.

Beath, C.M. (1991), Supporting the information technology champion, *MIS Quarterly*, September, 355–372.

Beath, C.M. and Straub, D. (1989), Managing information resources at the department level: an agency perspective, in: *Proceedings of the Hawaii International Conference on System Sciences*, vol. III, Honolulu.

Bedell, E.F. (1985), *The Computer Solution: Strategies for Success in the Information Age*, Dow-Jones Irwin, Homewood.

Belmonte, R.W. and Murray, J. (1993), Getting ready for strategic change: surviving business process redesign, *Information Systems Management*, Summer, 23–39

Bemelmans, T.M.A. (1994), *Management Information Systems and Computerization* (in Dutch), Kluwer Bedrijfswetenschappen, Deventer, The Netherlands.

Benbasat, I., Goldstein, D.K. and Mead, M. (1987), The case research strategy in studies of information systems, *MIS Quarterly*, September, 368–386.

Berg, R.J. van den and Renkema, T.J.W. (1994), Tackling information management issues through an information infrastructure, in: *Proceedings of the International Conference of the Information Resource Management Association*, San Antonio.

Berghout, E.W. (1997), *Evaluation of Information Systems: Design of a Decision Support Method*, Ph.D. dissertation, Delft University of Technology, The Netherlands.

Berghout, E.W. and Meertens, F.J.J. (1992), Investment portfolio for evaluating information systems proposals (in Dutch), *Informatie*, **34**, theme issue, 677–689.

Bierman, H. and Smidt, S. (1984), *The Capital Budgeting Decision: Economic Analysis and Financing of Investment Projects*, Macmillan, New York.

Björn-Andersen, N. and Davis, G.B. (eds) (1988), *Information Systems Assessment: Issues and Challenges*, North-Holland, Amsterdam.

Blackler, F. and Brown, C. (1988), Theory and practice in evaluation: the case of the new information technologies, in: Björn-Andersen, N. and Davis, G.B. (eds), *Information Systems Assessment: Issues and Challenges*, North-Holland, Amsterdam.

Bolwijn, P. and Kumpe, T. (1990), *Market-Driven Business: Management of Continuity and Change* (in Dutch), Van Gorcum, Assen.

Boonstra, A. (1991), Political aspects of information systems development, *Informatie*, **33**, no. 12, 857–864.

Bower, J.L. (1970), *Managing the Resource Allocation Process: A study of Corporate Planning and Investment*, Harvard University Press, Boston.

Boynton, A.C. and Zmud, R.W. (1987), Information technology planning in the 1990's: directions for practice and research, *MIS Quarterly*, March, 58–71.

Bradley, S.P. and Nolan, R.L. (1998), *Sense and Respond: Capturing Value in the Network Era*, Harvard Business School Press, Boston.

Brealey, R.A. and Myers, S.C. (1988), *Principles of Corporate Finance*, McGraw-Hill, New York.

Broadbent, M. and Weill, P. (1997) Management by maxim: how business and IT managers can create IT infrastructures. *Sloan Management Review*, **39**, no. 1, 77–92.

Brown, A. (1994), Getting value from an integrated IS strategy, *European Journal of Information Systems*, **3**, no. 2, 155–165.

Brown, A. and Remenyi, D. (eds) (1994), *Proceedings of the First European Conference on IT Investment Evaluation*, Operational Research Society, Birmingham.

Brown, A. and Remenyi, D. (eds) (1995), *Proceedings of the Second European Conference on IT Investment Evaluation*, Operational Research Society, Birmingham.

Brown, J.A. and Watts, J. (1992), Enterprise engineering: building 21st century organizations, *Journal of Strategic Information Systems*, December, 243–249.

Brynjolfsson, E. (1993), The productivity paradox of information technology, *Communications of the ACM*, **36**, no. 12, 67–77.

Brynjolfsson, E. and Hitt, L. (1993), Is information systems spending productive? New evidence and new results, in: *Proceedings of the 14th International Conference on Information Systems*, Orlando.

Brynjolfsson, E. and Hitt, L. (1994), The three faces of IT value, in: *Proceedings of the 15th International Conference on Information Systems*, Vancouver.

Brynjolfsson, E. and Hitt, L. (1998), Beyond the productivity paradox: computers are the catalyst for bigger changes, *Communications of the ACM*, **41**, no. 8, 1–18.

Buss, M.D.J. (1983), How to rank computer projects, *Harvard Business Review*, January–February, 118–125.

Butler, R., Davies, L., Pike, R. and Sharp, J. (1993), *Strategic Investment Decisions: Theory, Practice and Process*, Routledge London.

Butler Cox (1990), *Getting Value from Information Technology*, Research Report 75, Butler Cox Foundation, London.

Cairncross, C. (1997), *The Death of Distance: How the Telecommunications Revolution Will Change Our Lives*, Harvard Business School Press, Boston.

Canada, J.R. and Sullivan, W.G. (1989), *Economic and Multiattribute Evaluation of Advanced Manufacturing Systems*, Prentice-Hall, Englewood Cliffs.

Carlson, W.M. and McNurlin, B.C. (1989), *Measuring the Value of Information Systems*, I/S Analyzer Special Report, United Communications Group, Bethesda.

Carter, W.K. (1992), To invest in new technology or not? New tools for making the decision, *Journal of Accountancy*, May, 58–62.

CBS (1996), *Central Bureau Statistics of the Dutch Economy* (in Dutch), Staatsuitgeverij, The Hague.

Checkland, P.B. (1981), *Systems Thinking, Systems Practice*, Wiley, Chichester.

Checkland, P.B. (1985), From optimizing to learning: a development of systems thinking for the 1990's, *Journal of the Operational Research Society*, **36**, 757–767.

Checkland, P.B. (1989), An application of soft systems methodology, in: Rosenhead, J. (ed.), *Rational Analysis for a Problematic World: Problem Structuring Methods for Complexity, Uncertainty and Conflict*, Wiley, Chichester.

Checkland, P.B. and Scholes, J. (1990), *Soft Systems Methodology in Action*, Wiley, Chichester.

Ciborra, C. (1994), The grassroots of IT and strategy, in: Ciborra, C. and Jelassi, T. (eds), *Strategic Information Systems: A European Perspective*, Wiley, London.

Clark, T.D. (1992), Corporate systems management: an overview and research perspective, *Communications of the ACM*, **35**, no. 2, 61–75.

Clemons, E.K. (1991), Evaluation of strategic investments in information technology, *Communications of the ACM*, **34**, no. 1, 23–36.

Clemons, E.K. and Weber, B.W. (1990), Strategic information technology investments: guidelines for decision making, *Journal of Management Information Systems*, **6**, no. 2, 9–28.

Cohen, M.D., March, J.G. and Olsen, J.P. (1972), A garbage can model of organizational choice, *Administrative Science Quarterly*, **17**, no. 1, 1–25.

Coleman, T. and Jamieson, M. (1994), Beyond return on investment: evaluating all the benefits of information technology, in: Willcocks, L. (ed.), *Information Management: The Evaluation of Information Systems Investments*, Chapman & Hall, London.

Computable (1997), IT spendings of European Companies (in Dutch): Report on Information Strategy Research, *Computable*, **30**, no. 47.

Cron, W.L. and Sobol, M.G. (1983), The relationship between computerization and performance, *Information & Management*, no. 6, 171–181.

CSC Index (1993), *Building the New Information Infrastructure*, Report no. 91, CSC Index Foundation.

Cullen, R. (1995), *Executive Information Systems* (in Dutch), Ph.D. Thesis, Eindhoven University of Technology.

Currie, W.L. (1989), The art of justifying new technology to top management, *Omega*, **17**, no. 5, 409–418.

Cyert, R.M. and March, J.G. (1963), *A Behavioral Theory of the Firm*, Prentice-Hall, Englewood Cliffs.

Daft, R.L (1986). *Organizational Theory and Design*, West Publishing Co., St. Paul.

Darnton, G. and Giacoletto, S. (1992), *Information in the Enterprise: It's More than Technology*, Digital Equipment Corporation, Utrecht.

David, P.A. (1990), The dynamo and the computer: a historical perspective on the modern productivity paradox, *American Economic Review, Papers and Proceedings*, **1**, no. 2, 355–361.

Davenport, T.E. (1993), *Process Innovation: Reengineering Work through Information Technology*, Harvard Business School Press, Boston.

Davenport, T.E. and Short, J.E. (1990), The new industrial engineering: information technology and business process redesign, *Sloan Management Review*, Summer, 11–27.

Davis, G.B. and Olsen, M.H. (1985), *Management Information Systems: Conceptual Foundations, Structure and Development*, McGraw-Hill, New York.

Deitz, R.H.M. (1997), *IT Investments Between Intuition and Calculation* (in Dutch), Ph.D. Thesis, Eindhoven University of Technology, The Netherlands.

Deitz, R.H.M. and Renkema, T.J.W. (1995), Planning and justifying investments in information technology: a framework with case study illustrations, in: *Proceedings of the Second European Conference on IT Investment Evaluation*, Henley.

Deming, E. (1986), *Out of the Crisis*, Cambridge University Press, Cambridge.

DeSanctis, G. and Jackson, B.M. (1994), Coordination of information technology management: team based structures and computer-based communication systems, *Journal of Management Information Systems*, **10**, no. 4, 85–110.

Diebold Group (1990), *Evaluating Information Technology Expenses and Investments: Summary of Findings*, Report 246E, The Diebold Research Program, New York.

Dinther, M. van (1993), *Caught in a Web, Psychological Backgrounds of Investment Decisions* (in Dutch), AXA Equity and Law.

Dixit, A.K. and Pindyck, R.S. (1995), The options approach to capital investment, *Harvard Business Review*, May–June, 105–115.

Douglas, D.P. and Walsh, L. (1992), Basic principles for measuring IT value, *I/S Analyser*, no. 10.

Dos Santos, B.L. (1991), Justifying investments in new information technologies, *Journal of Management Information Systems*, **7**, no. 4, 71–90.

Dos Santos, B.L. (1994), Assessing the value of strategic information technology investments, in: Willcocks, L. (ed.), *Information Management: The Evaluation of Information Systems Investments*, Chapman & Hall, London.

Drucker, P.F. (1988), The coming of the new organization, *Harvard Business Review*, January–February, 45–53.

Drummond, H. (1996), *Escalation in Decision Making: The Tragedy of Taurus*, Oxford University Press, Oxford.

Dutch Ministry of Economic Affairs (1994), *Electronics Highways: From Metaphor to Action* (in Dutch), Ministry of Economic Affairs, The Hague.

Earl, M.J. (1989), *Management Strategies for Information Technology*, Prentice-Hall, London.

Earl, M.J. (1992), Putting IT in its place: a polemic for the nineties, *Journal of Information Technology*, **7**.

Earl, M.J. (1993), Experiences in strategic information systems planning, *MIS Quarterly*, March, 1–24.

Earl, M.J. and Runge, D.A. (1987), *Using Telecommunications Based Information Systems for Competitive Advantage*, Report RDP 87/1, Templeton College, Oxford.

Eden, C. (1989), Using cognitive mapping for strategic options development and analysis, in: Rosenhead, J. (ed.), *Rational Analysis for a Problematic World: Problem Structuring Methods for Complexity, Uncertainty and Conflict*, Wiley, Chichester.

Edwards, B.R., Earl, M.J. and Feeny, D.F. (1989), *Any Way Out of the Labyrinth for Managing Information Systems?*, Templeton College, Oxford Institute of Information Systems, Oxford University.

Engardio, P. (1994), Third World leapfrog, *Business Week*, June 13, 46–47.

European Union (1994), *Europe and the Worldwide Information Society*, European Union, Brussels.

Farbey, B., Land, F. and Targett, D. (1992), Evaluating investments in IT, *Journal of Information Technology*, **7**, 109–122.

Farbey, B., Land, F. and Targett, D. (1993), *How to Assess Your IT Investment: A Study of Methods and Practice*, Butterworth–Heinemann, Oxford.

Feeny, D.F. and Ives, B. (1989), In search of sustainability: reaping long-term advantage from investments in information technology, *Journal of Management Information Systems*, **5**, no. 1, 27–46.

FinTech (1992), Spotlight: business process reengineeering brings big benefits, *FinTech Electronic Office*, **2**, no. 4.

Fitzgerald, G. (1998), Evaluating information systems projects: a multidimensional approach, *Journal of Information Technology*, **13**, 15–27.

Frielink, A.B. (ed.) (1961), *Auditing Automatic Data Processing*, Elsevier, Amsterdam.

Frielink, A.B. (ed.) (1975), *Economics of Informatics*, North-Holland, Amsterdam.

Galbraith, J.R. (1973), *Designing Complex Organizations*, Addison-Wesley, Reading.

Galbraith, J.R. (1995), *Designing Organizations: An Executive Briefing on Strategy, Structure and Process*, Jossey-Bass, San Francisco.

Gerrity, T.P. and Rockart, J.F. (1986), End user computing: are you a leader or a laggard?, *Sloan Management Review*, Summer, 25–34.

Glasson, B., Hawryszkiewycz, I.T. and Underwood, B.A. (1994), *Business Process Re-engineering: Information Systems Opportunities and Challenges*, IFIP TC8 publication, Elsevier, Amsterdam.

Goodhue, D.L., Wybo, M.D. and Kirsch, L.J. (1992), The impact of data integration on the cost and benefits of information systems, *MIS Quarterly*, September, 293–311.

Gregory, A.J. and Jackson, M.C. (1992), Evaluation methodologies: a system for use, *Journal of the Operational Research Society*, **43**, 19–28.

Grover, V., Teng, J.T.C. and Fiedler, K.D. (1993), Information technology enabled business redesign, *Omega*, no. 4, 433–447.

Guba, E.G. and Lincoln, Y.S. (1989), *Fourth Generation Evaluation*, Sage, Newbury Park.

Gunton, T. (1989), *Infrastructure, Building a Framework for Corporate Information Handling*, Prentice-Hall, Hemel Hempstead.

Gurbaxani, V. and Kemerer, C.F. (1990), An agency theory view on the management of end-user computing, in: *Proceedings of the Eleventh International Conference on Information Systems*, Copenhagen.

Hagel, J. and Armstrong, A. (1997), *Net Gain: Expanding Markets through Virtual Communities*, Harvard Business School Press, Boston.

Hammer, M. (1990), Reengineering work: don't automate, obliterate, *Harvard Business Review*, July–August, 104–112.

Hammer, M. and Champy, J. (1993), *Reengineering the Corporation: A Manifesto for Business Revolution*, Nicholas Brealey, London.

Hammer, M. and Stanton, S. (1995), *The Reengineering Revolution: a Handbook*, Harper Business, New York.

Handy, C. (1994), *The Age of Paradox*, Harvard Business School Press, Boston.

Hardjono, T.W. (1995), Rhythmics and Organizational Dynamics, Ph.D. Thesis, Eindhoven University of Technology, The Netherlands.

Hares, J. and Royle, D. (1994), *Measuring the Value of Information Technology*, Wiley, Chichester.

Harrington, H.J. (1991a), *Business Process Improvement*, McGraw-Hill, London.

Harrington, H.J. (1991b), *Organizational Structure and Information Technology*, Prentice-Hall, London.

Harris, S.E. and Katz, J.L. (1989), Predicting organizational performance using information technology managerial control ratios, in: *Proceedings of the Hawaii International Conference on System Sciences*, Honolulu.

Harrison, E.F. (1987), *The Managerial Decision Making Process*, Houghton Mifflin, Boston.

Henderson, J.C. and Venkatraman, N. (1993), Strategic alignment: leveraging information technology for transforming organizations, *IBM Systems Journal*, **33**, no. 1, 4–16.

Henderson, J.C., Venkatraman, N. and Oldach, S. (1996), Aligning business and IT strategies, in: Luftman, J.N. (ed.), *Competing in the Information Age: Strategic Alignment in Practice*, Oxford University Press, New York.

Hickson, P.J., Butler, R.J., Cray, D., Mallory, J.R. and Wilson, D.C. (1986), *Top Decisions: Strategic Decisions in Organizations*, Basil Blackwell, Oxford.

Hirschheim, R. and Smithson, S. (1988), A critical analysis of information systems evaluation, in: Björn-Andersen, N. and Davis, G.B. (eds), *Information Systems Assessment: Issues and Challenges*, North-Holland, Amsterdam.

Hochstrasser, B. (1990), Evaluating IT investments: matching techniques to projects, *Journal of Information Technology*, **5**, 215–221.

Hochstrasser, B. (1993), Quality engineering: a new framework applied to justifying and prioritising IT investments, *European Journal of Information Systems*, **2**, no. 3, 211–223.

Hochstrasser, B. and Griffiths, C. (1990), *Regaining Control of IT Investments: A Handbook for Senior Management*, Kobler Unit, Imperial College, London.

Hogbin, G. and Thomas, D.V. (1994), *Investing in Information Technology: Managing the Decision-Making Process*, McGraw-Hill, London.

Hoogeveen, D. (1997), *The Long and Winding Road from IT Investments to Business Performance*, Ph.D. Thesis, Erasmus University, The Netherlands.

Huigen, J. and Janssen, G.S.H. (1991), The benefits of information systems (in Dutch), *Economic Statistical Briefings*, **76**, no. 3815, 673–676.

Huppes, T. (1990), Information management and organization management: the twain shall meet, in: Huppes, T. (ed.), *IT Deployment to Serve Effectiveness Improvement: A Promising Perspective* (in Dutch), Stenfert Kroese, Leiden, The Netherlands.

Idenburg, P.J. (1992), Bossa nova in strategy development (in Dutch), *Economic Statistical Briefings*, April 22, 398–403.

Irsel, H.G.P. van, Fluitsma, P. and Broshuis, P.N.A. (1992), Evaluating IT investments: aligning supply and demand, *Information*, **34**, theme issue, 716–726.

Irsel, H.G.P. van and Swinkels, G.P.J. (1992), Investing in information technology: take IT or leave IT (in Dutch), *Information*, **34**, theme issue, 624–636.

Ives, B. and Learmonth, G. (1984), The information system as a competitive weapon, *Communications of the ACM*, no. 12, 1193–1201.

Janis, I.L. and Mann, L. (1977), *Decision-Making: A Psychological Analysis of Conflict, Choice and Commitment*, The Free Press, New York.

Janssen, B.T., Koot, W.J.D. and Mutsaers, E.J. (1993), Information technology expensive? IT assessment: a validated method to evaluate the effectiveness and effeciency of IT deployment (in Dutch), *Compact*, no. 2, 3–11.

Johannson, H.J., McHugh, P., Pendlebury, A.J. and Wheeler, W.A. (1993), *Business Process Reengineering: Breakpoint Strategies for Market Dominance*, Wiley, Chichester.

Jong, W.M. de (1994), *The Management of Informatization*, Ph.D. Thesis, Groningen University, The Netherlands.

Jones, M. (1994), Don't emancipate, exaggerate: rhetoric, reality and reengineering, in: Baskerville, R., Smithson, S., Ngwenyama, O. and DeGross, J.I. (eds),

Transforming Organizations with Information Technology, North-Holland, Amsterdam.

Joslin, E.O. (1968), *Computer Selection*, Addison-Wesley, London.

Joslin, E.O. (1977), *Computer Selection: Augmented Edition*, The Technology Press, Fairfax Station.

Kambil, A., Henderson, J. and Mohsenzadeh, H. (1993), Strategic management of information technology investments: an options perspective, in: Banker, R.D., Kauffman, R.J. and Mahmood, M.D. (eds), *Strategic Information Technology Management*, Idea Group Publishing, Harrisburg.

Kaplan, R.B. and Murdock, L. (1991), Core process redesign, *McKinsey Quarterly*, 27–49.

Kaplan, R.S. (1986), Must CIM be justified by faith alone?, *Harvard Business Review*, March–April, 87–95.

Kaplan, R.S. and Norton, D. (1992), The balanced scorecard: measures that drive performance, *Harvard Business Review*, January–February, 71–79.

Kaplan, R.S. and Norton, D. (1996), Using the balanced scorecard as a strategic management system, *Harvard Business Review*, January–February, 75–85.

Keen, P.G.W. (1981), Value analysis: justifying decision support systems, *MIS Quarterly*, March, 1–15.

Keen, P.G.W. (1991), *Shaping the Future: Business Design Through Information Technology*, Harvard Business School Press, Boston.

Keen, P.G.W. and Cummins, J.M. (1994), *Networks in Action: Business Choices and Telecommunications Decisions*, Wadsworth, Belmont.

Kepner, C.H. and Tregoe, B.B. (1981), *The New Rational Manager*, Princeton Research Press, Princeton.

Kickert, W.J.M. (1979), *Organisation of Decision-Making: A Systems-Theoretical Approach*, Ph.D. Thesis, Eindhoven University of Technology, The Netherlands.

King, J.L. (1983), Centralized versus decentralized computing: organizational considerations and management options, *Computing Surveys*, **15**, no. 4, 319–349.

King, J.L. and Schrems, E.L. (1978), Costbenefit analysis in information systems development and operation, *Computing Surveys*, **10**, no. 1, 19–34.

Kleijnen, J.P.C. (1980), *Computers and Profits: Quantifying Financial Benefits of Information*, Addison-Wesley, Amsterdam.

Kling, R. (1994), *The Information Society*, ISWORLD Electronic Network, digest February 22–23.

Koopman, P.L. and Pool, J. (1992), *Management and Decision-Making in Organizations: A Strategic Perspective* (in Dutch), Van Gorcum, Assen.

Kumar, K. (1991), Post-implementation evaluation of computer-based IS: current practices, *Communications of the ACM*, **33**, no. 2, 203–212.

Kusters, R.J. and Renkema, T.J.W. (1996), Managing IT investment decisions in their organizational context, in: Brown, A. and Remenyi, D. (eds), *Proceedings of the Third European Conference on IT Investment Evaluation*, University of Bath, UK.

Landauer, T.K. (1995), *The Trouble with Computers: Usefulness, Usability and Productivity*, The MIT Press, Cambridge.

Lederer, A.L. and Sethi, V. (1992), Meeting the challenges of information systems planning, *Long Range Planning*, **25**, no. 2, 69–80.

Leeuw, A.C.J. de (1986), *Organization Management: A Systems Perspective on Analysis, Design and Change* (in Dutch), Van Gorcum, Assen.

Leeuw, A.C.J. de (1994), *Managing Change Processes* (in Dutch), Van Gorcum, Assen.

Legge, K. (1984), *Evaluating Planned Organizational Change*, Academic Press, London.

Lincoln, T.J. (1986), Do computer systems really pay-off?, *Information and Management*, no. 11, 25–34.

Lincoln, T.J. (ed.) (1990), *Managing Information Systems for Profit*, Wiley, Chichester.

Lincoln, T.J. and Shorrock, D. (1990), Cost justifying current use of information technology, in: Lincoln, T.J. (ed.), *Managing Information Systems for Profit*, Wiley, Chichester.

Lindblom, C.E. (1959), The science of 'muddling through', *Public Administration Review*, **19**, Spring, 79–88.

Loveman, G. (1988), *An Assessment of the Productivity Impact of Information Technology*, Sloan School of Management, MIT, Boston.

Lucas, H.C. (1995), *The T-Form Organization: Using Technology to Design Organisations for the 21st Century*, Jossey-Bass, San Francisco.

Luehrman, T.A. (1998), Investment opportunities as real options: getting started on the numbers, *Harvard Business Review*, July–August, 51–67.

Luftman, J.N. (ed.) (1996), *Competing in the Information Age: Strategic Alignment in Practice*, Oxford University Press, New York.

Luitjens, S.B. and Tas, P.A. (1995), Organization management for information management: an anticyclical view (in Dutch), in: Mantelaers, P.A.H.M. and Looijen, M. (eds), *Information Systems Organization*, Kluwer Bedrijfswetenschappen, Deventer, The Netherlands.

Lumby, S. (1991), *Investment Appraisal and Financing Decisions*, Chapman & Hall, London.

Lyttinen, K. and Hirschheim, R. (1987), Information systems failures, *Oxford Surveys of Information Technology*, **4**, 257–309.

Maes, R. (1990), Infrastructure: a key concept for information management (in Dutch), in: Truijens, J., Oosterhaven, A., Maes, R., Jägers, H. and Iersel, F. van. (eds), *Information Infrastructure*, Kluwer Bedrijfswetenschappen, Deventer, The Netherlands.

Malone, T.W. and Crowston, K. (1994), The interdisciplinary study of coordination, *ACM Computing Surveys*, **26**, no. 1, 87–119.

Markus, M.L. (1983), Power, politics and MIS implementation, *Communications of the ACM*, **26**, no. 6, 430–444.

Martin, J. (1989), *Strategic Information Planning Methodologies*, Prentice-Hall, Englewood Cliffs.

Martin, J. (1995), *The Great Transition, Using the Seven Disciplines of Enterprise Engineering to Align People, Technology, and Strategy*, Amacom, Brussels.

Martin, J. (1996), *CyberCorp: The New Business Revolution*, Amacom, New York.

McFarlan, F.W. and McKenney, J.L. (1983), *Corporate Information Systems Management: The Issues Facing Senior Executives*, Dow Jones Irwin, Homewood.

McGaughey, R., Snyder, C.A. and Carr, H.H. (1994), Implementing information technology for competitive advantage: risk management issues, *Information and Management*, **26**, 273–280.

McKay, D.T. and Brockway, D.W. (1989), Building I/T infrastructure for the 1990s, *Stage by Stage*, **9**, no. 3, 1–12.

Meel, J.W. van, Bots, P.W.G. and Sol, H.G. (1994) Towards a research framework for business engineering, in: Glasson, B.C. (ed.), *Business Process Re-engineering: Information Systems Opportunities and Challenges*, North-Holland, Amsterdam.

Miles, M.B. and Huberman, A.B. (1984), *Analyzing Qualitative Data: A Source Book for New Methods*, Sage, Beverly Hills.

Mintzberg, H. (1983a), *Power in and Around Organizations*, Prentice Hall, Englewood Cliffs.

Mintzberg, H. (1983b), *Structure in Fives: Designing Effective Organizations*, Prentice Hall, Englewood Cliffs.

Mintzberg, H. (1994), *The Rise and Fall of Strategic Planning*, Prentice-Hall, Englewood Cliffs.

Mintzberg, H., Raisinghani, D. and Theoret, A. (1976), The structure of 'unstructured' decision processes, *Administrative Science Quarterly*, **21**, June, 246–275.

Morgan, G. (1986), *Images of Organization*, Sage, London.

Morris, D. and Brandon, J. (1993), *Reengineering Your Business*, McGraw-Hill, London.

Negroponte, N. (1995), *Being Digital*, Alfred A. Knopf, New York.

Niedermann, F., Brancheau, J.C. and Wetherbe, J.C. (1991), Information systems issues for the 1990's, *MIS Quarterly*, December, 474–500.

Nievelt, M.C.A. van (1992), Managing with information technology, a decade of wasted money?, *Compact*, no. 2, 15–24.

Nolan, R.L. (1979), Managing the crisis in data processing, *Harvard Business Review*, March–April, 115–126.

Nolan, R.L. and Croson, D.C. (1995), *Creative Destruction: A Six Stage Process for Transforming the Organization*, Harvard Business School Press, Boston.

Nolan, R.L. and Koot, W.J.D. (1992), The currency of Nolan's stage model (in Dutch), *Holland Management Review*, no. 31, 77–88.

OECD (1992), *Main Economic Indicators 1960–1992*, OECD, Paris.

Oosterhaven, J.A (1990), Business units and IT deployment: bounded freedom (in Dutch), *Harvard Holland Review*, Autumn, no. 94, 105–111.

Oosterhaven, J.A. (1994), *Information Strategy*, Samson, Alphen aan den Rijn.

Orlikowski, W.J. and Baroudi, J.J. (1991), Studying information technology in organizations: research approaches and assumptions, *Information Systems Research*, **2**, no. 1, 1–28.

Parker, M.M., Benson, R.J. and Trainor, H.E. (1988), *Information Economics, Linking Business Performance to Information Technology*, Prentice-Hall, Englewood Cliffs.

Parker, M.M., Benson, R.J. and Trainor, H.E. (1989), *Information Strategy and Economics*, Prentice-Hall, Englewood Cliffs.

Peters, G. (1988), Evaluating your computer investment strategy, *Journal of Information Technology*, **3**, 178–188.

Peters, G. (1989), *The Evaluation of Information Technology Projects*, Ph.D. Thesis, Brunel University.

Peters, G. (1990), Beyond strategy, benefits identification and management of specific IT investments, *Journal of Information Technology*, **5**, 205–214.

Pettigrew, A.M. (1985), *The Awakening Giant: Continuity and Change in ICI*, Basil Blackwell, Oxford.

Pfeffer, J. (1981), *Power in Organizations*, Pitman, Boston.

Pike, R. and Ho, S. (1991), Risk analysis in capital budgeting: barriers and benefits, *Omega*, **19**, no. 4, 235–245.

Porter, M.E. (1985), *Competitive Advantage, Creating and Sustaining Superior Performance*, The Free Press, New York.

Powell, P. (1992), Information technology evaluation, is it different?, *Journal of the Operational Research Society*, no. 1, 29–42.

Pruijm, R.A.M. (1992), The added value of information technology (in Dutch), *Information and Information Policy*, **10**, no. 4, 51–58.

Reeken, A.J. van (1992), Investment selection of information systems: Eugene Bedell's method (in Dutch), *Handbook of Management Information Systems*, pp. C 1030-1–1030-32.

Remenyi, D., Sherwoord-Smith, M. and White, T. (1997), *Achieving Maximum Value from Information Systems: A Process Approach*, Wiley, Chichester.

Renkema, T.J.W. (1998), The four P's revisited, business value assessment of the infrastructure impact of IT investments, *Journal of Information Technology*, **13**, 181–190.

Renkema, T.J.W. and Berghout, E.W. (1997), Methodologies for information systems investment evaluation at the proposal stage: a comparative review, *Information and Software Technology*, **39**, 1–13

Renkema, T.J.W. and Dolan, T.J. (1995), Investment-based analysis of IT enabled business process re-engineering, in: Browne, J. and O'Sullivan, D. (eds), *Re-engineering the Enterprise*, Chapman & Hall, London.

Ribbers, P.M.A. (1996), The IT manager becomes a network manager (in Dutch), in: Oonincx, J.A.M., Ribbers, P.M.A. and Takkenberg, C.A.Th. (eds), *Organization, Control and Information: Development of Theory and Practice*, Samson, Alphen aan den Rijn.

Roach, S. (1991), Services under siege: the restructuring imperative, *Harvard Business Review*, September–October, 82–91.

Rockart, J.F. (1979), Chief executives define their own data needs, *Harvard Business Review*, March–April, 81–93.

Rockart, J.F. (1988), The line that takes the leadership: IS management in a wired society, *Sloan Management Review*, Summer, 57–64.

Rockart, J.F. and Short, J.E. (1991), The networked organization and the management of interdependence, in: Scott Morton, M. (ed.), *The Corporation of the 1990's: Information Technology and Organizational Transformation*, Oxford University Press, New York.

Rodden, T., Mariani, J.A. and Blair, G. (1992), Supporting cooperative applications, *Computer Supported Cooperative Work*, **2**, no. 1/2, 41–67.

Rosenhead, J. (ed.) (1989), *Rational Analysis for a Problematic World: Problem Structuring Methods for Complexity, Uncertainty and Conflict*, Wiley, Chichester.

Ross, J.W., Beath, C.M. and Goodhue, D.L. (1996), Developing long-term competitiveness through IT assets, *Sloan Management Review*, Fall, 31–42.

Ryan, B., Scapens, R.W. and Theobald, M. (1992), *Research Methods and Methodology in Finance and Accounting*, Academic Press, London.

Saaty, T.L. (1980), *The Analytic Hierarchy Process*, McGraw-Hill, New York.

Sager, I. and Gleckman, H. (1994), The information revolution, *Business Week*, June 13, 35–39.

Samuelson, P.A. and Nordhaus, W.D. (1985), *Economics*, McGraw-Hill, New York.

Sanders, F.M. (1994), *Infrastructure Planning and Sustainable Development* (in Dutch), Faculty of Civil Engineering, Delft University of Technology, The Netherlands.

Sassone, P.G. (1988), A survey of cost benefit methodologies for information systems, *Project Appraisal*, **3**, no. 2. 73–84.

Sassone, P.G. and Schäfer, W.A. (1978), *Cost–Benefit Analysis: A Handbook*, Academic Press, New York.

Schäfer, G. (ed.) (1998), *Functional Analysis of Office Requirements: A Multiperspective Approach*, Wiley, Chichester.

Schein, E.H. (1988), *Organizational Culture and Leadership*, Jossey-Bass, San Francisco.

Schön, D.A. (1983), *The Reflective Practitioner*, Temple Smith, London.

Schwartz, E. (1997), *Webonomics*, Broadway Books, New York

Scott Morton, M. (ed.) (1991), *The Corporation of the 1990's: Information Technology and Organisational Transformation*, Oxford University Press, New York.

Senge, P. (1990), *The Fifth Discipline: The Art and Practice of the Learning Organisation*, Doubleday Currency, New York.

Shank, J. and Govindarajan, V. (1992), Strategic cost analysis of technological investments, *Sloan Management Review*, **34**, no. 1, 39–51.

Sharp, D.J. (1991), Uncovering the hidden value in high-risk investments, *Sloan Management Review*, Summer, 69–74.

Silk, D.J. (1990), Managing IS benefits for the 1990's, *Journal of Information Technology*, **5**, 185–193.

Simon, H.A. (1977), *The New Science of Management Decision*, Prentice-Hall, Englewood Cliffs.

Simson, E.M. von (1990), The 'centrally decentralized' IS organization, *Harvard Business Review*, July–August, 158–162.

Spraque, R.H. and Carlson, E.D. (1982), *Building Effective Decision Support Systems*, Prentice-Hall, Englewood Cliffs.

Steiner, G.A. (1971), *Top Management Planning*, Macmillan, New York.

Stone, D.N. (1991), Language, training and experience in IS assessment, *Accounting, Managing and Information Technologies*, **1**, no. 1, 101–108.

Strassman, P.A. (1990), *The Business Value of Computers*, The Information Economics Press, New Canaan.

Strassman, P.A. (1997), *The Squandered Computer*, The Information Economics Press, New Canaan.

Swanson, E. and Beath, C. (1989), *Maintaining Information Systems in Organizations*, Wiley, Chichester.

Symons, V.J. (1990), *Evaluation of Information Systems: Multiple Perspectives*, Ph.D. Thesis, University of Cambridge.

Symons, V.J. (1991), A review of information system evaluation: content, context, and process, *European Journal of Information Systems*, **1**, no. 1, 205–212.

Tapscott, D. (1997), *The Digital Economy: Promise and Peril in the Age of Networked Intelligence*, McGraw-Hill, New York.

Tapscott, D. and Caston, A. (1993), *Paradigm Shift: The New Promise of Information Technology*, McGraw-Hill, New York.

Thurow. L.C. (1991), Foreword, in: Scott Morton, M. (ed.), *The Corporation of the 1990's: Information Technology and Organisational Transformation*, Oxford University Press, New York.

Tissen, R.L., Lekranne Deprez, F., Andriessen. E. (1998), *Value-Based Knowledge Management*, Addison-Wesley, Amsterdam

Truijens, J., Oosterhaven, A., Maes, R., Jägers, H. and Iersel, F. van (1990), *Information Infrastructure: A Management Instrument*, Kluwer Bedrijfswetenschappen, Deventer, The Netherlands.

Udo, G. and Guimaraes, T. (1992), Improving project selection with a socio-technical approach, *Proceedings of the International Conference of the Information Resource Management Association*.

aid-Raizada, V.K. (1983), Incorporation of intangibles in computer selection decisions, *Journal of Systems Management*, November, 30–36.

enkatraman, N. (1991), IT-induced business reconfiguration, in: Scott Morton, M. (ed.), *The Corporation of the 1990's: Information Technology and Organisational Transformation*, Oxford University Press, New York.

erschuren, P.J.M. (1992), *The Problem Statement of Research*, Het Spectrum, Utrecht, The Netherlands.

erzellenberg, L.N.J. (1988), *Investments in Hospitals: Model and Practice* (in Dutch), Ph.D. Thesis, Eindhoven University of Technology, Eindhoven, The Netherlands.

room, V.H. and Jago, A.G. (1988), *The New Leadership: Managing Participation in Organizations*, Prentice-Hall, Englewood Cliffs.

Jaes, R.M.C. van (1991), *Architectures for Information Management*, Ph.D. Thesis, Free University of Amsterdam, Amsterdam, The Netherlands.

Jalsham, G. (1993), *Interpreting Information Systems in Organizations*, Wiley, Chichester.

Jard, J.M. (1990), A portfolio approach to evaluating information systems investments and setting priorities, *Journal of Information Technology*, **5**, 222–231.

Jard, J.M., Griffiths, P. and Whitmore, P. (1996a), *Strategic Planning for Information Systems*, Wiley, Chichester.

Jard, J.M., Taylor, P. and Bond, P. (1996b), Evaluation and realisation of IS/IT benefits: an empirical study of current practice, *European Journal of Information Systems*, **4**, 214–225.

Jatson, R.T., Kelly, G.G., Galliers, R.D. and Brancheau, J.C. (1997), Key issues in information systems management: an international perspective, *Journal of Management Information Systems*, **13**, no. 4, 91–116.

Jeick. K. (1979), *The Social Psychology of Organizing*, Addison-Wesley, Reading.

Jeill, P. (1990), *Do Computers Pay Off? A Study of Information Technology Investment and Manufacturing Performance*, ICIT Press, Washington.

Jeill, P. (1993), The role and value of information technology infrastructure, in: Banker, R.D., Kauffman, R.J. and Mahmood, M.D. (eds), *Strategic Information Technology Management*, Idea Group Publishing, Harrisburg.

Jeill, P. and Olsen, M. (1989), Managing investment in information technology: mini case examples and implications, *MIS Quarterly*, March, 2–17.

Jeill, P. and Broadbent, M. (1998), *Leveraging the New Infrastructure: How Market Leaders Capitalize on Information Technology*, Harvard Business School Press, Boston.

Jeill, P., Broadbent, M. and StClair, D.R. (1996), IT value and the role of IT infrastructure investments, in: Luftman, J. N. (ed.), *Competing in the Information Age: Strategic Alignment in Practice*, Oxford University Press, New York.

Jeston, J.F. and Copeland, T.E. (1991), *Managerial Finance*, Dryden Press, New York.

Jijers, G.J. (1994), *Horizontal Synergy* (in Dutch), van Gorcum, Assen.

Jilkes, F.M. and Samuels, J.M. (1991), Financial appraisal to support technological investment, *Long Range Planning*, no. 6, 60–66.

Jillcocks, L. (1994), Introduction: of capital importance, in: Willcocks, L. (ed.), *Information Management: The Evaluation of Information Systems Investments*, Chapman & Hall, London.

Jillcocks, L. and Lester, S. (1993), How do organizations evaluate and control information systems investments? recent UK evidence, in: Avison, D., Kendall,

J.E. and DeGross, J.I. (eds), *Human, Organizational, and Social Dimensions of Information Systems Development*, Elsevier Science, Amsterdam.

Willcocks, L. and Lester, S. (1994), Evaluating the feasibility of information systems investments: recent UK evidence and new approaches, in: Willcocks, L. (ed.), *Information Management: The Evaluation of Information Systems Investments*, Chapman & Hall, London.

Willcocks, L. and Margretts, H. (1994), Risk assessment and information systems, *European Journal of Information Systems*, **3**, no. 2, 127–138.

Wilson, D.D. (1993), Assessing the impact of information technology on organizational performance, in: Banker, R.D., Kauffman, R.J. and Mahmood, M.D. (eds), *Strategic Information Technology Management*, Idea Group Publishing, Harrisburg.

Wilson, T. (1991), Overcoming the barriers to the implementation of information system strategies, *Journal of Information Technology*, **6**, 39–44.

Wiseman, C. (1985), *Strategy and Computers*, Dow-Jones Irwin, Homewood.

Wiseman, D. (1992), Information economics: a practical approach to valuing information systems, *Journal of Information Technology*, **7**, 169–176.

Wissema, J.G. (1983), *An Introduction to Capital Investment Selection*, Francis Pinter, London.

Witte, E. (1972), Field research on complex decision making processes: the phase theorem, *International Studies on Management and Organization*, no. 2, 156–182.

Wolstenholme, E.F., Gavine, A., Watts, K.M. and Henderson, S. (1992), The design, application and evaluation of a system dynamics based methodology for the assessment of computerised information systems, *European Journal of Information Systems*, **1**, no. 5, 341–350.

Yan Tam, K. (1992), Capital budgeting in information system development, *Information and Management*, **23**, 345–357.

Yin, R.K. (1989), *Case Study Research: Design and Methods*, Sage, Newbury Park

Zee, H.T.M. van der (1996), *In Search of the Value of Information Technology*, Ph.D. Thesis, Tilburg University, The Netherlands.

Zee, H.T.M. van der and Koot, W.J.D. (1989), IT-assessment, a qualitative and quantitative evaluation of IT deployment from a strategic perspective (in Dutch), *Information*, **31**, no. 11, 805–900.

Zmud, R.W. (1983), *Information Systems in Organizations*, Scott, Foresman.

Zmud, R.W. (1984), Design alternatives for organizing information systems activities, *MIS Quarterly*, June, 79–93.

Zuboff, S. (1988), *In the Age of the Smart Machine*, Basic Books, New York.

Zuurmond, A. (1994), *The Infocracy* (in Dutch), Ph.D. Thesis, Erasmus University, The Netherlands.

Subject Index

Printed and bound by CPI Group (UK) Ltd, Croydon, CR0 4YY

27/10/2024

14580366-0001